W9-AHB-835

STREETWISE

# DIRECT
# MARKETING

## Books in the Streetwise series include:

STREETWISE

# DIRECT MARKETING

How to Use the Internet,
Direct Mail, and Other
Media to Generate
Direct Sales

## by George Duncan

Adams Media Corporation
Holbrook, Massachusetts

Published by Adams Media Corporation
260 Center Street, Holbrook, MA 02343. U.S.A.
www.adamsmedia.com

ISBN: 1-58062-439-1

Printed in the United States of America.


J  I  H  G  F  E  D  C  B  A


Library of Congress Cataloging-in-Publication data
available upon request from publisher.

This publication is designed to provide accurate and authoritative information with regard to the sub-ject matter covered. It is sold with the understanding that the publisher is not engaged in rendering legal, accounting, or other professional advice. If legal advice or other expert assistance is required, the services of a competent professional person should be sought.
— From a *Declaration of Principles* jointly adopted by a Committee of the American Bar Association and a Committee of Publishers and Associations

Many of the designations used by manufacturers and sellers to distinguish their products are claimed as trademarks. Where those designations appear in this book and Adams Media was aware of a trade-mark claim, the designations have been printed in initial capital letters.

Cover illustration by Eric Mueller.

*This book is available at quantity discounts for bulk purchases.*
*For information, call 1-800-872-5627.*

**Visit our exciting small business Web site: www.businesstown.com**

# CONTENTS

## SECTION I: THE BASICS

## SECTION II: THE NUTS AND BOLTS

## SECTION III: THE CREATIVE PROCESS

## SECTION IV: THE SUPPORTING CAST

## SECTION V: THE INTERNET: MARKETING'S 800-POUND ELECTRIC GORILLA

## APPENDICES

# ACKNOWLEDGMENTS

**F**resh out of the service in 1960, I took a copy exam at *Esquire* magazine. The instruction for one of the exercises was written by Esquire/GQ/Scott Stamp direct mail pro Sheldon Sachs and was intended to help the candidate focus on benefits. "Talk about my lawn, not your grass seed," was Sheldon's admonition. Since I got the job, I feel I owe a debt of gratitude to Sheldon for his guidance then, and in any number of long lunches subsequently. Thanks, Shel, wherever you are.

The individual who got me seriously started in direct mail was Richard Steeg, then direct mail manager at Ziff-Davis, now CEO of the world-class, New York-based list brokerage Coolidge Company. One could not have had a more knowledgeable, more thoughtful guide to the intricacies of direct mail than Dick.

Going "out on one's own," as a freelancer is more than a little scary. But from the moment I arrived in Cambridge, the late Harvey Cinamon and his gracious wife Marcia made me feel welcome. They introduced me to the Boston direct marketing community, especially the New England Direct Marketing Association (NEDMA), and Harvey gave me my first official freelance project—which won for both of us the very first John Caples Prize, awarded in 1978. It sure helped ease the freelance willies.

Later I was privileged to be part of a trio—with Bob Sabloff and the late Larry Chait—to found the Vermont-New Hampshire Direct Marketing Group. Now in its twelfth year, the Group boasts some 1,000 members and a robust direct marketing program designed to help small businesses safely navigate the interactive waters. I'll always be deeply grateful to many members of the Group over the years, especially Carole Ziter (her catalog is profiled in Chapter 13) and her direct marketing guru husband, Tom, and to Amy Africa and Bill LaPierre for their support then and now.

One aspect of *Streetwise Direct Marketing* that sends a thrill up my spine is the lineup of direct marketing pros who have so generously contributed their expertise to its pages. Copywriters really don't have all the answers—we just talk as though we do. So to double-check my own understandings and to tap knowledge bases substantially more reliable than mine in special areas, I asked for help with some of the chapters.

> "Talk about my lawn, not your grass seed."

To have such industry stars as Leon Henry, Maxwell Sroge, Bernie Goldberg and Tracy Emerick, Ted Kikoler, and others contributing to a book with my name on the cover is to truly realize a dream.

Speaking of direct marketing pros, a genuinely heartfelt thanks to Pierre Passavant for his generous contribution in the Foreword and for his help, once again.

Thanks also to the DMA's Chet Dalzell for the use of the DMA Guidelines . . . to Hank Hoke for his encouragement and cooperation . . . to Cathy Kingery for her diligence and thoughtful suggestions in proofreading the manuscript . . . and to my editor at Adams Media, Jere Calmes, for his guidance and support.

On the home front, much love and gratitude to my sweet, wonderful wife Sally, who kindly let me off the hook for any number of onerous chores so I could keep typing, and an extra can of salmon for two of the world's pushiest cats, Marmaduke and Hathaway, for helping me keep my sense of humor.

But that's enough about me. Now let's talk about *you*.

—George Duncan

> A genuinely heartfelt thanks to Pierre Passavant for his generous contribution in the Foreword and for his help, once again.

# FOREWORD

George Duncan and I worked together at Xerox Education Publications in the mid-seventies. Our task was to sell classroom products like the *My Weekly Reader* student newspaper to schools throughout America, and spinoffs like the Weekly Reader Children's Book Club to parents at home. All of this selling to hundreds of thousands of teachers and to millions of parents was accomplished through direct mail, some print advertising, and telemarketing.

When I think back, it was really rather remarkable that our small promotion staff at Xerox Education could be in direct communication with so many individuals and schools—trying to get them to be our customers. And once they became customers, then the challenge was trying to get them to resubscribe to our classroom periodicals, or to keep their children in one of our book clubs. George had a special knack for creating direct mail packages and ads with just the right tone and content for our special audiences, and getting them to respond to our offers.

That's what his new book, *Streetwise Direct Marketing*, is about: using the power of direct marketing to acquire large numbers of new customers and then getting them to buy again. It will show you how to use the techniques of direct marketing to reach out to thousands of establishments and perhaps millions of people, going far beyond the few live sales calls, or phone calls, you can make yourself. George does this now for the clients of his very successful direct marketing consultancy, and his book explains how you can do it yourself.

In my 40-plus years in business, I have worked for several very large companies, and managed a couple of rather small ones. Currently I direct the Center for Direct Marketing at New York University, where we offer a Master's in Direct Marketing program. In every case, I have been involved in direct marketing—using it to acquire customers, retain them, and increase their value. I am convinced that the principles and techniques of direct marketing can be used successfully in any enterprise—service, manufacturing, retailing, education, and others.

> Techniques of direct marketing can be used successfully in any enterprise—service, manufacturing, retailing, education, and others.

The methods of direct marketing are precise and need to be applied professionally, whether you are trying to sell directly or generate leads. Amateurs who ignore what experienced direct marketers have learned over the years take a real risk of failure. George Duncan is a person who has both the knowledge and practical experience to guide you through the steps of professional direct marketing.

I wish you good luck in your efforts!

Pierre Passavant
Director, Center for Direct Marketing and
Clinical Associate Professor of Direct Marketing
New York University
School of Continuing and Professional Studies

> Amateurs who ignore what experienced direct marketers have learned over the years take a real risk of failure.

# PREFACE

The seeds for this book were sown six years ago when I established a Web site and began writing monthly articles on various direct marketing subjects in order to keep the content fresh. I had envisioned the site as a lead generator for copy and consulting projects, but very soon, I was receiving e-mails from people who had read the articles.

The posts came from newcomers to direct marketing, from small business owners in Europe and Asia as well as the United States, and even from direct marketing professionals with agencies or consultancies of their own. Without exception, they were highly complimentary, often thanking me for putting the information on the site, frequently asking if I had a book they could buy. It quickly became clear that these articles were helping a lot of people, and maybe a book needed to be written.

The articles built up over time, and by early 1999, I started calling publishers. With great good fortune I encountered Adams Media on my second or third call. Editor Jere Calmes had heard of me and he was interested in a book on direct marketing for small business. When he told me about Adams's Streetwise series, I was hooked. What perfect positioning for the work I was doing and writing about! Streetwise, indeed.

In my early years "streetwise" meant cashing in enough deposit bottles to take the "A" train from my block in Washington Heights to the streets of Times Square or the Village and getting back unscathed. Today it means getting the most out of every dollar a client spends on a direct mail package or ad, or brochure—and making sure he or she spends no more than is absolutely necessary to achieve a positive result.

During my sixteen years with direct marketers like Esquire, Columbia House, Grolier, and Xerox, there was always a production guy down the hall on whose desk I could dump the job and wait for samples. But as a freelancer, I'm it—production guy, list consultant, lettershop liaison, and all the rest depending on a client's needs—and it all has to fit within the client's budget. Budget? That was a department at Ziff-Davis, wasn't it? The end result was I've had to become "streetwise" in the strategies I recommend and the tactics I employ on behalf of clients.

And that's what *Streetwise Direct Marketing* is all about—helping small- to mid-sized businesses work wisely within limited budgets to achieve the very best results possible. From choosing an envelope format to writing a sales letter to designing a Web site, special attention is given to strategies and tools, techniques and technologies that give a marketer the biggest bang for the buck.

For years I've watched so-called gurus promise quick riches from the kitchen table or untold sales by applying the "secrets" of mail order. It is my hope that *Streetwise Direct Marketing* will cut through the baloney and explain the interactive dynamics of direct marketing in a way that small business marketers can understand and apply to help them effectively promote their businesses and avoid costly mistakes.

If I stress some of these dynamics to the point of repetition, it's because I see them as the key to understanding and successfully deploying all of direct marketing's diverse forces. It's a capability that has become even more compelling for businesses of every type and size as increasingly interactive, customer-centric marketing paradigms from "one-to-one" strategies to the Internet rapidly displace the mass marketing techniques of the past.

Small business owners, entrepreneurs, startups, and solos will find what they need in these pages to plan and supervise a successful direct marketing program. Marketing professionals will absorb the basics and use *Streetwise* as a stepping stone to more concentrated resources in specialty areas. I've long maintained that, the more arcane statistical techniques of data mining notwithstanding, there is no such thing as "advanced" direct marketing, any more than there could be an "advanced" conversation with a customer.

In today's technology-driven marketing environment, change is constant. In order to help readers track rapidly evolving Internet strategies, the latest database marketing technologies and more, I have established a place on my Web site where readers can sign on and update the information provided here. Details are on page 303.

Thank you for buying my book. As a how-to guide to specific strategies and techniques, as a dialog on marketing, as a platform from which to explore the technology-driven environments of the 21st century, I hope you'll make *Streetwise Direct Marketing* your roadmap to response.

—George Duncan

# The Basics

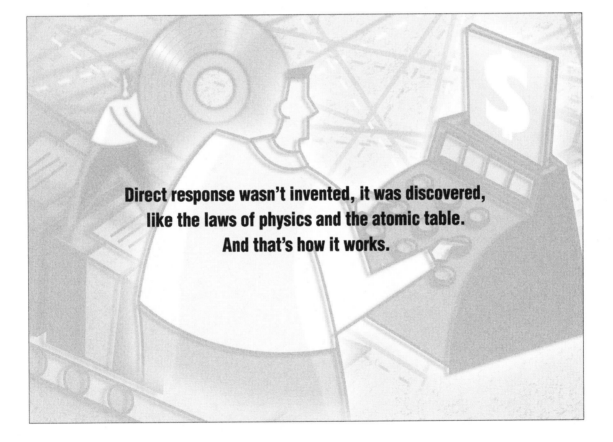

Direct response wasn't invented, it was discovered,
like the laws of physics and the atomic table.
And that's how it works.

# Chapter 1

# Introduction— Direct Mail and the Dynamics of Response

## Make Every Contact Interactive

For many years, a management consultant I know has been sending "prospects" a detailed study of New England businesses charting such metrics as sales growth, revenues, and performance estimates across a variety of functional areas including operations, marketing, sales, product development, and more. It also includes sales and profit projections for the coming year. Recently I asked him, "Why don't you send out a letter or brochure announcing the availability of the report to 'qualified' companies, and invite them to request it? That way, people interested in such information would raise their hand by requesting the report, giving you an opportunity to build a database of such prospects, call and see what interests them most, what special metrics they might want to have, and generally open up a dialog that could lead to consulting projects?" He thought that was a good idea. The point, of course, is that it turns a one-way communication into an *interactive* communication and allows prospects to identify themselves for sales follow-up. (I have put "prospects" in quotes above because that's how my consultant friend thinks of them. Actually, as we'll see later, they aren't prospects until they respond to an offer or inquire for more information.)

The last 20 years have seen dramatic growth in the use of direct response methods by an ever-widening constituency of marketers. From the book clubs, magazine publishers, and catalogers who pioneered most of today's successful direct marketing techniques to such relative newcomers as packaged-goods manufacturers and virtually the entire *Fortune* 500 . . . from the local merchant whose simple postcard announces an annual preseason sale to Dell's Internet juggernaut selling upwards of 16 million dollars worth of computers a day . . . more and more companies large and small are engaging in "targeted marketing," "database marketing," "relationship marketing," "accountable marketing," "closed loop" marketing, "one-to-one" marketing, or some similar designation.

Clearly, responsible marketers are increasingly turning to direct marketing or database marketing as a major player in the marketing mix. Indeed, given the increasing movement toward niche marketing generally, the difficulties of getting new products accepted by major retail chains—not to mention the major cut they take for their efforts—and the soaring costs with dubious results of traditional mass media, direct marketing arguably has become the hottest ticket in town!

This chapter is intended to help small- to mid-sized companies and entrepreneurs enhance their understanding of direct marketing generally, and of direct mail in particular. To help identify "direct's" unique dynamics. To understand what it is and what it isn't. To learn how it works in order to put it to work more effectively.

After more than 20 years applying direct marketing techniques to a wide variety of products and services, I believe there are some areas that still warrant clarification if small business owners and marketers are to reap the full benefits that database/accountable/relationship/targeted marketing has to offer. Here I will refer to it as direct marketing.

Entrepreneurs especially need to know the boundaries of direct marketing (and, more specifically, direct mail), including the cost of entry, realistic results projections, and how to maximize the medium to start and grow a business.

## Direct Marketing: An Interactive Process

Direct marketing is a comprehensive system of media and methods designed to elicit a response from a prospect or customer in order to develop or enhance a "client relationship."

In lead generation or "two-step" marketing, our goal is to convert a "suspect" into a "prospect" through list or individual qualification. Then we want to convert our prospect into a "customer" with an initial sale. Our customer is transformed into a "client" through repeat sales and, finally, if our customer service and follow-up methods are effective, our client becomes an "advocate"—a source of new sales to other prospects through word-of-mouth recommendation by providing testimonials, case studies, and more (See Figure 1-1).

In order generation or direct sales, many of the same qualifying dynamics apply. As we'll see in the following section, you gain nothing in direct marketing by selling one product to one user one time. The task is to create a database of customers to whom you can sell additional products at higher response rates and with greater cost-effectiveness.

The system we use to accomplish this process includes print and broadcast media, direct mail, and telemarketing, employed individually or in combination. Electronic media—including the Internet and online services like America Online and MSN—are growing factors in the media mix. The booming World Wide Web has rapidly become an ever-more-powerful medium both for direct sales and lead generation for most products and services.

In that vein, Leslie Laredo, Ziff-Davis Interactive's director of advertising development, once said, "Direct mail is the best place to learn the techniques that work best in electronic media." More recently, Seth Godin, founder of YoYodyne Entertainment and VP of direct marketing for Yahoo!, stated, "The Net . . . is the finest direct-marketing mechanism in the history of mankind. It is direct mail with free stamps." It is safe to say that the World Wide Web has become a prime direct marketing medium—another good reason to understand the interactive dynamics of direct mail and how they apply to online marketing.

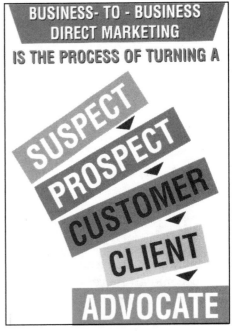

Figure 1-1

Direct mail is primarily a selling medium. It isn't advertising, and it isn't correspondence—although it borrows elements from both—it is direct marketing. Its task is to sell something or to obtain an inquiry. Right here, right now. Across time and space. A sale or invitation to an unknown person by an invisible salesman. And it is designed to receive payment or a request for information by return mail or telephone. (Fund-raising direct mail is a special case with its own unique dynamics.) Direct mail achieves this startling task by applying a variety of techniques, mostly proven over time in general terms, and tested as likely strategies in specific cases.

The most common applications of direct mail include:

- Selling products and services directly to prospects and customers (also the role of mail order or catalogs).
- Generating qualified leads for sales follow-up.
- Converting inquiries or leads into sales.
- Increasing sales to current customers (database marketing).
- Introducing new products and services, especially to specialized or vertical markets.
- Selling vertical applications of horizontal products.
- Building or promoting a dealer/distributor network.
- Selling follow-up or aftermarket products and services.
- Selling into marginal territories.

> The need for better qualified sales leads has become an increasingly critical imperative of responsible, cost-effective marketing.

As the cost of a sales call approaches the $500 mark, the need for better qualified sales leads has become an increasingly critical imperative of responsible, cost-effective marketing. In addition, the efficiencies of marketing to a database have made a compelling case for direct marketing. (Pareto's Law has been telling us for years that 80% of our business comes from 20% of our customers. In talking to my seminar attendees over the years, I have yet to find an exception.) (Fig. 1-2)

And while direct marketing may work *with* general advertising, PR, sales promotion, and other disciplines, it remains separate and distinct from all of those with its own unique strategies and techniques, and its own innate dynamics. It especially is not advertising.

## Why Direct Marketing Isn't Advertising—and Why It Matters

Most of us know—or think we know—advertising. We're raised with it. We're bombarded by it to the tune of some 600 ad impressions per day (or a few thousand, depending on whom you believe). Marketing people enjoy advertising. So does senior management. They especially like to write and design ads. It's fun. It's sexy. And it's a way of imprinting one's own personality on a product. But in so doing, many marketing people, designers, ad agency types, and others with overall marketing responsibility, untrained in direct response, tend to apply the same copy and design principles they learned in advertising to mail, space, and the other media.

A "bon mot" taped to the top of my computer screen reads, "Everybody thinks they're a copywriter." That's dangerous thinking. For in fact, about all advertising and direct marketing have in common is the English language. Here's why.

The primary functions of general advertising are to build brand awareness or to create demand for a new product category. To provide a context for a sale at a later time and place. General advertising does this through multiple impressions via a variety of media. TV, radio, newspapers, magazines, billboards, point-of-purchase, and more are orchestrated in a complex media mix to deliver $x$ millions of impressions over $y$ weeks or months. The information flow is transitive: from the advertiser to the market. The sales transaction is executed through a third party (e.g., dealer, distributor, supermarket) at a time and place chosen by the buyer, not by the seller.

The dynamics of direct marketing are exactly the opposite. First, direct marketing is structured to sell now—either immediately by phone or mail, or within an established time frame through a sales contact. (Even in lead generation, we expect the initial response to be immediate or nearly so.)

Second, in direct marketing, the information flow is *from* the prospect *to* the advertiser. It's interactive, not transitive. When we mail, we want to determine which lists—what segments of mail order buyers—will respond best to our offer. So we test lists and list segments. Then we research the responders to find out as much about them as we can, so we can duplicate them for further mailings.

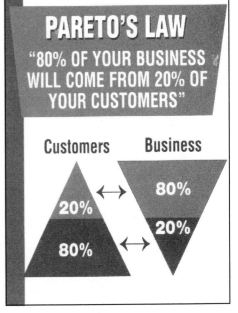

Figure 1-2

List testing is the single most significant element in any direct mail program's success. It represents roughly 40% of the success of your program. We start with mail order or direct mail buyers whenever we can, because experience shows that "response" lists—those that include the mail purchase behavior—yield significantly higher rates of response than "compiled" lists.

Lists compiled from telephone directories, membership rolls, and other such sources are lacking purchase behavior. Often, however, response lists are simply not available in sufficient quantities for effective marketing and compiled lists are the only way to go.

We want to learn what we have to offer these prospects and how best to present that offer. So we test offers (the proposition) and formats. (The offer is the second-most-important element . . . another 40%.) (Fig. 1-3)

We want to know how much our prospects are willing to pay for our product or service. So we test price.

Most important, we want to know what else we might profitably sell to these people once they become our customers, as well as where to find others just like them, so we segment them by common characteristics, model them, and attempt to replicate them from other sources.

Our ultimate purpose is to build our own personal marketplace—one that we can go back to again and again and sell follow-up, after-market, or new products at much higher rates of response than the 2%, 1%, or less we typically experience in the prospecting phase. I emphasize this fact because it is the single greatest barrier to entry into direct mail marketing for the start-up entrepreneur. Many entrepreneurs have just one product that they hope to sell by direct mail. Often the price point is below $100. It is difficult, if not impossible, to sell such a product to cold lists at sufficiently high rates of response to show a profit. Direct mail just costs too much, and "cold" lists simply do not respond much beyond 2% gross—often much less. Naturally, company identity, price point, offer, and more all impact the rate of response. But forget the dreams of 10% response. It probably won't happen for a "cold" sale. In fact, direct marketers often prospect at a loss in order to build a customer file that will later respond at rates of 10%, 15%, 25%, or more. We want to get Pareto's Law working *for* us instead of *against* us. Think of direct response as a process of obtaining marketing information, paid for (in whole or in part) by sales.

> Direct response is a process of obtaining marketing information, paid for (in whole or in part) by sales.

We do that by building a database—a comprehensive, interactive record of the customers, prospects, and even the suspects that make up our marketing universe (by itself, a customer file is not necessarily a database).

Following are several more key ways in which direct marketing differs from general advertising.

Where advertising uses many impressions and a mix of media, the typical direct marketer uses one. Either space or mail, perhaps with telemarketing follow-up. Some mega-marketers use several: space, mail, TV, telemarketing, etc. But they are the exception rather than the rule. (A recent phenomenon is the extensive use of television advertising by the dot-coms designed to drive traffic to their sites where interactive marketing can take place.) For most marketers, that ad or mailing typically must do the job alone. And whether it's a solo mailing or ad, or a three-part or five-part campaign, it has to work *now*.

Advertising builds awareness for a sale at some other time and place, under the control of the buyer, whereas direct marketing makes the sale or contact now, directly with the customer, at a time and place controlled by the seller.

Advertising is only vaguely measurable, usually in terms of "market share," which is affected by a great deal more than just the advertising. Indeed, many top advertising pros acknowledge that general advertising's effectiveness really isn't measurable at all. Direct marketing, conversely, is fully accountable. Every response is measured. Cost per order, cost per lead, and the lifetime value of a customer are common calculations in direct marketing. You know exactly what your money is doing for you . . . or not doing. And you know now, so you can take appropriate action. The story is often told of the retail magnate John Wanamaker who is alleged to have said, "I know half of all I spend on advertising is wasted. I just don't know which half!" Had he been using direct marketing, he would have known!

Advertising creates markets; direct marketing discovers them (through the testing process described earlier).

Advertising sells masses, whereas direct marketing sells niches and segments of niches. For example, a newsletter publisher approached me with a publication that provided recent court rulings in medical injury cases. It was called *The Malpractice Reporter*. In

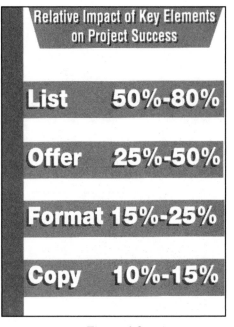

**Relative Impact of Key Elements on Project Success**

| List | 50%-80% |
| --- | --- |
| Offer | 25%-50% |
| Format | 15%-25% |
| Copy | 10%-15% |

Figure 1-3

researching his material, I suggested he segment the cases by specialty and create *The Surgeon's Malpractice Reporter, The Anesthesiologist's Malpractice Reporter, The OB/GYN Malpractice Reporter,* and several others. Eventually we tested six newsletters of which four survived and grew, each with its own vertical constituency. And when he went to sell the business several years later, he had four publications to sell instead of one.

Advertising seeks to change behavior; direct marketing seeks to repeat or model it. (If you think your current word processor is great, try ours—with our special competitive upgrade offer!)

Advertising sells products. Direct marketing sells offers. (In lead generation, for example, we may actually want to conceal the product or service, at least initially.)

Advertising deals largely in emotional imagery; direct mail deals almost exclusively in facts (specific benefits derived from enumerated features, backed by proofs, including performance comparisons, user testimonials, etc.).

Advertising design is complementary, often image-driven. Art and photography are frequently the primary communicators.

Response design must be functional and disruptive. It supports the copy as the primary communicator.

In summary:

- Advertising sells products—direct sells offers.
- Advertising creates markets—direct discovers them.
- Advertising changes behavior—direct models it.
- Advertising is heavily emotional—direct is heavily factual.
- Advertising copy tends to be short—direct copy tends to be long.
- Advertising design is complementary and image-driven—direct design is disruptive and functional.
- Advertising creates sales—direct creates customers.

There are always exceptions to these parameters, of course, but basically, those are the differences. Keep them in mind when some general ad agency tells you—as they will—that they "do direct."

> Advertising sells products. Direct marketing sells offers.

Ask questions—armed with a thorough understanding of the essential dynamics that make direct marketing work. Above all, ask to see some of the "direct" they've done, and demand the results. Also be sure to ask to see the pieces they tested against that mailing. If they can satisfy you on that score, great.

The trend in recent years to "integrate" general advertising and direct marketing techniques is one that any direct marketer must examine closely in light of the conflicting functions outlined earlier. Personally, I always considered it an attempt by the general ad community to co-opt the direct marketing function and slip it in under the door so they wouldn't lose clients to their direct marketing agency competitors. Most of the larger agencies solved the problem simply by buying up the direct agencies, lock, stock, and indicia.

If advertising is an art, direct mail is a science. Clearly, the functions of advertising and direct marketing could not be more different. In fact, you can think of a direct mail campaign as a scientific experiment. We want to document all the variables, test them, and turn them into constants so we can "replicate" the experiment with the same or better results again and again, to larger and larger lists.

If I seem to belabor these points, it's because as direct marketing has grown as a medium and become more and more commonplace, many business owners and others tend to take it for granted. Write a cover letter, "buy" a list, mail it. Fold a product sheet, put it in an envelope, mail it. Do a postcard. It's cheap, no envelope. Response of .005%? Oh, well, we tried direct mail. It didn't work. Offer? What do you mean, "offer?"

That's an all-too-typical scenario, especially with marketers who can't afford big budget agencies and direct marketing shops, and have to do it themselves. Unfortunately, I know from my own clients that finding reliable freelancers and consultants isn't all that easy either. Between the arrogant blowhards and talented youngsters who mean well, but just haven't lived long enough yet to understand the realities of the marketplace, there aren't that many capable independents.

I know from talking and working with dozens of designers over the years that many of them have no desire to do what they think of as "junk" mail. Indeed, they will actively resist attempts to get them to use response design techniques. They prefer to bend direct marketing

> If advertising is an art, direct mail is a science.

to fit their preconceived, often egotistic notions of what constitutes "creative" copy and design rather than learn and apply the proven, often more prosaic techniques of direct response.

A designer I worked with once had a series of squiggly lines running right through the text of a media kit. Not near it, or around it, but *through* it! He called it a "design element." When I helped the client to see the plain stupidity of such an approach, they had the lines removed and the job reprinted. As the client, you may pay the price of this creative arrogance if you aren't sufficiently well grounded in direct marketing principles to know the difference and/or if you aren't sufficiently motivated to demand response design in your response promotions.

Some folks—client and agency alike—have a personal antipathy for direct mail. They may dislike the so-called "bells and whistles"—the copy teasers, the tokens, the simulations, the banners, and other visual devices that direct mail employs so effectively.

Some years back a magazine owner for whom I was recommending a token in a 6" × 9" subscription package told me, "I'd rather take 1% or 2% lower response than use one of those things!"

That may have been very erudite on his part, but it isn't responsible marketing.

To be sure, in corporate or business-to-business marketing we need to tread lightly, and monitor how aggressively we employ these tools. However, many of these techniques can frequently be used as effectively in business-to-business marketing as they are every day in consumer direct mail.

Furthermore, as professionals, we are charged with doing our job, regardless of personal prejudices. Our responsibility is to do what works for our company, our product, and our customer, not our own egos.

In the coming chapters, we'll explore each of these dynamics and show the many ways they are played out through copy and design, through the structuring of offers, the use of the database, interactive Web techniques, and more so you can effectively conduct your own direct marketing program, or supervise and evaluate the work of your agency or consultant.

> As professionals, we are charged with doing our job, regardless of personal prejudices.

For more information on this topic, visit our Web site at www.businesstown.com

# The Offer—
# Key to Response

> The stimulus isn't the product—it's the offer!

**M**ost marketers begin with the seemingly logical assumption that they are selling a product (or service) and that's what they have to describe in order to sell. Well, yes. And no.

Remember that direct mail is an interactive medium. In psychological terms, it is a stimulus/response transaction. We have to get a response—not just agreement. You could describe your product in glowing terms in a 10-page letter, illustrate it up one side and down the other in an award-winning brochure, and if all you get is "Gee, that's a great idea. When's my next meeting?" your effort has failed. In order to get our prospect to act, we must provide a mechanism for action. A stimulus. And the stimulus isn't the product—it's the offer!

When some folks think of the offer, they assume it means price. The offer includes the price, but it is much more than that. The offer consists of everything that impacts the value or perceived value of the product or service and everything that impacts the process of getting it from the seller to the buyer.

It's the "deal." The quid pro quo. I'll give you a free trial, a demo, a free issue, a free report, an on-site needs assessment, a video, a calculator, a sweepstakes prize (if you win), a special, limited-time price—if you'll complete the enclosed order form or tuck the token in the slot and mail it today in the postpaid envelope provided, or call the toll-free number. Charge it to your credit card, bill it to your company, enclose your check with complete assurance that you'll get every nickel back if you're not satisfied. No risk, no obligation, of course.

Some popular consumer offers include:

- Free trial (15 days, 30 days, etc.)
- Buy one, get one free (often better than 50% off, or 2-for-1)
- Sweepstakes prize
- Negative option (customer must say "no" to discontinue)
- Volume discount
- Payable monthly
- Buy two, get a third item free
- Free gift or premium (a) just for ordering, (b) upon payment

Premiums can make or break a promotion. They should be extensively tested, but in my experience, they rarely are. A premium should be tangible. An item designed for instant gratification, together with the process by which the prospect can receive it now . . . or promptly upon payment for his order.

In lead generation (mostly business-to-business [BTB]), information related to the product (e.g., a special report, a series of case studies, a free cost-benefit analysis, an industry study or survey, a white paper, etc.) is often a good premium. We'll take a closer look at BTB offers in the section on lead generation.

When selling directly (mostly consumer), a special gift such as a watch or tote bag, or the possibility of a big sweepstakes payout, can add involvement and boost response.

In both cases, a stated time limit will often improve response, as will a yes/no option on the order form. (In consumer marketing a yes/no/maybe option has frequently proved most effective. "Maybe" is essentially the same as "Yes," but projects a greater degree of choice.)

Taken together, it is the offer that you stick in the window. It is the offer that you "sell" to your prospect as a quick and easy, guaranteed way to explore for himself the various claims you've made for the product. Or, in lead generation, it is used as a way of indicating interest in a particular product or service category.

This assumes, however, that you've done your homework on your lists and that you're offering your prospect something he or she wants.

True "junk mail" is an offer sent to the wrong person.

Inviting the prospect to send for "more information," which we often see in business-to-business ads, is not an offer. At best, it's a weak offer because it's too open-ended and it only promises another sales pitch. There's nothing tangible for the prospect to want—nothing for him to visualize, like a special report with a descriptive title that promises some specific type of related information.

An offer is a form of neutral turf. It's a place where the prospect and the marketer (buyer and seller) can meet without obligation and where the prospect feels he can obtain some sort of value, usually in the form of information. Information that's altruistic in nature. Facts, tips, data that will be useful independent of the product.

> True "junk mail" is an offer sent to the wrong person.

## Make Me an Offer—but Guarantee It!

Whatever your offer, a guarantee is essential. Contrary to what some entrepreneurs think, offering a guarantee in no way diminishes or denigrates your product. The guarantee has nothing to do with the product. Rather, it speaks of you and your company and the honest, fair, and open manner in which you do business. It's designed to build trust and mitigate risk.

Further, most direct marketers have found that they rarely get ripped off by guarantees. Most people are honest, and most businesspeople especially are just too busy, too distracted, or too professional to spend time ripping off a mailer. Sure, it happens, but it's not a major consideration.

In stating your guarantee, "Money back if not satisfied" is unnecessarily negative. "Try it for 30 days without risk or obligation" is the same thing put more positively. And longer guarantees—60 days, 90 days, or life-of-the-product—usually pull better than 15 or 30 days. The recipient often becomes acclimated to the product during the longer trial period, and you can get good old human inertia working for you, instead of against you.

## The Quantity/Quality Ratio

One dynamic you'll want to consider in framing your offer is the universal truth that you can't have it both ways. The higher the quantity (volume) of response, the lower the quality (interest level) of the respondents.

There are "hard" offers and "soft" offers, and several levels in between. The harder the offer, the more highly qualified your prospects will be, but there will be fewer of them. Vice versa with a soft offer.

Give away a free introductory issue of a newsletter, for example, with a "bill me later" option (i.e., soft ), and those subscribers will renew at lower rates than those who simply entered a paid subscription in response to a straight, no-risk offer. Magazine subscribers who are given free premiums or who buy into mega-sweepstakes will be less likely, on average, to renew their subscriptions without the same or similar inducements. A free demo or video will attract more "tire kickers" than a paid one, even if the prize is just a few dollars. But it should attract more prospects in the aggregate. In general, the more difficult you make it for your prospect to buy—the more hoops you make her jump through—the more highly qualified she will be. That should translate into higher response rates downstream.

Under FTC rules, you can't say that something is "free" if the prospect has to send payment to obtain it—or without some clear statement of the deal in close proximity to the word "free." For example, "Yours FREE with offer inside" implies that the prospect has to do something in order to get the "free" gift.

Thus a "free trial" must include a "bill me" option (no payment up front). A "no-risk" or "risk-free" trial, however, can require payment with a refund option clearly stated.

A free trial (i.e., no payment required up front) may prompt more returns than with cash on the barrel head, but you should realize sufficiently higher gross sales to justify the offer. Net sales will depend on a variety of factors including list quality, price, product positioning, and more. Testing is essential to determine the most profitable option. (In positioning your product, never make a promise that it can't keep. You'll end up paying for it on the back end, both in immediate returns and in lost additional business.)

A common offer mistake, in my opinion, is to offer a reduced rate on a second, usually related product, as an inducement to purchase the primary product. For one thing, it dilutes the sell. Now the prospect has to weigh the merits of two products, not one. However, the second product almost never receives the sales push that the primary product gets. The relationship may be clear to you, but it's rarely that clear to the prospect. To her, you're simply trying to sell two products instead of one. This kind of double offer often provides the prospect with an excuse to put off the purchase decision until "later," a.k.a., never.

If experience shows that you are likely to convert a high percentage of respondents into customers, then open wide the offer door with "FREE" product trials, free gifts, etc.

In most cases—and this applies to direct selling as well as to lead generation—you want buyers who are well qualified, involved,

> In general, the more difficult you make it for your prospect to buy—the more hoops you make her jump through—the more highly qualified she will be.

active. Customers who will purchase additional products and services from you when added to your marketing database. So be sure to crank those considerations into your offers.

## The "Assent Without Action" Trap

Another important role of the offer is to give the prospect something tangible to act upon. As we touched on earlier, general advertising's primary goal is to foster "awareness" and "acceptance" of the product advertised. This is accomplished through a mix of media producing many millions of impressions over a period of time, so that when you or I go to a supermarket, or a drug store, or a car dealer, we will be favorably predisposed toward the product. The actual purchase involves many more elements, including timely distribution, in-store display, local sales promotion tie-ins, aggressive pricing strategies, and more.

In direct marketing, that "favorable disposition toward the product" can kill us. Because we can create a direct mail or direct response advertising appeal that gets us to that point, that succeeds in getting the prospect's agreement with our proposition, and . . . nothing. No response. "Gee, that's really great," our prospect thinks to himself as he puts our piece aside and gets on with his day. Meanwhile, our mailing is dead in the water. Assent without action strikes again.

However, by making a concrete offer, we give the prospect something tangible to respond to, rather than merely creating an image in his or her own head, however favorable. We answer the question, "So what am I supposed to do about it?"

The bottom line in direct marketing is that we need a response (an order, an inquiry, a donation), and we need it *now*! Assent is not enough. And that dynamic is what makes direct response the challenging form of marketing that it is. It's why direct marketing is different from general advertising, and it's why direct marketers are different from general ad people. It's why we do most of what we do in direct mail, from brown kraft envelopes to tokens . . . simulated checks to credit cards . . . little red dots you punch out to signify renewal of a

> The bottom line in direct marketing is that we need a response (an order, an inquiry, a donation), and we need it *now*! Assent is not enough. And that dynamic is what makes direct response the challenging form of marketing that it is.

subscription . . . blow-in cards that drop out of your magazine onto the floor . . . computer personalization . . . and all the other bells and whistles that characterize direct marketing today and have done so for more than 50 years.

No one "invented" the many response techniques we use in direct marketing. Rather, over the years, savvy direct marketers discovered them—occasionally through trial and error, but more often through rigorous testing, modeling, and retesting. If advertising is an art, direct marketing is a science in which key components are tested, evaluated, and run again at higher, more profitable rates of response.

I like to compare general advertising design versus direct marketing design to a Maserati versus a lawn mower. I say to the Maserati designer, "I love the aerodynamic muffler, Gino, but does it cut grass?" The lawn mower may not make it into the Museum of Modern Art collection, but it cuts grass. Direct marketing has to cut the grass.

## "Times Change, People Don't."

About once a year, some young direct marketing type pens an article in one of the trade magazines that is highly critical of the "traditional" methods that have driven the industry since its inception. One just appeared as I was writing this. Chafing under the disciplines described here, these iconoclasts presume to lead us all to a brighter world of increased response through more "contemporary" approaches. They are especially amusing now, as we move into electronic marketing methods on the Internet with Web and e-mail, and find the same proven techniques working once again at the speed of light.

For more information on this topic, visit our Web site at www.businesstown.com

# Chapter 3

# Interactive Design

**W**hat do we mean by "interactive" design and copy? What's a copywriter doing preaching about design anyway? To answer the second question first, a copywriter will see that the design supports the marketing message without upstaging or disrupting it. He or she will put your best foot forward and make sure no self-serving designer steps on it.

The problem is that most of our information comes through our eyes. Visual images are extremely powerful and difficult to overcome with copy. If the design component does not closely support the marketing message, but rather leads the reader in a tangential direction, that's the way the reader will go—and nothing the copy can say will prevent it. The result is a mixed—or missed—communication, and a loss of response.

As to the first question, response-driven copy and design is interactive. At times even proactive. Why? Because if you need a response, agreement with your message (the goal of general advertising) isn't enough! You must prompt an action . . . now! An order. An inquiry. A donation. Whatever. That, in turn, requires the prospect's involvement, which we create by (1) getting the prospect's Attention, (2) arousing his or her Interest, (3) stimulating Desire, and, finally, (4) directing him or her to Action. The time-honored mnemonic is known in direct marketing as "AIDA."

## Disruption and Interaction

Imagine walking into an art gallery. As you enter the room, there are four pictures immediately visible. Each is the same approximate size, shape, etc. Which would draw your attention? Hard to say, isn't it?

Now in your mind's eye, turn one of those pictures slightly askew. Now which one would you notice first? Of course. The crooked one. That's the principle of direct mail design. It's the unexpected that gets attention.

In order to prompt a response, design must be disruptive. It must be proactive. It must reach out to the reader and involve him or her. Here again we want to avoid the, "Gee, that's nice . . . When's my next meeting?" syndrome. Predictable straight lines and white

> If you need a response, agreement with your message isn't enough!

space don't do that. As former *Target Marketing* editor Denny Hatch once put it, "Neatness rejects involvement." He also compared direct marketing design with Piet Mondrian's painting, "Broadway Boogie Woogie," with its network of colored rectangles. It's an apt comparison, except it omits the diagonal. Mondrian's painting is all vertical and horizontal lines, albeit engagingly juxtaposed. The diagonal is even more intrusive. Add one diagonal line to that painting, and that's exactly where the reader's eye would land.

Direct mail design must cut through the clutter of all the other mail your prospect received that day (more than 200 pieces a week for some executives). And when it does, it must then interrupt that incessant conversation she has going on in her head—just as you and I and everyone else has. It must override daily concerns about the morning meeting . . . the unanswered e-mails, the phone messages waiting on the desk . . . and that guy at the party last night. And we must make all that happen in the next five seconds! Following are some proven tools and techniques, used and used again by savvy direct marketers.

Personalized envelopes get attention, for all the reasons that our own name gets our attention. How much more attention they get than addressing straight titles depends on the market, the product, and other factors. Some positions turn over so rapidly that titles can be more reliable than individual names.

A copy teaser—if it's the right teaser, and if the recipient is a valid prospect—will help target the prospect and offer her an immediate reason to open the envelope. Further, it gives the prospect something to agree to—right up front. So even before she's seen your proposition, you have her saying "yes" at least to your teaser statement. That's a valuable edge. I often try to include both a user benefit and a reference to the offer on the envelope. As mentioned previously, however—and it bears repeating—teaser-laden envelopes, Cheshire labels, and other indications of advertising mail may be self-defeating in certain environments. (Teasers are discussed in detail in Chapter 9.)

Size and shape can play a role. These days, 9" × 12" envelopes seem to be working for many marketers, although these are considerably more expensive than No. 10s. Size is often associated with

> A copy teaser will help target the prospect and offer her an immediate reason to open the envelope.

importance. Even mailers who regularly use No. 10s are testing larger No. 12s and No. 13s. Poly envelopes appeal to the tactile and visual senses, providing a tempting, "peek-a-boo" hint of the contents, as do multiple windows in paper envelopes with stickers, tokens, and illustrations showing through.

Brown or gray kraft stock signifies monetary or informational value, while copy written on a slant raises the reader's anxiety level . . . to be resolved by the copy inside. Phrases highlighted by bullets (e.g., benefits, features), get read before body text, and are retained longer.

A headline "group"–a headline with a subhead that immediately expands upon the headline statement, followed by two or three short, bulleted extensions–gives the reader more information and greater involvement in roughly the same amount of space than a headline alone, no matter how well written it may be.

Simulated checks don't fool anyone–but they project a value image nonetheless, as do stamps. In recent years, AT&T and other major telcos have been using checks–real ones–in their attempt to get people to switch their long-distance provider.

Tokens help focus the prospect's attention and provide a stand-alone response mechanism. It's like handing the prospect a pen after he or she has read the contract. They also give the prospect something concrete to do–an action to take to signify assent. Copy snipes and bursts, on the other hand, introduce unexpected visuals into your design to seize and hold attention and promote involvement.

Let me repeat: Don't dismiss these tools and techniques just because you personally may consider them beneath you or your audience. While we want to introduce these techniques carefully in business-to-business applications, consider what you're trying to achieve in the face of all that inertia, inattention, distraction etc., and test these proven stimulus/response mechanisms. Then let the market tell you what works and what doesn't. Business publications like *Fortune, Inc., Business Week,* and others, have historically used all the techniques above to so-called "busy" executives with great success.

That said, we also need to be alert to the changing moods of prospects and the public in general and monitor reactions to what they perceive as "junk." The business publications referred to earlier, for example, switched to simple Monarch and No. 10 outer envelopes in 1998 and 1999 with a simple, official-looking order form offering a "professional courtesy" rate. No letter, in most cases.

A direct mail package doesn't pull 2% because 98% of the recipients said "no" to your offer. As Mary Kay Ash has pointed out, only about 35% of any population is open to new ideas at a given point in time. And then there are all the people who, for one reason or another, never saw your package to begin with.

## Just Your Type

Typography is a very creative art. That's one reason there are so many typefaces available, with more being created as you read this. But leave those faces to the posters and display ads and annual reports and packaging and sales promotion pieces, where they belong. For response design, stick with the tried and true for maximum readership and retention.

## Serif Typefaces for Text

The purpose of the serif, or the little knob on the ascenders and descenders of each letter, is to create a line across the page for the eye to follow like a track. It allows the eye to relax as it moves across the page, since it doesn't have to work so hard to keep its place in the text.

Ease of reading translates into more thorough reading of the material, with higher retention of the content. It's a law of the universe, not my opinion, that any energy expended to understand copy will leave the reader with less energy for retention.

Sans-serif faces (those with no serifs) can be used in headlines for some variety, so long as the headline is short and the typesize is large enough so the eye doesn't have to work to capture it. (I have an 85-page "Handbook of Direct Response Production" in my library, published by a major paper manufacturer no less, with all the text set in a sans-serif typeface, and captions for the illustrations screened down to about a 50% gray against a gray-tinted background. Very cool. And very unreadable.)

**Stamps Signify Value**

Several years ago, I tested stamps in an insurance package to a very conservative military market. It outpulled the control at the time, and, as a policyholder, I received the same mailing myself several years later, so I know it was successful.

> Just because there are a million typestyles available on a CD-ROM doesn't mean you have to use them.

The two most reliable and widely used typestyles are Times Roman (serif) for text and Helvetica (sans-serif) for heads. Other text faces include Century Schoolbook, Garamond, Caslon, Goudy, and Palatino. Display or headline faces include Antique Olive, Avant Garde, Futura, and Univers. You can find many variations on those, but don't stray too far from the basics. In fact, in studies conducted by IBM when they were developing their famous electric typewriter, Courier proved to be the easiest to read and has the highest retention levels. It became better known as IBM Executive.

Just because there are a million typestyles available on a CD-ROM doesn't mean you have to use them. Above all, type should never call attention to itself. It should be "transparent" to the reader. Reverse type (white type dropped out against a black or dark background) is especially hard on the eyes and uses up a lot of the reader's energy just to comprehend what's been written. It also, not surprisingly since it is the opposite of a positive, creates a negative image. Don't do it—unless you deliberately want to create a negative emotion with the copy.

Do not mix more than two typefaces or families on a page or panel, or possibly even for an entire direct mail package. Use bolds, lights, mediums, Roman, and extended styles of the basic typeface for variety. Use italics sparingly, for emphasis. Do NOT set entire copy blocks in italics, for the same comprehension problems reasons that apply to reverses.

Set body copy in 10- to 12-point type, never less than nine points. And if your market is "mature," consider setting body copy larger than 12 points. Headline copy should be several points larger, depending on length.

For promotion letters, stick to Courier, 10 to 12 pitch, as un-creative as that may seem (I hate it myself!). Again, don't be afraid to go larger for older audiences. You're after readability, not design awards.

## What Color Is Authority?

Not surprisingly, color plays a role as well. Warm colors are perceived "warmly" (i.e, inviting and friendly). Not surprisingly, cool colors are perceived "cooley" (i.e., distant and authoritarian). Let's say you happen to love the color teal (lots of people seem to these days). If you use it on your stationery and business card (and lots of people seem to these days), it will project an attitude of distance and aloofness . . . whether you like it or not! But hey, you may want to do exactly that if you're a business-to-business consultant, for example. You want to be the expert, bestowing wisdom to the unwashed from on high. That's how you support that hefty fee at the end of the day.

In most consumer businesses, you want to be warm and inviting. Friendly and trusting. So use reds and oranges with black and maybe another warmish color just for accent. Yellow is too hard to work with; it's almost invisible in text. Remember "Roy G. Biv" from grade school? Stands for the basic spectrum: red, orange, yellow, green, blue, indigo, violet. Warm to cool. More significant, it goes from the most active part of the spectrum to the least active. That means red gets people's attention, violet doesn't.

In an ongoing series of tests, a major envelope manufacturer consistently shows that, in head-to-head tests, colored envelopes out-pulled plain white envelopes by a significant margin. Why? Because color is more emotional than colorless white.

> Red gets people's attention, violet doesn't.

## Ted's Ten

Among the few designers I've met who understand the unique dynamics of response design and communication design in general is "the man from Toronto," Ted Kikoler (416-444-6631). Following are "Ted's Ten"—admonitions to writers, designers, and others for "Graphics That Sell."

1. Get the product into the reader's hands. This does not mean give him a sample, but visually get the product closer to him. People need to take a car for a test drive, try on a dress, or walk through a house before purchasing it. The

closer they can get to the product, the closer they get to wanting it. Do this by:

- Making photos and illustrations as large as possible. Crop them to show the essence. Cut away all unnecessary material. Leave the part of the photo that still tells the whole story. The reader will automatically fill in the missing part of the product in his mind. This technique saves valuable space and can make unexciting photos appear more dynamic.
- Involve the reader in the picture. Have life-size hands coming in from the side of the page that could be his.
- Show the product in actual use if possible.

2. Make the reader's eyes go where you want them to. His mind will follow.

Here are some things that work:
The eye normally goes from
- Dark areas to light areas
- Large objects to small ones
- Bright areas to drab areas

The eye zeroes in on things that are out of place, color, size, shape, or position (as with our art gallery exercise earlier).

Have photos and illustrations face the copy or be in the direction you want the reader to go. Every photo has direction.

The further along you get in the sales pitch, the smaller the type size can be. The more interested the reader gets, the easier it is to keep him with you. Therefore, the smaller the type size can get. Have your largest type at the beginning for the headlines and lead-in paragraphs.

Captions and call-outs get high readership. In fact, it's best never to run a photo without a caption.

If everything in a direct mail package looks alike, the reader can make the mistake that he's already seen one of your messages. Make each side of a two-sided piece look different.

3. Handwritten messages get noticed. It's an effective way of highlighting special thoughts or teasing a reader into a long letter. But don't overuse it.

> Captions and call-outs get high readership. In fact, it's best never to run a photo without a caption.

4. Make things move. Don't let anything be static. This can be dangerous, though. Too much movement on the page or in the wrong direction can hurt readability.

5. Break up large areas into smaller visual ones. These smaller chunks are easier to digest and add noticeability. Large, massive blocks of copy look like a lot of work to the reader. Make it easy for him.

6. Make different sections look different. The reader gets bored easily and if he sees something with the same style throughout, it will look like a lot of reading, which means work.

7. Talk the reader's language. Use colors, layouts, and overall appearances that the reader can relate to.

8. Talk the product's language. Masculine products have to look masculine, female products have to look feminine, etc.

9. Warm colors get a warm response, and cold colors get a cold response. Use bright, warm colors such as red on order cards.

10. Keep things simple. Make the eye move easily from one block of information to another. Line up as many things as possible. This reduces eyestrain and distraction.

> Talk the reader's language. Use colors, layouts, and overall appearances that the reader can relate to.

Those are the basics of good, response-driven design, from a copywriter and from a designer. There are many other design considerations involved in the creation of a direct mail package and its various components, including format, paper stock, action and involvement devices, and more. But if you understand what we've said here, they will make much more sense to you as you continue to explore the dynamics of direct response.

For more information on this topic, visit our Web site at www.businesstown.com

# The Nuts and Bolts

Putting all the pieces together—*before* you mail!

# Chapter 4

# What Does It Cost to Do a Mailing?

One of the most frequently asked questions I get in regard to direct marketing is, "What does it cost to do a mailing?" So let's take a look at the costs involved and other considerations, such as testing, that affect costs.

Recently, a young man whose smarts in the area of developing and marketing shareware I greatly respect and admire, maintained that one could do a direct mail test for about $10,000. I took issue, making a few of the points I'll get to in the following section. He said, "But what if $10,000 is all someone has to fund a mailing?" I suggested that person take his ten Gs, spend a week in Vegas, and see if he can quintuple it at the tables. If not, he'll at least have had a week in Vegas, and he won't have blown his $10,000 on a likely bomb of a mailing. After all, what would you tell someone who wanted to enter the Grand Prix de Monaco if all he could afford to drive was a VW Beetle? The point is that there are certain minimum thresholds in direct mail that must be reached or all that will happen is you'll join the ranks of those who say, "We tried direct mail once. It didn't work."

The most you can mail for $10,000 today is about 15,000 pieces, assuming you do the creative work yourself at no cost, and your list is carrier-route certified for maximum discount. That's for a simple direct mail package: outer envelope, letter, two-color brochure, order card, and business reply envelope (BRE).

So let's say you want to mail the 20,000 pieces. That means you'll be limited to mailing, at best, four lists, because you need to test at least 5,000 names per list for any kind of statistical assurance. If your anticipated return is around 1%–a safe bet for budgeting purposes most of the time—you really should test 10,000 names per list, which means you can test two lists.

OK, you have this exciting new widget and $10,000, and you're determined to test this great list someone sold you (rented for a one-time use, that is), and maybe one other. You prepare your package and mail it in expectation of the infamous 2% response. But when you count the order cards, you only have 1%. Now you've spent $10,000, and what have you learned? That your widget is a winner? No. That it's a dog? No. All you know for sure is that those lists didn't work. Costly answer.

> There are certain minimum thresholds in direct mail that must be reached.

# WHAT DOES IT COST TO DO A MAILING?

Of all the considerations that go into a mailing, list testing is far and away the most critical. If you can't find your market, it doesn't matter what your widget is. And the only way to find your market is to test lists. The more lists you test—at a minimum of 5,000 names each—the better. With each additional list you test, you're buying yourself valuable insurance, especially since only about 30% of the lists you test are likely to prove out. Now you see the odds you're playing with a single list mailing. You're better off in Vegas.

An exception could be made if you had a list that was so on-target you could accurately say to yourself, "If I can't sell my widget to this list, I can't sell it anywhere." But even then, you'd also have to look at the offer, the format, the timing, and more to be sure.

Recently I did a personalized, web press package for a local bed and breakfast. We mailed 10,000 names for $6000 and pulled a 3% response. The list was a geographic selection (based on the owner's registrations) of *Country Inns* magazine subscribers. These are upscale travelers with a clear preference for inns and B&Bs. At these prices, the package had its limitations, however. It was printed in one color, for example (black on a tan stock). But because the package projected the warmth and friendliness of the inn, and because the list was dead-on for a historic B&B, it worked, and the client started building a mailing list at better response rates than they (or I) expected.

A web press package is one that's printed on a single, continuous roll of paper, then cut and folded into a direct mail package. It offers the opportunity for personalization, but with the budget I had to work with in this case, I couldn't do color, so I chose a colored stock with black ink. As we'll see in the following section, a standard package costs considerably more.

> If you can't find your market, it doesn't matter what your widget is.

| COMPONENT | 5K | 10K | 20K | 50K |
|---|---|---|---|---|
| Outer env., #10, 2C* (24# white wove) | $610 | $1,029 | $1,558 | $3,511 |
| Letter, 8½" × 11", 2C/1C (24# white wove) | 489 | 610 | 875 | 1,465 |
| Brochure, 8½" × 11", 2/2 (80# cover) | 866 | 1,244 | 2,045 | 4,336 |
| Order card, 2C (4" × 9", 7pt.) | 441 | 510 | 665 | 1,121 |
| BRE, 1C (#9, 20# white wove) | 228 | 386 | 679 | 1,540 |
| Printing, total | $2,634 | $3,779 | $5,822 | $11,973 |
| Lists** (90/M) | 450 | 900 | 1,800 | 4,500 |

| LETTERSHOP | 5K | 10K | 20K | 50K |
|---|---|---|---|---|
| Inkjet address envelope (1.60/M) | 8 | 16 | 32 | 80 |
| Inserting, bagging, mailing (1.70/M) | 8.50 | 17 | 34 | 85 |
| Postage, @ $.33 | $1,650 | 3,300 | 6,600 | 16,500 |
| Subtotals, lists & mailing | $2,116 | 4,233 | 8,466 | 21,165 |
| Total Costs*** | $4,750 | 8,012 | 14,288 | 33,138 |

* 2C = two color. 2/1 = two colors one side, one color the other.
** Lists vary from $50/M (compiled) to $120/M (response).
Special selects (Title, Geo select, etc.) can add $5/M to $15/M.
If your list needs to be "merge-purged" or de-duped, or otherwise enhanced with other data, the service bureau or data processing costs can vary from $10/M for large lists to $25/M for smaller volumes.
Postal qualification is critical to costs. These lists are assumed nonqualified. A carrier-route qualified list can mail for as little as 15.6¢ each.
***This is your incremental cost. Creative is a fixed, one-time cost. Assuming simple graphics, copy and design for this package should be approximately $5,000.

## A Direct Mail Cost Model

Following is an estimate matrix for a "bare bones" direct mail package at four quantity levels. This is based on an actual printer's quote.

As you can see, the best we could do for $10,000 with our "bare bones" example is 8,000 pieces in the mail. Even assuming you take some chances on statistical reliability and mail fewer than 5,000 names per list, the best you'll do here is test three lists. Actually, if you anticipate a 1% response, which is wise, you'd be better advised to mail 10,000 names per list to be sure you have a valid result.

You're unlikely to get the same numbers from any two printers for the same mailing. It's critical to shop around. Use only printers with deep experience in volume mailing. Most so-called "job shops" can't do this kind of work efficiently. Also, the cost of paper—which sometimes skyrockets for periods of time—will heavily impact prices.

If you're inexperienced in pricing jobs, find a direct mail package (you should be keeping a direct mail "swipe file") that closely resembles what you plan to mail and take it to two or three printers so they can question you on paper stock, colors, bleeds, photos, etc. The person who designs your package should also be able to give you a set of specs to take to printers.

You can save time and money by using a printer/mailer—someone with both capabilities under one roof. But always get and check references.

### Prototype Package for List Approval

Another point to consider is that the list owners whose lists you rent will want a "sample package" to look at before they approve your rental request. Frequently, rough layout and copy may do the trick, but you will need to have your package written and mostly designed before you can submit list rental requests.

### How Long Does It Take?

Timing considerations include two weeks for the printer, two weeks for the mailer, and a month for the copy/design/list/approval process. Custom envelopes can take six to eight weeks to deliver. Some printers can deliver quicker, but for raw planning, allow time.

### How Not To Save Money

I saw a would-be newsletter publisher ruin a job trying to save money by going to a small local printer who gave him a low quote. He printed on available stock, a coated paper that imparted a glossy or "slick" image to what was supposed to be a heavily information-based product. He printed and folded the 8" × 11" order forms so they were all interwoven like Kleenex in a box. The letter-shop had to spend hours pulling them apart, and then the coated stock kept sliding off the inserting machines. YIKES!

## Make a Budget

Here's a simple budget format that will help you determine whether you're ready to do a test mailing.

| Function | Cost/M | Total Cost |
|---|---|---|
| 1. Copy & Creative* | N/A | $_____ |
| 2. Total Package Costs | $_____ | $_____ |
| 3. Total Cost | $_____ | $_____ |
| 4. Cost of Product | $_____ | $_____ |
| 5. Fulfillment (Shipping, Postage) | $_____ | $_____ |
| 6. Total Fulfillment, Product Cost per order (Line 3 + line 4) | $_____ | $_____ |
| 7. Number of orders received (Estimate several rates of response) | | $_____ |
| 8. Total Cost for Orders Received (Line 5 × line 6) | | $_____ |
| 9. Allocated Overhead (Salaries, phone, rent, etc.) | | $_____ |
| 10. Guesstimate Cost of Refunds/Returns | | $_____ |
| 11. Total Uncollectibles × Selling Price | | $_____ |
| 12. Mailing Grand Total (Add lines 3, 8, 9, 10, 11) | | $_____ |
| 13. Number of Orders/Inquiries | | $_____ |
| 14. Per-Order/Per-Inquiry Costs (Line 12 divided by line 7 or 13) | | $_____ |
| 15. Cash Received Per Order | | $_____ |
| 16. Total Cash Received (Line 7 × line 15) | | $_____ |
| 17. Net Profit (Subtract line 12 from line 16) | | $_____ |

* Remember that creative is a one-time cost.

### "Gathering Information, Paid for by Sales"

That's my definition of direct marketing. If you make money on each sale, great! But even if you don't—and many marketers go into a mailing knowing they won't show a profit—remember that you're looking for information that you'll capitalize on later.

Your mailing and your tests should be structured so that when all the numbers are in, you'll know which lists worked (and maybe what segments of individuals on each of those lists) . . . what price worked . . . what premium . . . etc.

You can't test all those variables in a single mailing, so test lists and offer first. That's where you'll get the biggest bang for your buck. Until those two factors are working for you, you really don't have a program. Premiums, copy appeals, format, color of the stamp (just kidding), etc., can all be tested later.

> You're looking for information that you'll capitalize on later.

## What Will You Do For an Encore?

Whether you make a profit on that first mailing or not, remember that you are buying names—at a profit maybe, or at some cost tempered by sales. That customer list is your store. It's your database. It's your treasure chest. You make it grow by remailing your best list/offer panels and testing new lists incrementally in each successive mailing.

Even if you make a profit, there's not a lot of money to be made in selling one thing one time (granting the usual exceptions). Especially not at typical "cold" list response rates of 2%, 1%, and lower. You want to grow that customer list and market to it at significantly more profitable response rates of 5%, 10%, and more (and at lower costs). But what will you market?

I often hear from folks who want to do a mailing, but have only one product to sell. If that's your case, you might be better off on the Internet, where you can reach large numbers of people for very little cost per contact. Even there, if you can't upsell more costly versions of your product to customers, or cross-sell upgrades, related products, training, support, or whatever . . . think it through carefully.

---

**For more information on this topic, visit our Web site at www.businesstown.com**

# Chapter 5

# What Kind of Results Can I Expect?

## List Accuracy Matters

The very first element your direct marketing promotion depends on is the list.

The accuracy of the list is credited with roughly 40% of the success of the mailing. I once pulled 13% for a magazine specifically edited for the short-lived Radio Shack Color Computer. The list we mailed was a "hotline" of people who had just paid close to $2000 for that machine over the last six months or so.

# Three Answers to Every Question in DM

It's been said there are two answers to every question in direct marketing: "It depends," and "Test it." To those, I'd like to add a third: "I don't know." Let's take a look at each.

## It Depends . . . on What?

**The very first element your direct marketing promotion depends on is the list.** I've met would-be marketers who had a very clear idea of who their ideal customer was, but when it came to actually finding those people on available, mailable lists, they weren't there! Others, when asked who their target market is, will say, "Everyone!" (I was once told this by a fellow who marketed pricey collectible coins . . . "Everyone!" Good grief.) Needless to say, neither situation is very helpful.

**The Color Computer magazine package was designed as a square, to look as though it contained a floppy disk, and it stood out smartly in silver Mylar. And because I knew the recipients had just purchased that particular computer, I was able to tease them with, "O.K. You have your Color Computer, your User's Guide, and Desk Mate (an included program disk) . . . NOW GET THE REST OF IT!" It would be hard not to think that there might be a critical additional program for the Color Computer in that envelope . . . and it appears most people did, to the tune of a 13% response. (Lest I be accused of subterfuge, the magazine, of course, was a form of Color Computer "software," packed with user tips and actual programs exclusively for use with that machine.)**

Magazine subscription response rates typically run from 1% to 5% or 6%, so 13% was considered a hit, and it successfully launched the magazine. Yet, brilliant as the package was ;-), most of that response was due not to the copy and design, but to the accuracy and immediacy of the list.

There are also such factors as whether you use response lists or compiled lists . . . even whether you direct-address or use labels, which we'll discuss further on.

## One-Step or Two-Step?

No, that's not an invitation to dance. It's another factor that response rates depend on. Are you selling directly out of the direct mail package? Or are you seeking inquiries? If your product is costly or especially complex, you may not be able to sell it directly, but you can use direct mail to obtain qualified leads for sales follow-up. This is a classic database marketing situation.

## A Rule of Pinkie

Is there any "rule of thumb" for guesstimating lead generation response rates? Not really, but there is what I call a "Rule of Pinkie."

A restaurant consultant contacted me to see whether direct mail might work for him. He shows restaurant owners how to measure menu revenues and then modifies those menus to generate significantly greater profit, he claims.

I put together a proposal for a three-part direct mail campaign, and his first question was, "What kind of results can I expect?" I knew his response could run anywhere from .05% to 20%. But that's a pretty wide range, so I called one of the industry's leading consultants in business-to-business marketing and lead generation and described the situation. Mind you, this fellow is an author and an internationally renowned consultant in this field. The short answer was he didn't know. "I tell clients to estimate 1% per mailing," he said. And he confirmed my guesstimate of a worst case at .05%, with a possibility of generating up to 20%.

I felt vindicated that there wasn't some magic answer out there that I didn't know about. My Rule of Pinkie today is to estimate 1% response, and if the numbers don't work at that response rate, re-think the project.

But why the range? Why can't we get closer than that to an educated estimate of response? In the menu consultant example, there are lists of restaurants one can mail to, but (a) Who gets the mail? The owner? A clerk? (b) How many restaurant owners believe they need this kind of help to improve their menu profitability, versus those who believe they can do it themselves? Remember, direct mail works best when we identify a behavior and model it . . . not when we try to change it.

> My Rule of Pinkie today is to estimate 1% response, and if the numbers don't work at that response rate, re-think the project.

Actually, this consultant had a good chance of success, I thought, because of his offer—a free menu analysis without obligation. Meaning he'd come pretty close to showing them what he was going to do before he did it. He also had excellent credentials, in terms of his client list and selected testimonials. Those, too, are important factors in determining a response rate. Who are you? What's your track record? What level of risk do I have to accept in order to be able to make a decision?

### Make Me an Offer . . . Please!

I mentioned the offer earlier. The offer represents another 40% of the success of the mailing.

Naturally, a key factor in the offer is the price. After the lists and the offer, the price is the most tested element in direct mail. Note that the offer includes price, but it also takes into account the terms and/or guarantee, plus any premiums that might be offered. There are several psychological "stops" in pricing, starting at $50, then $100, $150, and so on. The higher the price, the more "push" you need behind it, in terms of both the package itself (you likely won't sell a new or complex idea at $200 with a postcard, for example), the proofs or testimonials, the illustrations, and so on.

In direct marketing, we use extensive testing to try as much as possible to let the customers tell us what they are willing to pay for our product or service and how they prefer to pay it.

Offer testing is also strongly recommended. Changing the premium can easily boost response 30% or more. So can an extended guarantee (unlimited guarantee vs. 15- or 30-days). So can paying in installments, and paying after a 30-day trial rather than up front. Each of these carry their own dynamics in terms of the "Quality/Quantity Ratio." (See Chapters 2 and 7). In direct response advertising, just changing the headline can alter response by 30% to 50% one way or the other.

> After the lists and the offer, the price is the most tested element in direct mail.

## Test It

### Format Dynamics

After deciding on the list and the offer, you'll want to seriously consider and/or test format. I say "and/or" because format testing is more costly, and frankly, I don't see marketers of any kind doing a whole lot of it. Magazine publishers are the most aggressive in this area, partly because magazine subscriptions depend so heavily on direct mail, and a winning package can make a big difference on the bottom line.

Many first-time marketers want to use self-mailers because they appear to be so much less expensive than envelope packages. But, all other things being equal, you can measure self-mailer response in tenths of a percent compared with envelope packages that typically start at 1%.

First, in one-step marketing, it's very difficult to sell anything substantial directly from a self-mailer. They just don't carry enough clout. Offering a free trial of a book or magazine is OK. You've no doubt seen most trade shows and conferences using self-mailers, but they're typically multipage mailers, and promoters have to mail them in the gazillions in order to fill a show.

In two-step marketing, self-mailers can frequently be a good choice, if they are designed in series of three or more. For example, a software marketer had been getting about .05% response with his own self-mailer. He later realized a 1½% response with just the first of a four-part series I wrote for him. The series eventually pulled 3%. The secret? No secret, just strong user testimonials, color, and, most of all, a coherent offer.

But it's still just an 8½" × 11" piece folded to 5½" × 8½". Here I believe repetition is the key. As with most space ads, you need to think in terms of three. Prospects see the first one, consider the second one, and act on the third. That's an oversimplification of some complex dynamics perhaps, but it's as close as anyone has come to explaining it.

Other format considerations include the amount of real estate you need to tell your story. Maybe you need a 9" × 12" outer envelope to pull off a certain type of appeal. I just did one of those in

> In one-step marketing, it's very difficult to sell anything substantial directly from a self-mailer.

brown kraft for a certification testing software product in order to create an "official testing" environment. It's a vertical package with the window in the upper-left quadrant. If it works in that format, I've recommended retesting it in 6" × 9" or No. 10 formats to reduce costs, hopefully without losing the response rate.

Another reason for the size in this case is the need to show program screens and explain how they work. That usually means an 11" × 17" brochure. With that brochure, you already have one fold to 8½" × 11". Folding it once more to fit 6" × 9" isn't too bad, but folding it in thirds to fit inside a No. 10 envelope turns it into a dog's breakfast. Sometimes a simpler, 8½" × 11" brochure (two sides) will do it, but it's a judgment call.

### Dimensional Mailings

A critical factor in boosting response rates is, of course, getting the package opened. You may have a socko offer, but no one will know it if they don't open the package. Dimensional mailings are a near sure-fire, if expensive, answer to the problem of getting attention and getting the package opened. They also win many awards in the various direct mail and advertising competitions.

Few people can throw away an item interestingly packaged in a custom box, or even in a jiffy bag, without opening it. Three-dimensional objects, however, whether custom designed or purchased in volume, can be quite expensive, and the packaging adds more cost. But for high-gross-margin products (a $10,000 database software product or promoting a Web site to advertisers, for example), they work quite well. They're often tightly targeted to relatively small lists of select decision makers.

Other techniques include paying for FedEx or Express Mail delivery, either real or one of the simulated packages that are commercially available.

### It's For You

Another way to boost response rates is to support your direct mail with telemarketing. While it adds to your cost, the often dramatic increases in response—up to 300% and more—make telemarketing well worth testing.

> Few people can throw away an item interestingly packaged in a custom box, or even in a jiffy bag, without opening it.

Indeed, any time you're trying to get people to alter their behavior (and "do" something other than send for a free trial), you'll need to provide lots of push, either with a more substantive package, a series of mailings, or a blend of mail, phone, and Web site, or some other combination.

### The 2% Solution

The standard answer one gets when asking what kind of response to expect is "2%." No one knows where that came from, but it really doesn't mean much, other than as a warning not to expect 50% response rates. Actually, any newsletter promotion (for a $200+ newsletter) that pulled over 1% would be response heaven for the publisher. Conversely, 2% for a $25 to $30 magazine isn't anything to shout about.

Then there's the matter of payup. A major business magazine once had me rewrite their billing series because their super-duper, "low-cost" double postcard ("FREE ISSUE!") was netting just 40% payup. Of course, magazines have unique financials. Their revenues come primarily from advertising, not circulation.

Magazine circulation directors learned long ago that the only way to know what response rate you're going to get is to test your options in the mail.

A major West Coast publisher, for example, wants to test a double postcard (actually a triple) against their current control package. Even within that narrow format choice, there are options. The first is a straight-offer sell (make the free issue a no-brainer); second, a content sell (you must know this stuff to survive!); third, an action device test (remove the sticker and place where indicated).

## Answer Number Three

What the magazine marketer in the accompanying sidebar (page 48) calls a "fishing expedition," most publishers know as testing, something he clearly hadn't time for. I suggested he stick to the telephone until he learned more about direct mail. Clearly, this was a case for answer number three: "I don't know what kind of response you'll get," since he obviously wasn't up for "it depends," or "test it."

### A Mailing About a Mailing

Working with a direct marketing agency, I once had great success getting electric utility CEOs to attend a day-long conference on electric security using Certified Mail. It was preceded by a postcard alerting them to the Certified envelope that was on the way. They were on the phone to the agency before the Certified package even arrived!

Few consultants want to admit they don't know, I guess, and do what they can to avoid the issue. Some freelancers will tout their ability to increase your response rates by various breathtaking percentages. They put this promise in their ads, aimed at anyone selling anything, presumably. How can they make that claim, I often wonder, before they even know what you sell, and to whom? My guess is they play the odds and "forget" the losers.

### Figure the Break-Even and Go from There

There are lots of formulas for calculating response rates—once you have a testing history to work from. But in a first-time-out situation, the best you can do is figure your break-even rate. Add up all your costs (see Chapter 4), take your net revenue per sale, and determine what response rate you need in order to break even on the mailing. If it comes to 10%, you're in trouble. As I said earlier, if you can't make it at 1%, take another look at the project.

But keep in mind that direct mail is a database business. Your purpose is to build a list of happy customers to whom you can sell, cross-sell, or up-sell related products, upgrades, whatever. Marketers are often willing to give a little on the front end in order build a database for back end profits. "Direct mail is a process of gathering information, paid for by sales." It doesn't say "fully" paid for, and your job is to be sure the information you buy is worth the cost.

For more information on this topic, visit our Web site at www.businesstown.com

# Finding Your Way Through the Mailing List Swamp

## Chapter 6

*I would to God thou and I knew where a commodity
of good names were to be bought.*

WILLIAM SHAKESPEARE, *KING HENRY IV*

### Web Tip

These list resources—and many others—are available online. See the URLs at the end of this chapter.

To appreciate the importance of the list to your overall marketing effort, consider the oft-quoted 40-40-20 rule: 40% of the success of your mailing depends on the quality of the lists. (The other 40% is the offer, and 20% is the creative.

But even Shakespeare himself couldn't write a successful mailing if it were sent to inaccurate lists. "Junk mail," I like to say, "is an offer sent to the wrong person."

Further, the cost of list rental has skyrocketed in recent years, making list testing considerably more expensive. We can no longer throw another three or four lists into the test matrix just for the heck of it as we once did when lists were $25 per thousand and gas was 32 cents a gallon.

## How Many Lists Are There?

Standard Rate and Data Service, a mainstay of the list marketing industry and publishers of the *SRDS Direct Marketing List Source,* recently announced some 16,000 lists in its database, available to subscribers who purchase their proprietary software. Dun & Bradstreet's DB Marketplace boasts more than 10 million U.S. businesses on CD-ROM (Slice and dice it into as many segments as you need. Sixty percent of that total are companies with four or fewer employees.), and Database America's business file touts 11 million companies.

In his landmark guide, *The Complete Direct Mail List Handbook* (Prentice-Hall, 1988), list guru Ed Burnett estimates there are some 20,000 lists available commercially. So obviously there are lists and there are lists, and most mailers experience their share of dogs on a regular basis. I'll cover some of the basics here, with the caveat that I'm not a list broker, and your best chance of assembling an effective list matrix is by working with a reputable broker. More about brokers in a bit.

## Types of Mailing Lists

You should be aware of the different types of lists and list compilation methods. They yield substantial differences in results. Basically, there are five categories of lists:

### House List

Your house list is composed of your customers. They have bought something from you at least once. They can be presumed to be familiar with your company and your product, and satisfied with both. Your house list will always be your best responding list for the same reason a $5000 political contributor gets his phone call returned: they know you. If you're not aggressively building your house list and maintaining it on a computerized database . . . maybe you'd be happier driving a cab. A house list may also consist of inquirers if you're primarily into lead generation—people who have written or called directly to obtain information. If you're a fund raiser, your house list is your donor file.

> Your house list will always be your best responding list.

### Response Lists

A response list is composed of people who have responded to a direct marketing offer, preferably by buying something, but perhaps also by requesting information, or businesspeople who have said "OK" to a free subscription to a controlled-circulation business publication.

Already you can detect differences in quality here. The person who paid cash for a product is clearly a more valuable prospect than either of the others . . . unless the business publication subscriber happens to be director of jet engine procurement for United Airlines and you're the jet engine marketing director at GE. Everything is relative.

Actually, multimagazine publishers, like McGraw-Hill, Chilton, Cahners, CMP/Miller Freeman, and Penton offer large, unduplicated databases of their business/trade publication subscribers as "direct mail buyers" because they said "Yes" to a free subscription, or otherwise qualified themselves via a questionnaire. You'll have to decide if you want to consider that a response list. They did take the time to fill out the Qualification Form, and for them, time is money. These companies also offer a variety of marketing tools and services.

A list of similar businesspeople who paid for their subscriptions may be expected to produce better-qualified prospects, all other factors being equal. Indeed, that holds true for response lists generally— but then, all other factors are seldom equal. Also, response lists cost more to rent than compiled lists.

Surprising as it may seem, your best bet for selling a bible by mail is a person who just bought a bible by mail. You may have a problem getting hold of that list, however, since the owner likely won't rent it to a competitor (although they might trade with you if the list universe is close).

In many niche markets, however (especially business markets), the availability of high-quantity response lists can thin out quickly, which means if you're going to sustain any kind of volume mailing program you'll need to rely on compiled lists.

> Surprising as it may seem, your best bet for selling a bible by mail is a person who just bought a bible by mail.

## Compiled Lists

Compiled lists are those that are assembled from existing data sources, either public or proprietary. They can also be custom compiled from special sources or combinations of sources. Compiled lists start with phone books from which names and addresses are captured in volume, then spot-verified by telephone. White pages yield consumer names (three-line addresses), and yellow pages yield businesses (four-line addresses). R.H. Donnelly/Metromail is the principal compiler of phone book lists.

Other sources of compiled lists include trade show attendees, automobile registrations (which are currently under fire for privacy concerns and may become tightly regulated), association memberships, product warranty cards, sweepstakes entrants (choose "Yes" or "No" respondents), occupant lists, and more.

Largely because the purchase behavior is missing, or cannot be quantified, compiled lists usually pull at lower rates than response lists—but then, they usually cost less.

## Data Banks

Both business and consumer lists, response and compiled, are available in data banks. These are large databases of lists that have been compiled, combined, deduplicated, and enhanced. Enhancing means the files have been overlaid with census data and various other types of demographic and psychographic (i.e., lifestyle) data.

Consumer lists can be enhanced with such demographic overlays as driver's license data, median age, median home ownership and value, make and value of car, dates of birth of household members, and more.

Psychographic characteristics include hobbies, special interests, product ownership, and more. (Demographic data may show I own an expensive car. But is it a Lincoln Continental or a Porsche? The difference may be important to you.) Psychographic data is collected via mail and telephone for inclusion in various "lifestyle" lists or overlays to lists.

SRDS and the Polk Company jointly publish *The Lifestyle Market Analyst*. As their ad puts it, "You'll find out who owns a dog, who attends cultural events, who uses home video games, and who uses a personal computer." The *Analyst* identifies magazines and mailing lists that target these special interests. They claim to profile 19 million households.

Another primary source of consumer lists is catalog buyers. The Millard Group in Peterborough, N.H., is a major source of catalog lists and manages many of the leading catalog and publishing lists. Some large data banks consist of catalog multibuyers, unduplicated and enhanced with other data.

Business enhancement is more limited. SIC codes and phone number are two key pieces of information most users seek. The SIC code tells us what business or industry the company is in, and the phone number facilitates the call we often need to make to determine the individual's decision-making functions and purchase intentions . . . or to (hopefully) get referred to the right person in the company. Other data enhancements include number of employees, sales volume, and various county, city, and metro codes.

> Data banks are large databases of lists that have been compiled, combined, deduplicated, and enhanced.

Among the richest data banks for this kind of information are the business publishing databases mentioned above. McGraw-Hill, Cahners, et al. put big bucks into gathering the kind of marketing data mailers seek, and it's usually dependable. Some list brokers manage large data banks as well.

Companies like Dun & Bradstreet that publish specialized lists can add credit information and both Market Data Retrieval and CMG Group provide enhanced school lists.

## E-Lists

The newest addition to the list universe is the e-list, gathered either from e-mail or directly from the World Wide Web. The common standard for e-lists today is the "opt-in" list, indicating that the individual has agreed to have his or her e-mail address available for mailings. However, there are many slips between the "opt" and the "in," so tread cautiously. E-lists are covered in greater detail in Chapter 16.

As with hard copy lists, e-lists are being used most effectively when they are customer lists or at least inquirers to the mailer. The cost of mailing your own e-list is virtually free, so begin gathering customer e-mail addresses ASAP.

## List Rental Costs

Speaking of costs, I frequently hear someone say they "bought" a list. You should understand that lists are rented for one-time use only. List owners protect their lists by seeding them with dummy names and otherwise monitoring their usage. Mail a list a second time without paying for it, and you'll be hearing from an attorney pretty quick.

Most lists are rented in minimum quantities of 5,000 names, which for most mailers is about the right test quantity per panel. Some very popular lists double that minimum to 10,000. You don't need to mail to all the names you rent, however.

Today, for budgeting purposes, estimate lists at $100 per thousand ($100/M) and you'll be pretty close. Some are more, some are less. Compiled lists may average slightly less, from $85 to $90/M. High-tech lists tend to start at $100/M and can double that.

> The common standard for e-lists today is the "opt-in" list, indicating that the individual has agreed to have his or her e-mail address available for mailings.

For a current project, for example, a client plans to mail IBM AS/400 computer locations. A list of 5,900 locations (32,290 names or an average of 5.5 names per location) on CD-ROM costs $19,425 or $329 per *location*. Each file includes detailed sales and contact data for each location.

Whatever the base price, special selections can increase that price quickly. State selections, male/female, income, and other segmentations each add $5, $10, or even $15/M to your base cost. Some negotiation on price may, however, be possible.

## Net Names and Net Net Names

If you're renting a number of lists from one source, you may be able to negotiate a "net names" agreement, paying only for those names that survive a "merge-purge" or deduplication process.

A "net net name" agreement runs the lists against certain specified screens for bad debt, certain zip code suppression, income, and other factors. Usually, you need to be mailing large quantities to make these types of screenings pay out.

## Hotlines

"Hotlines" are those names that have come onto the file in the last 30 days or 60 days or whatever, depending on the list. That is, they are the most recent names on the file. Most list data cards will indicate the monthly hotlines available. Because hotlines normally pull at higher rates than the core list, they cost more.

If you determine that you can successfully mail a particular list's hotline exclusively, and are willing to pay the premium, that's fine. But beware the "hotline test," where a broker or list owner provides hotline names exclusively for a test, where you're planning to mail the core list. You'll get a skewed result in your test. It would be better, in my view, to mail the core list and anticipate a bump in response when you add hotline names later. Including both in your initial test will give you some indicators.

If there are sufficient hotline names coming on line each month for you to use them exclusively, use them. Lucky you.

> Whatever the base price, special selections can increase that price quickly. State selections, male/female, income, and other segmentations each add $5, $10, or even $15/M to your base cost.

## Names vs. Titles

In mailing business lists, you'll need to decide how reliable your names are. If you're satisfied the names are accurate, mail them. If the names are doubtful, use the title instead, since the title will likely still be there, even if the person isn't, and the piece may get passed along to the new person using that title.

## N.C.O.A. and List Hygiene

N.C.O.A. stands for National Change of Address, a constantly updated database generated by the USPS and administered by selected service bureaus around the country. Wherever you get your lists, you want to be sure they have been run against the NCOA database for accuracy. Approximately 20% of Americans change their addresses every year, and any list deteriorates at about 50% per year.

You also want to be sure you run your own lists against the NCOA file to save mailing costs and improve deliverability. Other forms of "list hygiene" include the following:

- **CASS** (Coding Accuracy Support System)**.** This is a software program that will standardize your addresses, especially where lists have been enhanced. Make sure your data processor uses only CASS-certified software.
- **ZIP+4.** To take full advantage of carrier sort discounts, you must append ZIP+4 and carrier route data with CASS-certified software.
- **PAVE** (Presort Accuracy, Validation, and Evaluation)**.** Your list must also be presorted according to the Domestic Mail Manual. PAVE is another software program that will save you much time, aggravation, and money.
- **Barcodes.** The USPS requires that reply envelopes be barcoded if they are being carried by an envelope that is itself getting barcode discounts. Also try to use delivery point barcodes whenever possible. This is an extension of the ZIP+4 barcode in which the last 10 bars represent the first two digits of the street address. Since the barcode is read instead of

### If "Break-Even" is 10% or More, Re-Think It!

A software developer had put much time and money into a contact management/calendar program and after learning what it would take to get the product on the shelves in the retail channel, decided to go direct. I created a direct mail package, selected lists, and generally supervised a mailing that pulled close to a 4% response. I was delighted—until the client told me, after the fact, that he had needed a 10% response to make enough to keep mailing. Oops.

the printed address, the mail needn't meet OCR standards—granting you some additional leeway in envelope design.

- **ACS.** Here is a less costly alternative to ACR (Address Correction Requested) It provides electronic return of an undeliverable piece for 20 cents instead of the 50-cent rate for hard-copy address returns.

## Costs and Testing

As I said in Chapter 4, there are certain thresholds one needs to reach in order to have a valid test. Test one list and all you'll know when you're done is that it was a good (or bad) list. Is that enough for further marketing decisions? I don't think so.

A rule of thumb for statistical reliability in list testing is to mail sufficient names to obtain at least 50 responses. If you anticipate a 1% response, that would indicate a 5,000 name mailing. If you anticipate fewer responses, increase the quantity accordingly.

Other "musts" include:

- Key code every list so you can track results.
- Test no more than one variable at a time so you'll know where the spike or drop came from.
- Mail all tests at the same time.
- Test, in order of importance: lists, offer, price, creative, format, and season.

You can expect that only about 30% of the lists you test will pay out, so the more lists you test, the more insurance you're buying, and the more you're learning about your market.

Also, if you go into the mail expecting that the revenue from your initial test will fund the next level of testing, you're likely to be disappointed. You should have sufficient capital to test mail, adjust lists, offer, or creative based on results; and remail and remail again before seeing any substantial revenue.

In fact, if a "break even" analysis shows you need a 10% response in order to succeed, it probably won't happen. Rethink the project.

> If you go into the mail expecting that the revenue from your initial test will fund the next level of testing, you're likely to be disappointed.

## A List Selection Model

In constructing a test mailing from list data sheets, I use a letter-number system for prioritizing lists. Letters–A,B,C, etc.–designate the list's closeness or compatibility with my customer profile. Since an exact fit would likely be available only from a direct competitor, and since they probably won't rent to you, your "A" designation will have to be approximate, but as close as you can get with the list selections you have.

For example, if I'm promoting a newsletter on the subject of recruiting, I probably will have to live without subscribers to a hypothetical *Recruiting* magazine (unless I can work out a swap, which is always worth a phone call). But a compiled list of "corporate recruiters" would rate an "A."

A list of human resources managers might also rate an "A," but a list of human resource directors or VPs wouldn't. Why? Because human resource managers often do the actual recruiting work. HR directors and vice presidents are somewhat removed from the day-to-day recruiting process (been there, done that) and probably wouldn't think they need hands-on advice on recruiting.

## Watch Out for Fuzzy Logic

OK, you might say, but wouldn't HR directors want their people to know as much as possible about recruiting and pass the mailing piece along to them? Or, might not some of these HR VPs make hiring decisions? Sure, some might. But that's not a primary and normally anticipated behavior for this group. Be careful of that kind of fuzzy logic, tempting as it can be. It will have you selecting marginal lists, which will tend to drag down your aggregate response. If the promotion or offer isn't directly related to the person receiving it, your odds of a sale drop dramatically.

The numbers are assigned according to the total size of the list. Relative to the lists I have to choose from, the largest lists rate a "1," next largest a "2," etc. Smaller lists (3) can always be added to a continuation or rollout later at low incremental cost, rather than claiming a spot in the initial test. You don't want to mail too many small

> If the promotion or offer isn't directly related to the person receiving it, your odds of a sale drop dramatically.

lists, since even if you get a good hit on some of them, there won't be many names to go back to.

I then construct my test list: A-1s first, then A-2s, B-1s, B-2s, and so on. If you find yourself getting down into "C" lists rather quickly, you may have a list problem, or need to look further.

## Of List Brokers and List Managers

**List brokers** have access to all or almost all lists available for rent. They consult with you, determine your needs, and make recommendations. Their fee is paid by the list owners in the form of a commission, roughly 20%. If they subrent from "exclusive" list representatives, they split some of that. Whatever the case, the list broker represents you and your interests.

**List managers** handle a wide variety of lists. That is, they market them to the list rental marketplace, either directly to you, or through a broker. They represent the list owner in maximizing the revenue from his or her list.

If you're a relatively small mailer, say 200,000 pieces a year or less, find one broker and give him or her all your business so the broker has an opportunity to learn more about your business and the lists that serve your needs. He or she will also have a stake in your success. By all means, talk to list managers, too. You can learn a lot about lists that way. And if you can develop a good relationship with the list manager, great! Just don't forget that the list manager has a vested interest in the lists he or she represents. That may work well for you, if the management is large enough to encompass your needs.

It is sometimes difficult to find a broker who will give his or her full time and attention to a person needing only 10,000 names for a test. But they do exist, and they hope your business with them will grow as you grow. When you find one of these, hold on. One thing a broker cannot do is tell you a list's rate of response for another mailer. They can, however, tell you the list usage; who rented the list, and, more important, who came back for continuations (2nd or 3rd test mailings to larger quantities of names) and rollouts (large-volume campaigns).

> One thing a broker cannot do is tell you a list's rate of response for another mailer. They can, however, tell you the list usage.

## List Formats

Lists are provided in several forms: Cheshire labels and pressure-sensitive labels, and magnetic tape, diskette, or CD-ROM for direct (ink jet) addressing.

Cheshire labels telegraph "advertising mail" to recipients and are the least desirable. By far the best addressing strategy is to use magnetic tape and direct-address—ink jet or laser—on the order form (to show through a window envelope), on the top of the letter (ditto), or on the outside of a closed face envelope. (One direct marketing agency I know refuses to take a client who insists on using Cheshire labels.) In some mail formats, you can have computer personalization in more than one place.

Some additional points to remember when renting and using lists:

- Be sure all lists are coded by test panel (or order forms are coded if the record is not on the return piece) so you can record results by list.
- Make list selections by "nth" name to spread your test evenly across the list.
- Always eyeball the list before you mail. You might even want to pull some names at random and call them to verify that they are who you think they are.
- Remember that the list owner will require a sample mailing piece before approving the list rental. Plan ahead.

> Cheshire labels telegraph "advertising mail" to recipients and are the least desirable.

## List Resources

So where do you find all these great lists? Following are some places to go, at least initially. As mentioned earlier, your best bet, especially for response lists, is to work with an experienced broker.

You'll find brokers and other list sources (along with tons of helpful how-to information on direct marketing and list dynamics) listed in several direct marketing publications and on their Web sites, including:

*Target Marketing* Magazine, 800-777-8074
(*www.targetonline.com*)

DM News, 212-925-7300 (*www.dmnews.com*)

*DIRECT* Magazine, 203-358-9900 (*www.mediacentral.com/direct*)

*Direct Marketing* Magazine, 800-229-6700

Marketing Tools, 800-828-1133 (*www.marketingtools.com*)

Catalog Age, 203-358-9900 (*www.catalogagemag.com*)

Also check your local yellow pages under Advertising, Direct Mail, and Lists, the Manhattan yellow pages, or check with your local direct marketing club or association. There's a comprehensive listing of associations and local clubs in the Appendix. The Direct Marketing Association (DMA) can also provide referrals in your area: 212-768-7277 (*www.the-dma.org*).

Some other major list compiler/brokers include:

Standard Rate and Data Service (All list sources)
800-851-SRDS (*www.srds.com*)

The National Directory of Mailing Lists
800-955-0231 (*www.mediafinder.com*)

American List Council (all SICs, compiled lists, and response lists)
908-874-4300 (*www.amlist.com*)

Worldata (Especially big in high-tech lists, plus all SICs)
800-331-8102 (*info@worldata.com*)

Acxicom/Direct Media (high-tech lists, response lists and all SICs)
203-532-1000 (*www.acxicom.com*)

TRW (Consumer databases, automobile databases, financial lists)
800-527-3933

Metromail (Consumer databases)
800-527-3933 / 800-541-0524

Database America (All SICs, major business and consumer
    databases)
800-223-7777 (*www.databaseamerica.com*)

Dun & Bradstreet (Corporate and Executive databases)
800-624-5669 (*www.dnb.com*)

The Lifestyle Selector (Consumer psychographics)
800-525-3533

**Figure 6-1: Numeric References**

1. List size
2. Hotlines
3. List description
4. Minimum order
5. Source and/or percentage generated by direct mail
6. Demographics
7. Cost per thousand
8. Selections available
9. Formats available
10. Update frequency

## 12 Vital Questions to Ask Your List Broker

Your broker should provide you with a "Data Sheet" for each list that answers some or all of the following questions.

1. Who is on the list?
2. Is it a list of everyone who responded, or of actual buyers?
3. How recent is the list? When was the list last updated?
4. If it is a list of actual purchasers (response list), how recently were the purchases made?
5. Can you get a "hotline" select?
6. How often has this list been rented?
7. Has the list been tested?
8. After testing, did the renter continue to rollout?
9. Did the mailer rent the list for a follow-up mailing?
10. Where did the list come from? ("100% Direct Mail" is the best source.)
11. If the list came from the company that compiled it, ask for a sample of the mailing. This may be the best way to determine the relevance of the list for your mailing.
12. Is the list clean? How often does the owner clean it? Has it been NCOA'd? CASS certified?

—Direct Mail by the Numbers, USPS

**1** →

*TIME LIFE MASTERFILE*

11/30/99 66621
**Page 1 of 1**

```
 4,796,240  TOTAL FILE                          80.00/M        THRU: 10/99
 3,511,560  ACTIVES                             85.00/M
 1,029,240  30 DAY HOTLINES                     85.00/M   ——— SEX ———
   906,900  MULTIBUYERS                         85.00/M   45% F / 43% M
    55,220  LAST 12 MONTH COMPLETERS            95.00/M
 1,272,360  LAST 12 MONTH RESIGNS               70.00/M   ——— MATERIAL ———
            FUNDRAISER/MEMBERSHIP               65.00/M   4-UP CHESHIRE / NC
                                                          9-TRACK 6250 BPI
                                                          PRES. SENS. $10/M
```

**2** (points to 30 DAY HOTLINES)
**7** (points to price column)
**9** (points to MATERIAL)

TIME LIFE, A DISTINGUISHED NAME IN THE DIRECT
MARKETING INDUSTRY, CONTINUES TO BRING QUALITY BOOK,
MUSIC AND VIDEO PRODUCTS TO THE CONSUMER MARKETPLACE.
THIS DATABASE IS AN UNDUPLICATED MASTERFILE OF ALL
THEIR BOOK, MUSIC, AND VIDEO PRODUCT BUYERS. UPDATED
MONTHLY, THIS FILE ENABLES MAILERS TO CUT ACROSS ALL
OF THE VARIOUS LISTS FOR MAXIMUM UNIVERSES WITHIN
SOURCE, TYPE OF BUYER, HOTLINES, ACTIVES, COMPLETERS,
MULTIBUYERS, AND CHANGE OF ADDRESS INFORMATION.

**3** (points to description paragraph)

——— KEY CODING ———
$2.00/M

— MINIMUM ORDER — **4**
5,000 MINIMUM

— UPDATE SCHEDULE — **10**
UPDATE: MONTHLY

```
SELECTS: STATE, SCF, ZIP, $6/M    $25+            $6/M
         SEX               $6/M    $50+           $11/M
         SOURCE OR PAID    $6/M    $100+          $16/M
         30 DAY H/L       $11/M    $200+          $21/M
         3 MONTH          $11/M    CONT/SINGLE    $11/M
         6 MONTH           $6/M    MULTIBUYERS    $11/M
         INTEREST          $6/M    COA             $6/M
```

**8** (points to SELECTS)

SOURCE:  DIRECT RESPONSE

**5** (points to SOURCE)

PROFILE: AVG INCOME $45K+; AVG AGE 42; 81% MARRIED

**6** (points to PROFILE)

FOR INCREASED TARGETING, PLEASE SEE THE TIME LIFE
BOOK, MUSIC, OR VIDEO LISTS, AS WELL AS THE
AFFINITY FILES.

HOTLINES ARE LAST 30 DAY TRANSACTIONS; ACTIVES ARE
LAST 12 MONTH TRANSACTIONS; MULTIBUYERS HAVE
PURCHASED MORE THAN ONE TIME LIFE OFFER;
COMPLETERS HAVE RECEIVED AND PAID FOR A COMPLETE
SERIES; RESIGNS HAVE PURCHASED ONE OR MORE
SELECTIONS WITHIN A SERIES AND ARE NO LONGER
ACTIVE.

— NET NAME POLICY —
85% + $7.50/M RUN
CHARGES ON ORDERS
OVER 50,000 NAMES

— MAG TAPE INSTR —
$25.00 NON-
REFUNDABLE CHARGE
DO NOT RETURN TAPE
$50 FLAT CANCEL
FEE ON ALL ORDERS

— RECOMMENDED BY —

MILLARD GROUP, INC.

Figure 6-1. Please see page 62 for numeric references.

# Chapter 7

# Database Marketing—the Camel in the Dark

After years of working with marketers building (or not building) databases, and having read numerous books and articles on the subject, it's clear to me today that defining *database marketing* is the classic example of a committee describing a camel by having each member touch a different part in the dark. Indeed, the authors of one hefty reference baldly state in their introduction, "There is no universally accepted definition of database marketing."

Nevertheless, any attempt to employ direct marketing techniques without an understanding of the role of the database is likely doomed to failure. For one thing, the very definition of *direct marketing* (faithfully inscribed in each monthly issue of *Direct Marketing* magazine) includes the word *database*:

> "Direct Marketing is an interactive system of marketing that uses one or more advertising media to effect a measurable response and/or transaction at any location, with this activity stored on database."

That last phrase was added some years ago as computerized databases took customer information out of the shoe box and put it online. Remember the shoe box? Back when I was growing into a 38 short in New York, I was a regular customer at the formerly upscale men's clothing store, Rogers Peet & Company. The salesman there had a 3" × 5" card in a box with my name, phone number, and size written on it. When the fall shipment came in, he called me (!) to alert me to the fact that he now had some seven or eight crisp new suits in my rather difficult size, and suggesting I stop by before they were sold. I went.

That box of 3" × 5" cards was the salesman's database. He had a record of when I was in last (recency), how often I shopped at the store (frequency), and the average price range of my purchases (monetary). Recency, Frequency, and Monetary (RFM) still form the backbone of many database marketing systems—although there is some back and forth among database gurus about RFM's continued relevance and value amid today's more sophisticated statistical analysis methods.

Any attempt to employ direct marketing techniques without an understanding of the role of the database is likely doomed to failure.

More recently, I received a self-mailer from a business forms and stationery supplier from whom I had purchased some imprinted labels. "Dear Mr. Duncan," the card said. "It has been 18 months since you purchased your imprinted, pressure-sensitive labels (Item #00043), and your supply may be running low. Just check the replacement quantity you prefer on the card below, detach, and drop it in the mail. Your new supply of labels will arrive within two weeks." Same thing as the suit salesman, except now the cards are on a hard drive and they can automatically spit out a personalized letter on a timely basis. Automated sales follow-up is just one use of a marketing database—but it's a good one!

And just a few weeks before my last birthday, I received a birthday card with a $10 "Gift Certificate" from Radio Shack. You bet I used it.

## Some Fad!

In a posting to an online database marketing listserv to which I subscribe, another subscriber wrote: "I see DB marketing becoming yet another fad only surviving through the proselytizations of soapbox opportunists eager to get in on the action of training and seminar circuits. What long-term value does it give us to know what colour underpants our customers wear or when their pet canary has its birthday. I guess my point is that we can't get carried away with gathering information just for the sake of gathering information."

Well, I agree with the last part—as would most database architects, since gathering and storing information are time consuming and costly. But Victoria's Secret might love to know what color underpants their customers wear, both for product research purposes and in order to give frequent purchasers of colored undies a special offer next time they introduce a hot new color. And if you stop into any Petco store, they'll happily record your pet's birthday and mail out a subsequent invitation to come in and get a 10% discount. Think Petco is doing that out of the goodness of its heart? Probably not.

As for the "fad" rap, tell that to the folks at Land Rover, Ltd., who used their marketing database to invite 4,000 Range Rover owners to a

> Automated sales follow-up is just one use of a marketing database— but it's a good one!

special marketing event that eventually sold 1,000 new vehicles at $52,000 each. Yes, a $52 million winner (and a DMA Gold Mailbox award to boot) for an investment of about $150,000. Some fad!

Today's marketing case histories are filled with examples of successes similar to the Land Rover extravaganza for companies of all kinds pouring big bucks into their databases and into the marketing promotions they slice, dice, and spin off from the data. These range from the airlines' frequent flyer programs to Sears' mail order database, which helps the catalog and retail giant profitably target nearly two billion direct mail pieces a year to the company's 24 million shop-at-home customers.

> Today's marketing case histories are filled with companies of all kinds pouring big bucks into their databases and into the marketing promotions they slice, dice, and spin off from the data.

## Building an Effective Direct Marketing Database

### From Suspect to Advocate

What we want our database to help us do is to move names through the pipeline and along the way move them up the food chain from "suspect" to "advocate." Following are the primary stages:

**Suspect:** This is someone we have reason to believe may be interested in our offer by reason of their title, or their company's SIC (Standard Industrial Classification) Code for business mailings, or their income level for consumer mailings, or their buying history in either case.

This could be the CFO at a *Fortune* 1000 company if you're selling a financial services product or service to companies, for example. Or it could be a CEO in SIC Code 6020, which is banks. Or SIC 4724 (travel agencies) if you're promoting a hotel. It might be any family with a median income of $75,000 living in a single-family house if you're selling swimming pools, or subscribers to *The Wall Street Journal* if you're a financial planner.

**Prospect:** So you rented the list and mailed an offer, and you received 1,150 requests for your special report. The suspects are now prospects because they have replied directly to you, and they have raised their hand to say they are interested in reading the material you offered.

**Customer:** You sent out the Report along with a fulfillment kit offering your product. Maybe you called first to "qualify" the prospect further. And perhaps you called again after you sent the material to close the sale by phone. The prospect bought, and thus became a customer.

**Client:** Along with the product the customer bought, you sent a catalog with other products your company markets, and the customer purchased three products, thereby becoming a client. (Some marketers might wait for another sale to dub the customer a client.)

**Advocate:** Included with the catalog was a "Member-Get-A-Member" card, which offered a free gift if the client provided the names of three neighbors or colleagues. The client did so, thus becoming an advocate. (In a business-to-business setting, the client might have responded to a questionnaire with a testimonial, which you duly captured.)

Suspect to prospect, to customer, to client, to advocate—a quintuple play combination that helps feed a healthy business.

## The Relationship Marketing Database: First Step in Acquiring and Keeping Business-to-Business Customers

For business-to-business marketers, the cost of an industrial face-to-face sales call grew from about $97 in 1977 to more than $500 in 1999. Using a 20% cost of selling/marketing as an average percentage of the gross revenue, there is a significant disparity between the rising cost of the sales call and the revenue required to support that call.

> Suspect to prospect, to customer, to client, to advocate—a quintuple play combination that helps feed a healthy business.

In 1977, according to database consultant Bernard Goldberg, the revenue necessary to sustain the average sales call, assuming a 20% cost of selling, was under $500. Today, almost $2,000 in revenue is required to support that same sales call, using the same 20% criterion.

There are a number of possible solutions to this problem. The easiest is to increase prices to maintain profits. However, competitive pressures make it difficult to increase prices at a level high enough to deal with the escalating costs of selling. Another, more popular method, has been to curtail or abandon selling efforts to smaller customers or for less expensive products.

The escalating cost of sales requires companies to explore alternatives to address smaller customers and less expensive products. Many companies cannot afford even one sales call to any customer who is not spending at least $2000.

## Recreate the Salesperson's Customer Relationship

Historically, as we have pointed out earlier, it was the salesperson's responsibility to maintain the relationship with a company's customers. Successful salespeople develop a vast inventory of information about their customers. Like my friend at Rogers Peet, each maintains a file containing the past and current relationship between his or her company and its customers. In some cases, the salesperson's file is the most complete historical record available within the company concerning the relationship between the customer and the company.

All salespeople understand that the key to selling is establishing an ongoing relationship with their customers and prospects. The files are reminders and a documentation of those relationships.

Good salespeople will continue to record the history of their relationships in their own files. And they often guard them jealously. I once wrote a promotion for a leading high-end computer hardware manufacturer designed solely to get their salespeople to provide client information to the company's own aftermarket telesales team, of which, it seems, they knew little and trusted less—even though they received full commission on anything the telesales team sold to their customers!

> In some cases, the salesperson's file is the most complete historical record available within the company concerning the relationship between the customer and the company.

The real question, says Goldberg, is "How can you develop the same historical record for all your customers?" Some companies rely on their clerical staffs to develop and maintain complete customer files. Over time, however, there are limits to the amount of information these files can contain, and older information is often purged. In addition, these files often contain contact information only where the customer has initiated the contact. The file may not contain all the contacts initiated by the company.

It is quite common to have a customer file in accounting or administration detailing order and billing information. Another customer file in sales and marketing may detail correspondence and contacts with the customer. And still another customer file maintained by the salesperson contains all of that information plus other notes and miscellaneous information the salesperson has developed about that customer.

The files maintained by accounting and sales administration will generally be well organized and standardized—but likely incomplete. The salesperson's files will be complete but individualized by the salesperson and hard to use by someone else—there will be little organization or standardization. There may be scarce information available on smaller customers.

There is a direct relationship between how frequently a customer is contacted and how often he or she buys.

As selling costs continue to grow, the number of customers that a company can afford to have salespeople deal with will continue to decline. Smaller customers have and will continue to become too expensive to service with a salesperson. As a result, the historical record of the relationship with that customer, maintained by the salesperson, will be lost, exactly at the time it is most critical to moving the customer to a direct mail or telesales channel.

It is almost a self-fulfilling prophecy that smaller customers remain small or even become non-customers over time. The company ultimately loses its relationship with these customers. The best opportunity for a company is to establish long-term relationships with their customers. You can see how vital an effective direct marketing database is to that effort.

> There is a direct relationship between how frequently a customer is contacted and how often he or she buys.

An effective direct marketing database will:

- Contain the names, addresses, titles, and phone numbers of contacts we want to reach via direct mail, telephone, or some other direct marketing format.
- Have the capability to record all responses.
- Have the capability to record all purchases.
- Provide the capability to sustain communication and selling activity to all names on the database and record each contact.
- Be flexible and expandable to add new fields as needed.

## Lead Management Process

| Trade Shows | Space Ads | Direct Mail | White Mail |

Leads in →

Lead evaluation and qualification

Telephone verification

Database Program: Data entry/ Query/Fulfillment

Telephone/direct mail followup fo fulfillment — Input to database

Sales Reps (SALE!)

Customer Service

Aftermarket Sales [Upgrade, add-ons, cross-sell List rental]

**Figure 7-1**

## A Database For the Rest of Us

Now that we've touched a few of the humps, let's go back to the front of the camel and see if we can identify what kind of animal this is. The diagram in Figure 7-1 is a snapshot of a simple lead generating process using a database.

Your product/offer is seen at a trade show or in a magazine ad or direct mail piece, picked up through "word of mouth," or prompted by a news story on your company or product. (Add trade magazine, bingo card, TV ad, the Internet, etc.).

First, you'll want to verify the inquiry and determine the level of qualification before entering it into the database or passing it to the sales force.

Once the information is entered, the database can be programmed to pop out a label or a personalized "welcome" or acknowledgment letter to accompany the product, the special report, the demo, or whatever you must fulfill.

From there, the Telephone Sales Representative (TSR), salesperson, or marketing folks access the database and follow up to continue the dialog (in long sales cycle products) or upsell the customer and enter the results of that contact in the database. Or, the lead may go directly to a sales team, who acts on it and enters that result in the database.

Once you've made a sale, the information goes to customer service for support or for whatever other reason they may need a record, and the information again is entered in the database.

By now you've no doubt noticed that whatever happens, the activity is entered into the database. (No-sales can also be evaluated, coded, and entered in the database for a different kind of follow-up in, say, six months or a year.)

In allocating resources, you'll want to match your communications strategies to your market:

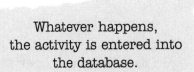

Whatever happens, the activity is entered into the database.

- Advocates may be candidates for special treatment in your loyalty/frequency program.
- Customers and up (clients, advocates) should get first dibs on your salesperson's time and attention, or at least hear from your TSR. (An exception would be a magazine's subscribers– but maybe not a more expensive newsletter's.)
- Prospects can be contacted by mail unless you have some highly targeted prospects that deserve a higher level of attention.
- Suspects should be communicated with primarily through your advertising and public relations efforts. You may want to keep them on your mailing database for one or two additional efforts, but purge them from your database as quickly as you're comfortable in doing so. They're costing you money.

## What a Database Does

If we can't define a database, we can at least identify its key functions. More accurately, we can describe the functions of a Database Management System (DBMS), which today is not a box of index cards, but a sophisticated database software program residing on a client/server platform, a minicomputer, or a mainframe. If you have a Web presence, you may want certain functions of the database on your Web server as well.

Database consultants and authors of *Business-to-Business Direct Marketing* Tracy Emerick and Bernard Goldberg spell out the primary ways in which a database is used:

1. **Provides names of customers or prospects.**
   The original name and address list is an important part of the database, but all of the activity relating to each of the names on the list is also essential.
2. **Stores and measures responses.**
   Once you reach the targets you identified and they respond to your offer, the database should provide the ability to track each contact and each response.
3. **Stores and measures purchases.**
   Now that you know if a prospect has responded to your direct marketing program, you want to track whether these respondents actually become buyers. "The back end conversion of respondents to orders is the key measurement in evaluating the success of the direct marketing program," state Emerick and Goldberg. "By tracking the actual respondents who purchase, you can establish the cost per order and the average order size."
4. **Facilitates continuing communication with prospects, respondents, and customers.**
   The database should allow you to have a sustained and complete ability to contact the initial list of prospects, the group that responded, and the group that became customers.

In the business stationery example described earlier, the company had stored on their database my name and address, what I purchased, and when and how much I paid. They also coded me as a customer and programmed in the resell date. They input appropriate copy to their database and programmed it to print and mail the self-mailer offer for a new supply of labels on a preset date. Then they went to lunch.

The key point of this description is that, unlike some others I've seen that seem to relate mostly to mega-mailers, it applies to any mailer, regardless of size. The four functions outlined above will work as well for my local pet store as it does for Sears' mail order buyers file.

> The database should allow you to have a sustained and complete ability to contact the initial list of prospects, the group that responded, and the group that became customers.

## The Family Jewels

Basically, what you put in your database are the family jewels—all of your contacts and the results of those contacts with all of your customers. Finally, the power of data processing is bringing us back to the days of the guy with the box of 3" × 5" cards who could call me personally and tell me he had some suits in my size!

According to a survey conducted by *DIRECT* magazine, the following types of customer data were maintained on the databases of 50% or more of the companies surveyed:

- Names of prospects
- Length of time each has been a customer
- Number of purchases annually
- Dollar value of purchases (monetary)
- Recency (date of most recent purchase)
- Frequency (how often he/she buys)
- Source of original lead or contact

In addition, the following types of customer data were maintained by less than 50% of those surveyed:

- Age/date of birth (didn't mention pets)
- Other purchase influencers at same address (critical for many types of long-sales-cycle B-T-B products)
- Rentals of customer's name
- Sociodemographic info by survey
- Sociodemographic info by overlay (See reference to demographic overlays in Chapter 6)
- SIC code (Essential to B-T-B marketers)
- Promotional history
- Company info by overlay
- Company info by survey
- Tracking of nonresponders
- Tracking of database usage by category

### Price Can Be a Powerful Qualifier

PC Age is a computer training school. The network certification course they offer costs around $9,000. The owner has learned to use the course price like an on/off toggle switch for inquiries. He includes it in his fulfillment material when he has all the leads his staff can handle, and omits it when his lead volume slows to a trickle.

## Push the Reply that Works the Best

In writing a "magalog" for a financial newsletter, we added an extra bonus for people who replied by phone instead of mailing the reply form. The reason is that phone responders were more involved generally and renewed at higher percentages than did mail respondents.

In addition, every record needs to have a customer code, account number, or other unique identifier.

These last 11 items might be considered "gathering information for the sake of gathering information" by my discussion list colleague mentioned earlier, but each marketer must determine the data that is critical to his or her particular marketing environment, and the amount of the investment he/she is prepared to make in the data.

The survey also reported that 40.5% of respondents use their database to cross-sell, 54.1% use it to prospect, and 54.7% use it to reactivate customers.

## Feeding the Database: Fine Tuning for the Quantity/Quality Ratio

The so-called "Quantity/Quality Ratio" is another way of saying you can't have it both ways. If you require a high degree of qualification for your leads, you will likely get fewer of them. Conversely, if you prefer a high volume, you'll have to settle for lower quality.

There are a number of elements that you can work into your direct mail or ad program that are much less costly than list modeling (discussed later in this chapter) and which will help push the quantity/quality game in one direction or another, depending on your sales strategy. Generally speaking, the more difficult you make it for the prospect to respond, the better qualified he or she becomes. As I sometimes say in my seminars, if you were to omit your company address and require the prospect to write on his letterhead, you might only get one reply—but boy, would he be qualified! Seriously, however, let's look at some of the ways you can structure your package and your offer to fine-tune the quality of the respondents.

Assuming you want high quality and are willing to accept a lower response rate, one of the first ways to discourage response and allow only top-rated inquiries through is to mention the price of the product or service in the offer, especially if it's costly. Since a prime reason for responding is to learn the price, stating it up front eliminates that necessity.

Other techniques include telling the prospect to expect a phone call or visit by a salesperson. Only someone truly interested in the product will voluntarily invite a sales call. Requiring a signature on the reply form also raises the anxiety level a bit, since most folks don't like signing things. It feels a little too contractual. Requiring a telephone reply can also raise the qualification level.

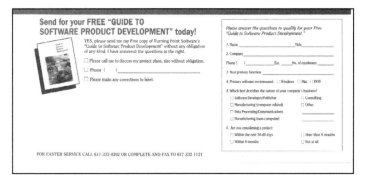

**Figure 7-2**

## The Qualification Questionnaire

By far the most reliable way of qualifying prospects is to include a brief questionnaire on the order form and require that it be completed—and maybe signed (this doesn't preclude any of the above tactics). Keep it short but to the point you're trying to determine—the respondent's qualifications.

**Figure 7-2** shows the reply form for a software development team seeking to qualify corporate software project directors; people who have the authority to outsource development projects. (See Case Study "A" on pg. 92 for more details.) Note that it states the prospect must answer the questions "to qualify for your Free *Guide to Software Product Development*." Note also that it includes a question relating to the anticipated timeframe in which the prospect might be considering a project. This allows you to assign priorities for your follow-up program. These same questions were asked of inbound callers as well.

**Figure 7-3**

**Figure 7-3** is an example of how the same techniques can be used to qualify consumer prospects. In this case, a travel wholesaler with a huge list of people needed to get the qualified travelers on the list to raise their hands. A free booklet on travel tips was offered only to "travelers age 50 and over." People over 50 represent the largest

## THE QUANTITY/QUALITY RATIO
### Generating Orders

| Lower Response / Higher Quality | Higher Response/ Lower Quality |
|---|---|
| Cash with order | Bill 30 days, credit cards |
| Add shipping and handling | Include shipping and handling |
| No examination period | 30 day free examination |
| No guarantee stated | Emphasize money-back guarantee |
| Computer personalized letter | Form letter |
| No brochure | Large, full-color brochure |
| No order form | Enclosed order card |
| Courtesy envelope (stamp required) | Business reply envelope |
| No premium | Premium or discount with purchase |

Figure 7-4

## THE QUANTITY/QUALITY RATIO
### Generating Leads

| Lower Response / Higher Quality | Higher Response/ Lower Quality |
|---|---|
| Reveal product and price | Omit product and price |
| Refer to salesman's visit | No sales reference |
| No interim step | Special report, related to |
| Charge for report/demo | Free report/demo |
| Require title, signature | Omit qualifiers |
| Telephone response only | Mail response |
| Toll call | Toll-free number |
| Require letterhead sample | Pre-addressed order form |
| Complete questionnaire | Require no data |

Figure 7-5

demographic for overseas travel (see Case Study "B" on pg. 93). In this example, as well as the first, note the *specificity* of the offer: the age requirement and the timeframe question.

In both cases the sales letter sold the *offer*– the travel guide and the development guide, not the ultimate product or service. Figure 7-4 shows some of the other elements you can include or omit in order to improve either the quantity or the quality of consumer respondents. Figure 7-5 shows the same for business-to-business markets.

## A Lead Generation Checklist

The following Lead/Inquiry Checklist is designed to help you organize your thinking and direct planning for a more effective lead-generation and database marketing program. It will help alert you to information that you do not yet have and provide a focus for more effective use of information you do have. It is also an effective starting point for lead generation planning for your advertising or marketing agency or consultant.

1. Description of Product(s)/Service:
2. Price point(s)

> Average sale: $_____
> Initial sale: $_____
> Ultimate sale: $_____

3. Average timeframe, contact to initial sale:
4. Title and function of Primary Purchase Decision-Maker:
5. Titles and functions of other purchase influencers:

6. How large do you estimate your universe to be?
7. How many inquiries can you effectively follow up in a week? In a month?
8. What are your main sources of leads right now?
9. What other sources are available for testing?
10. Who in your company closes the sale?
11. How many sales/installations to date?
12. How many transactions are in the sales pipeline at any one time?
13. How large is your house list? How is it maintained?
14. Do you have or can you get favorable Case Studies?
   Testimonials?
   Other types of customer recommendations?
15. What outside lists have you used successfully?
   Unsuccessfully?
16. What other media have you used successfully?
   Unsuccessfully?
17. Do you have a Web site?   Y ☐   N ☐
   If not, do you plan to have one soon?   Y ☐   N ☐
18. What is your current cost-per-lead? $____
   Cost-per-sale? $____
   Conversion rate? ____%
19. What is the lifetime value of a customer? $____
20. Do you market through vertical channels? Name them:
   Business Partners? Who?
21. If not, can the product/service be "versioned" for niche markets?   Y ☐   N ☐
22. What marketing support do you get from other sources?
23. Do you have a written marketing plan?   Y ☐   N ☐
24. Does it include a defined marketing budget?   Y ☐   N ☐
25. Do you have a written business plan?   Y ☐   N ☐
26. What are your immediate objectives?
27. Timetable:
28. Long-term objective:
29. Timetable:
30. Who are your primary competitors?
31. What are they doing that's worth noting?

> When you're selling direct, especially with cold mailings, every order is a lead. You want that customer to become a client—to come back and buy again and again, and buy other products.

32. Do you have a file of their advertising/promotion?
33. Have you done any market research? Describe.
34. Do you have a file of all advertising and promotion to date with results for each effort?
35. Who heads up market planning?
    Who handles creation and execution?

## Every Order Is a Lead

Don't assume that qualification techniques apply only to business-to-business leads.

You can qualify product purchasers (consumers) as well by applying the same basic concepts. Except with orders, the elements are a bit different. Remember that when you're selling direct, especially with cold mailings, every order is a lead. You want that customer to become a client—to come back and buy again and again, and buy other products. So the first sale is really a lead—a qualifier that tells you this customer may be worth pursuing.

In consumer transactions, there are factors that hype response and factors that inhibit it. If you want customers who are more likely to become repeat buyers, keep the hype to a minimum. Don't use a sweepstakes, for example, or give away a Palm Pilot. Keep your copy and creative on the lean side and put a few small roadblocks in the way of the purchase.

On the other hand, if you want as many buyers as you can get, regardless of quality, promote "Free" everywhere you can, give away a neat premium, offer a 30-day or even 60-day trial period, provide a handsome "Intro" offer or discount, and so on. The "How to Use Your Database" list later in this chapter spells out similar techniques you can use to fine-tune the consumer side. To be sure, these techniques are not 100% exact in their effects, but used together they can affect the volume and quality of your respondents and help you get more of the right kinds of names into the database to begin with. And unlike pricey modeling methods, they're free or almost free to implement.

### Slicing and Dicing for Fun and Profit

Most direct marketers are familiar with such P&L metrics as Break-even Analysis, Gross Response, Net Response, Cost-per-Inquiry, Cost-per-Order, Contribution to Overhead, Return on Investment (ROI), and other basic measurements that define financial success or failure.

Less familiar, and much less often computed, is Lifetime Value of a Customer. That is, how much revenue you can expect from a particular customer from acquisition until the relationship terminates. It's an important number because it tells you how much you can afford to spend to acquire a customer, how much to budget for subsequent marketing activities, how much data you should collect on your database, and it provides vital guidance for many other critical decisions.

The formula will vary with the circumstances, but it's a matter of computing total marketing expenditures and matching that against total revenues per customer, including present value of future profits.

Database technology helps improve the bottom line in several other ways as well. Predictive modeling is often a major reason for the care and feeding of a database, because it provides a way to find additional profitable customers with some reliability.

Say, for example, my travel agency client wanted to set up a predictive model of those "prospects" I mentioned—folks who said they traveled overseas. They would start with a demographic analysis of those customers (age and income), possibly including purchase behavior ("Hey, guess what! 92 percent of them bought jogging suits in the last 12 months!"), and other factors.

To that might be added a number cruncher's stew of lifestyle data, predictive variables, and so on, and out would come a computerized model against which to run all new prospect lists. The "hits" would be culled out and added to the "suspect" portion of the database.

Among the statistical tools at the modeler's disposal are such exotica as:

**CHAID** (Chi-Squared Automatic Interaction Detector)—an algorithm that predicts both response and profitability.

> The Lifetime Value of a Customer is an important number because it tells you how much you can afford to spend to acquire a customer.

**Regression Analysis**—compares data from those who responded to an offer to data from those who didn't and creates a formula that can measure a prospect's odds of responding.

**PRIZM**—classifies all U.S. households into one of 62 unique neighborhood types or "clusters" to help you identify, locate, and target your customers and best prospects.

**Neural Networks**—a statistical trick that identifies relationships in segments of data and adjusts itself as new data becomes available.

**Fractals**—a type of math that searches for patterns in data.

The point that needs to be made about these modeling techniques is that they are expensive. If you're not mailing around 200 million pieces a year, you probably can't afford them. It takes heavy usage of modeled databases to recover the costs of the technology. For the rest of us, RFM works just fine.

## ACT! Now—and Start Reaping the Database Goldmine

Another way to understand database management is to study the programs that are designed for it.

You don't have to be mega-mailer to put your customer information on popular contact managers like ACT! 2000® and Goldmine© 4.0. Even dentists have office management systems (one package I worked on locally I dubbed "Dental DOS") that kick out a personalized postcard reminder when your pearly whites are due for cleaning. My veterinarian's contact system even gets my cats' names right when it prints out their shot appointment letters.

Like ACT! 2000, many of today's contact managers are branching out into customer relationship management (CRM) tools (see the following section). Other contact managers in this general category include Janna Contact Professional 99, Maximizer Enterprise 5.0, and Telemagic Enterprise 4.0. Telemagic is a popular choice for integrating the database with the call center.

---

### Web Tip

When considering database technologies today, you'll want to strongly consider programs that interface with your Web site and provide seamless integration of data between the Web and your marketing database. Two tools that can assist in the translation from the database to HTML are Allaire's Cold Fusion and Microsoft Active Server Pages.

An e-commerce solution for online catalogers is Mail Order Manager, which integrates data from mail order, phone orders, and the Web.

---

A big brother to ACT! 2000 is SalesLogix®; also created by
ACT!'s developer, Pat Sullivan, it could be called "ACT II!." It boasts a
robust contact manager and is designed as a sales force automation
(SFA) tool. With custom configuration by business partners and systems integrators like GuideMark Systems (*www.guidemark.com*),
SalesLogix can make all the data in the sales pipeline and database
available to whomever needs it, around the office or around the world.

After the contact manager types of database program come
PC-based database programs: "flat file" and "relational." Clearly,
relational databases are more powerful and flexible and will do more
of the heavy lifting for larger mailers. But flat files work fine for
smaller mailers.

PC-based DBMS programs include Microsoft Access, dBase,
Lotus Approach, and Paradox. Mainframe and client-server programs
include FoxPro, Oracle, and others. Note that these are databases.
There is also a slew of mailing list management programs out there,
like Arc Tangent; catalog programs, like Mail Order Wizard; and
postal related programs, like Group 1. You may well want to consider
any of these programs, but be sure to understand the differences, or
work with a consultant who does.

Whatever system you use, even if you have to start with the
proverbial shoe box for now, capture those names, and include as
much data as you can afford to collect and manage. Be sure to select
a system that's "Web-compatible." As we'll see in Chapter 15, traditional marketing channels will play an ever-growing role in Web promotion. You'll also want to allow for expansion because changing
systems in midstream is painful and costly.

# One-to-One Marketing, Relationship Marketing, Data Warehouses, and CRM

### One-to-One
A few years ago, Don Peppers and Martha Rogers whetted
everyone's appetites for even stronger customer relationships with
their book *The One-to-One Future*, which championed what is essen-

> Whatever system you use, even if you have to start with the proverbial shoe box for now, capture those names, and include as much data as you can afford to collect and manage.

## The One-to-One Relationship

Peppers and Rogers suggest four steps to implementing a one-to-one relationship:

1. IDENTIFY customers by their buying patterns. Some are worth more than others. Work to separate the losers from the winners.
2. DIFFERENTIATE customers according to the reasons they buy—their needs and values. Addressing individual needs builds loyalty.
3. INTERACT by asking what customers want and getting a response. Then ask again.
4. CUSTOMIZE like my friend at Rogers Peet who knew my size and shape and called or sent a postcard when he had a new shipment of suits "made for me."

tially retention marketing—selling more to fewer customers since, as noted elsewhere in this book, it costs seven to nine times more to get a new customer than it does to keep an old one. Since then, Peppers and Rogers have been showing companies how to exploit the online communications capabilities of e-mail and the Web to tailor offers and deliver what amounts to customized products and services.

Basically, the idea comes back to the guy at Rogers Peet with his box of 3" × 5" cards, treating each customer individually. With the Internet and database technologies of the new century, that kind of one-to-one customer service becomes possible again

## Relationship Marketing

Today's ever-more-sophisticated database technologies and computing power have pushed the envelope to create ever-more-sophisticated relationship models and data analysis opportunities for companies. One of these is so-called relationship marketing. The airlines' frequent flyer programs are often cited as prime examples of relationship marketing. The Petco and Radio Shack birthday schemes mentioned above are sort of low-tech examples—more manageable than the frequent flyer programs and useable by just about any business.

A better term for Relationship Marketing might be "retention marketing," since it's really aimed at keeping customers longer and moving them up the RFM ladder. Driven, quite understandably, by the fact that it costs seven to nine times more to get a new customer than it does to keep a current one.

While programs with the heft of the frequent flyer deals may be a tad costly for most small businesses, the idea behind them has led to many successful "frequent buyer" and other types of loyalty programs. One danger here, of course, is incentivising a customer to do something he or she would have done in any case . . . buy yet another widget from you. Or worse, bribing a customer to buy, based not on the quality of your product, but on the bribe itself. Some feel that sweepstakes are a form of this kind of marketing. The sweepstakes quickly becomes a tar baby. Once you've used it, try selling something without it, and response drops precipitously. So you have to keep it going.

There is a lot of controversy surrounding the efficacy of frequency and loyalty programs. Some studies have indicated that they don't produce loyalty at all. That once the rewards stop, or even diminish in value, the customer moves on to another program. In addition, the complexity of some programs seems to invite disaster or thoughtlessness on the part of the marketer.

In designing a frequency or loyalty program, you should also be sure you're not relying on the customer to keep records, figure out awards, or do any other form of paperwork in order to take advantage of your largesse. Most won't. The few that will are folks who know how to work the system—not your best customers.

Other caveats include:

- Adding new layers of entitlement that slice the benefits thinner for people at the top of the food chain.
- Changing the rules.
- Failing to keep the program creative and innovative after it's launched.

You'll want to survey your members continually to keep close track of how your program is doing, what types of rewards your customers want most, what kinds of glitches are happening out there, and, of course, you'll need to monitor the ROI carefully to be sure you're meeting your plan.

Finally, keep in mind John Naisbitt's admonition in his book *Re-Inventing the Corporation*: "Today, there is no such thing as customer loyalty. To succeed in business, companies have to be loyal to their customers."

## Data Warehouses and Data Marts

As you might expect from the term, data warehouses are huge computer disks filled with customer data that has been mixed and matched with data from other sources such as lifestyle analyses, census data, behavior models, and more. Marketers then go "data mining" for nuggets of information that will make future mailings more accurate and more profitable. Data mining techniques are designed

### Give Your Assumptions a Reality Check

I flew to South Asia a few years back and earned a significant number of air miles. I have received several promotional mailings from that airline since, all assuming I'd be headed back to Singapore any day now. If the airline flies anywhere else, they're not telling me about it, and, in fact, I haven't flown that airline since. One-to-one and loyalty programs need to be carefully assessed to be sure they are adding sufficient present or potential future value to justify their considerable cost.

to uncover patterns and connections in data that might have otherwise gone unnoticed and unused.

The average data warehouse in 1999 was about 270 gigabytes. According to a study from Palo Alto Management Group, Inc., that's expected to grow by a factor of 24 by 2002, to 6.5 terabytes. The market is expected to grow from $15 billion in 1997 to $113 billion in 2002. The average number of users will grow from 2,200 people today to almost 100,000 in 2002.

Data marts are smaller "packages" of data that can be accessed and used by different sales and marketing teams within the enterprise. Here again, you need to be a major mailer dropping more than 100 million pieces a year before these tools become cost-effective. The same is true for CRM.

## Customer Relationship Management (CRM)

The mother of all data warehouse applications is customer relationship management (CRM), which seeks to integrate all of the functions of the enterprise—customer/marketing database, sales force automation, campaign management, business intelligence, and more—into a single "unified theory" of marketing and customer relationship control. In fact, the One-to-One Group uses the terms "one-to-one," "relationship marketing," and "customer relationship management" interchangeably.

The software created for CRM applications thus far costs in the hundreds of thousands of dollars to purchase and implement with much downtime and many integration problems along the way. Only the biggest spenders have been able to afford it, but that appears to be changing.

A recent study of the Direct Marketing Association indicates that companies are gradually implementing enterprise-wide CRM systems, turning call centers into customer integration centers, integrating it all into e-commerce functions, and using datamining and modeling to get a better handle on their customers. Cost and complexity are still a problem, but the move of these systems to the Internet may be making them more affordable for some companies.

> The One-to-One Group uses the terms "one-to-one," "relationship marketing," and "customer relationship management" interchangeably.

According to the study,

- One-fifth of marketers have implemented an enterprise customer database and 29 percent plan to do so.
- Fifty-five percent have integrated at least a part of their customer information across all sales channels.

While smaller businesses are unlikely to be able to utilize CRM packages cost-effectively, the concept of customer-driven data to support marketing decisions is essential to success.

## How to Use Your Database

### Consumer
As I've said before in these pages, "junk mail is an offer sent to the wrong person." A database system can help you target the right person, the first time. And when your database is up and running, here are some of the ways you can use it (in addition to seasonal sale announcements, special events, promotions, etc.):

1. Send timely reminders of needed services: doctor/dentist appointment, oil change/tuneup, service contract expirations. "Your imprinted labels will be depleted soon; order now with the attached reply form . . . "
2. Send a card or letter on the anniversary of a purchase.
3. Send customers' kids birthday cards, if you can get that information on your database.
4. Periodic surveys.
5. Invite customers/prospects to a product demonstration or educational seminar. (Free to customers, slight fee for prospects.)
6. Using careful segmentation, send:
   –Price changes, product changes, policy changes.
   –New product announcements ("Preview" for customers).
   –Product samples to customers—or OFFERS for product samples for prospects with qualifying information.

> While smaller businesses are unlikely to be able to utilize CRM packages cost-effectively, the concept of customer-driven data to support marketing decisions is essential to success.

> Items you offer through cyberspace or mail should be of intrinsic value, tangible, and carefully targeted to the status of the recipient, whether it's a suspect, prospect, customer, client, or advocate.

7. Contests and sweepstakes opportunities (Supports mail order sales and in-store traffic building programs).
8. Frequent buyer programs.
9. Newsletter (especially as part of Frequent Buyer Program).
10. Annual Report.

**Note:** In addition, ALWAYS include such items in the products you ship to customers along with discount certificates, etc., designed to spur repeat business.

## Business-to-Business

Always include in ads—and press releases—an offer for something other than "more information." Items you offer through cyberspace or mail should be of intrinsic value, tangible, and carefully targeted to the status of the recipient, whether it's a suspect, prospect, customer, client, or advocate.

1. Special report or "white paper" on technology or industry dynamics related to your product. Give it a title and offer it by name.
2. Case studies of successful implementation of your product. (Get permission early and have these on file.) "Seven Ways xyz Widgets have saved companies like yours more than $2 million!" Note the specificity of "Seven Ways" and "$2 million."
3. Profiles of successful client companies. "Meet the pros who are making a difference in astrophysics today!" (Can be any level, CEOs, engineers, etc.)
4. Test results of product performance—trade publication reviews and articles on such performance.
5. Conduct an annual industry survey on some vital issue (executive salaries, corporate marketing practices, product or corporate performance benchmarks, research expenditures), publish the results, and mail to customers.
6. Send press releases on new product announcements to customer/prospect segments. Include information for requesting product brochures.

7. Reprints of articles on your company or products.
8. Reprints of your ad campaign with note. (In case you missed our ads when they ran in xyz and abc. We're sure you'd want to see them.)
9. Contests (customers only). Integrate with sales incentive contest for sales reps.
10. Invitation to informational (product or industry) seminar.
11. Product video (this can be integrated into all of the above mailings and offers, when properly targeted).
12. Newsletter.
13. Annual Report.

## Setting a Good Example: Marketing with Case Studies

Items two and three in the previous list are important enough to consider separately in any discussion of successful BTB marketing methods.

Case studies are especially effective in business environments because they act as an automatic third-party endorsement—even if the company involved has not formally offered a testimonial. Assuming your project with the company was successful, it offers a clear example of how your product was deployed—one that your prospect can quickly understand and apply to his or her own circumstances. It may even suggest techniques and solutions he or she hasn't thought of.

But more than that, it gives the prospect executive *permission* to follow up with an inquiry. The case study validates your initial promises at least, and tells the prospect he won't be barking up a wrong tree by making the call . . . or returning the reply card. In a highly specialized niche market, he or she may even know the people involved in the case study, at least by reputation, which begins to create a relational loop to be closed by your information.

The moral is to begin collecting hard data on client projects if you haven't already done so, and when the time is right, ask the client company if you can use the information in a case study. There may be confidentiality considerations to deal with, so make an effort

> Case studies are especially effective in business environments because they act as an automatic third-party endorsement.

to have a solution to those before you ask. Disguising the company name, while not ideal, may be acceptable to other executives in similar situations. They wouldn't want you blowing their secrets, so it's important that they see you're protecting the clients you have. Using approximate numbers, averages, or percentages in place of actual metrics may also help.

You may have also noticed the inclusion of a newsletter in both database usage lists. In business-to-business applications especially, a newsletter can be a valuable marketing tool.

## Turn Prospects into Customers and Keep Both in the Loop—with a Promotional Newsletter!

How long are the sales cycles for your company's products? Three months? A year? Eighteen months? In today's business-to-business marketplace, long lead times are the rule rather than the exception. And the higher the price point, the greater the complexity of your products, and the longer their sales lead time will be.

How do you keep a prospect interested over a course of 18 months? How do you head off competitors' inroads into the prospect while your sales rep is working through the steps in the sales cycle?

One answer being discovered by companies in every industry is the promotional newsletter—often used in conjunction with other promotional mailings.

Part gentle reminder, part public relations tool, part sales device, the promotional newsletter gives you an entry into the prospect company when your salesperson can't be there. It helps keep the prospect informed on product features and benefits, company successes, and more, and it generally maintains a favorable impression of your company in the prospect's mind between sales calls.

As for customers, a newsletter is the perfect "follow-up sales call" whether it's published on a weekly, monthly, bimonthly, or quarterly basis. It keeps customers "in the loop" on new products, informs them on effective product use through case studies involving your company and products, and provides opportunities for product research, aftermarket sales of support and training, cross-selling of related products, and upgrades of the products they purchased.

> Part gentle reminder, part public relations tool, part sales device, the promotional newsletter gives you an entry into the prospect company when your salesperson can't be there.

## Include Case Studies

One of the most effective features you can include in a newsletter is the case history. Real-world examples of how other companies are successfully using your products—and innovative new ways to use them—can provide powerful peer approval of your product and give your prospect permission to inquire further. Successful case studies also reaffirm customers' purchase decisions and help keep them sold on your products and your company.

## "News" Stories

New products and services are, of course, naturals for news stories in your newsletter. Be careful, however, not to write about them in a promotional or hard-sell context. Rather, "report" on them objectively, almost as though they were some other company's.

You can use your newsletter to announce new white papers or special reports. But don't just announce that they are available. Write about them as news.

Prominent new customers can be featured in news stories as well, together with profiles of key customer end users.

Product performance test results can be reported as news, and you can include announcements of product reviews in the trade press. (You can also use your newsletter to correct or explain any unfavorable reviews that might have appeared in the trade press.)

## A Research Tool

You can also use your newsletter to publish occasional questionnaires designed to acquire information about readers' business needs and interests . . . trade publication reading habits . . . even salary and computer usage surveys.

## Industry Digest

It can be genuinely helpful to readers if you excerpt "news briefs" from your industry's trade publications. Be sure to observe "fair use" laws and ask permission for any verbatim or other reproductions you may use from other publications.

---

### 5 Benefits of a Promotional Newsletter

Basically, a newsletter can:

1. Create an awareness of your company and its capabilities

2. Burnish your company's image

3. Establish your expertise and credibility in the marketplace

4. Show your competitive strengths

5. Demonstrate the superiority of your products and/or service

In some cases, including an order form for readers to recommend peers and colleagues who might have an interest in your newsletter can increase circulation.

## Keep It Professional

Features to avoid include "Employee of the Month" and other "house" information . . . pictures of the building . . . pictures of the president. In short, keep it a newsletter and not thinly disguised flackery.

## Business-to-Business Case Study A: An Offer They Couldn't Refuse

### The Situation

A team of software engineers were having significant success developing software programs for major software companies, like Lotus and Microsoft, as well as for corporations like Xerox and DuPont. Current projects were drawing to a close, and they wanted to get more work into the pipeline before things wound down completely.

After reviewing their material, I determined that they had nothing readily available that they could offer to suspects to prompt an inquiry. I suggested they create a "Guide to Software Development" based on the belief that corporate software developers would be drawn to such a document if we could make it sufficiently tempting.

### The Solution

The letter was just over a page, appropriate for busy and harassed software project directors. It promoted the Guide almost exclusively, introducing the development team itself only in the P.S.

Also enclosed was a trifold brochure offering "Seven proven tips for keeping software development projects on time and on budget." There was no traditional company brochure. We used the color teal as a narrow border element and in a few headlines to provide visual continuity between the pieces.

---

**Web Tip**

Capture customers' e-mail addresses and send them an e-mail newsletter or e-letter keeping them up to date on your products and/or company. Provide a clear and easy way for the customer to "opt-out" or unsubscribe from the e-letter. Or invite customers to visit your Web site to sign up for an e-letter.

### The Result

More than 12% response, resulting in several new contracts and their "most successful promotion ever."

### Dynamics

While one can seldom document these things, I believe the package worked first because the teaser targeted the prospect/buyer very directly with a "hot button" offer that spoke directly to his or her primary interest—software development.

The package in fact promised *two* payoffs: The "seven ways, etc." in the envelope challenged the prospect's professional know-how and provided instant gratification of his curiosity. It also served to demonstrate the expertise of the company. Any software development project leader reading that brochure could not fail to see that this was a team of pros.

The second payoff was the more substantial Guide which, especially since it was free, any responsible project leader would have difficulty passing up. As the letter promised, the Guide would be "helpful in staffing and managing your next development project." Not a small matter.

The offer was sufficiently well qualified and the package overall had a crisp, professional look.

> The package worked first because the teaser targeted the prospect/buyer very directly with a "hot button" offer that spoke directly to his or her primary interest— software development.

## Consumer Case Study B: Travel Agency

### The Situation

A travel wholesaler in Boston had obtained a list of several million "senior citizens." Older Americans are known to travel abroad in greater numbers than their younger—and presumably more tied down—sons and daughters. This list, therefore, represented several million suspects—people the company had reason to believe—mostly because of their age—might be interested in their various travel programs.

In order to determine exactly who on that list were so inclined, I was asked to create a lead-generating direct mail piece. The criteria were quite specific. They wanted only people who were (1) over 50 years old, who (2) traveled overseas, not just domestically. My further charge was to produce highly qualified respondents. There was no wiggle room in the qualification requirement.

### The Solution

I started with a booklet the company had pretty much lying around the office which I retitled and teased on the envelope: "Go abroad in safety and comfort with 'Going Abroad: 101 Tips for Mature Travelers'—FREE to Travelers 50 and over!" That put the overseas travel and age requirements right up front.

Inside, I further qualified the respondents by asking them to answer four pointed questions about their age (again) and travel habits. They could also check off three destinations that interested them and receive free brochures on those locations.

The package was personalized on the envelope, letter, and response device, both to impress older recipients and to eliminate their need to write out any documents.

### The Result

Clients don't always share response rates with freelancers, but I was told it had been a "very successful mailing."

### The Dynamics

In my view, the primary dynamic was the tight qualification and the no-nonsense insistence on only respondents who were 50 or older and who had traveled abroad. The premium booklet was also tightly targeted to this population.

Personalization throughout added credibility, and the qualification questions provided just enough of a barrier to prevent a lot of "tire kickers" and deliver well-qualified prospects.

> The qualification questions provided just enough of a barrier to prevent a lot of "tire kickers" and deliver well-qualified prospects.

## Resources

Database development, marketing, and computer technology are highly complex areas. I strongly recommend reading a variety of books and magazine articles on these topics and talking with database consultants and service vendors before venturing into the database underbrush. It's a jungle in there! Following are some places to start.

- The 1-to-1 Group, *www.1to1.com.*
- *Direct Marketing* magazine, 1-800-229-6700
- *DM News, www.dmnews.com*
- *Target Marketing* magazine, *www.targetonline.com*
- *Marketing Tools*, 607-273-6343, *www.marketingtools.com*
- *Business to Business Direct Marketing*, by Bernard A. Goldberg and Tracy Emerick, and *The Lead Generation Handbook* by Bernard A. Goldberg Direct Marketing Publishers, Inc. 1304 University Drive, Yardley, PA 19067. (215) 321-3068.
- Claritas (for PRIZM analysis), *www.connect.claritas.com*
- Also check the Direct Marketing Bookstore at *www.netplaza.com.*
- The database Listserv I referred to is available at this Web site: *www.argo-navis.com/dm-digest/index.htm*

Finally, there are several conferences and trade shows where you can not only learn database marketing from the seminars, but meet with the service bureaus and other suppliers to the industry for firsthand information on the various technologies. These include:

- The National Center for Database Marketing and Direct Marketing to Business Conferences, 800-927-5007 or by e-mail at NCDMinfo@cowlesbiz.com, and Direct Marketing to Business Conference, at *www.dmbshow.com*
- The Direct Marketing Association conducts a variety of seminars and two semiannual conferences.
- *www.the-dma.org.*
- Direct Marketing Day in New York is always a biggie: *www.dmdny.com.*

Direct Marketing Day in New York is always a biggie: *www.dmdny.com.*

## Newsletter Resources

- Newsletter Association, 1401 Wilson Blvd. Suite 403, Arlington, VA 22209.
- International Association of Business Communicators, 870 Market Street, Suite 940, San Francisco, CA 94102.
- The Newsletter on Newsletters and Communicators Bookstore, PO Box 311, Rhinebeck, NY 12572.

For more information on this topic, visit our Web site at www.businesstown.com

# The Creative Process

"If it doesn't sell, it's not creative,"
David Ogilvy once said.

# Writing for Response: Direct Mail Copywriting

est I be accused of false pretenses, let me begin this chapter with a disclaimer. I don't believe that I can teach you how to write. Whether writing is a talent or a skill is beyond my understanding, except to say it's likely a little of both. Beyond that, however, direct mail writing is a learnable process, and, as guitar pickers say to a colleague who wants to learn a tune, "I can't teach 'ya . . . but I can show 'ya."

In the chapter that follows I'll show you how to structure your information and your thinking for writing response copy, and how to get them on paper in proven, effective ways. Keep in mind, this isn't the Great American Novel. It's writing for dollars. Mrs. Grundy or Sister Mary Elizabeth won't be around to rap your knuckles if you split an infinitive. And if your copy reads more clearly that way, go ahead and split it! Not sure which punctuation is best after a statement? Use an "em" dash—like that—and to heck with it.

The point is, we want our writing to be crystal clear to the reader, whatever it takes. We also want it to move smoothly from the outer envelope teaser to the order form (or telephone, or Web site). Any major interruption in our reader's train of thought, and chances are we'll be derailed. A confusing sentence, an illogical statement, an unclear description of how the product works or what we want the prospect to do, and it's all over.

Good copywriting also has a rhythm that helps move the reader along. Alliterations in text, short statements and comments, use of contractions ("you'll" instead of "you will"), rising and falling inflections, all contribute to a sort of iambic pentameter for copy that makes reading more of a pleasure, and less of a chore.

This would also be a good time to recall that agreement with our proposition is failure. We have to get a response or we're dead in the water.

The noted direct mail writer and author Robert Collier once said that we all walk around with a conversation going on in our heads, and the task of the copywriter is to break through that conversation and make himself heard. The topic of that conversation is, of course, oneself. That's why response writers use the second person almost exclusively—to join the conversation the prospect is already having with himself. And that idea is nothing new. No less a

> This would also be a good time to recall that agreement with our proposition is failure. We have to get a response or we're dead in the water.

personage than Alexis de Tocqueville recognized the American obsession with self back in the early 19th century. According to Alex, here's what you're up against.

> "In democratic communities, each citizen is habitually engaged in the contemplation of a very puny object: himself. If he ever raises his looks higher, he perceives only the immense form of society at large or the still more imposing aspect of mankind. His ideas are all either extremely minute and clear or extremely general and vague; what lies between is a void. When he has been drawn out of his own sphere, therefore, he always expects that some amazing object will be offered to his attention; and it is on these terms alone that he consents to tear himself for a moment from the petty, complicated cares that form the charm and the excitement of his life."

And if you'd like to take that idea even further back to the great Roman orator, Cicero, here's how he put it: "If you wish to persuade me, you must think my thoughts, feel my feelings, and speak my words."

As we'll see in a bit, that's why we stress *benefits*, the language of the *buyer*, rather than *features*, the language of the *seller*.

Having said all that—and notwithstanding all that follows—we've seen that copy and creative are about 10% to 20% of the success of a direct mail campaign. The list and the offer do the heavy lifting at 40% each.

Well-written copy will always enhance the results of any offer, but the right offer to the right list at the right time will likely survive even mediocre copy. On the other hand, no copy can save the wrong offer to the wrong list, not even if you brought Claude Hopkins back from the dead.

Further, all copy and creativity is a compromise with time. I've known top writers who agonize over every word and phrase and revise, revise, revise through sleepless nights and others who do a first draft, polish it, and let it go. Which you are will depend on who you are, and nothing I can say here will change it.

> All copy and creativity is a compromise with time.

## Preparing to Write: Researching the Product and the Market

The first preparation for writing direct mail is to pack in at least 30 years' of life experience and, somewhere along the line, do some selling—if it isn't already too late to suggest that. It will also help if you diversify your experience as much as possible. Young people looking to get into "direct" as copywriters should get a liberal arts degree and suck up all the media they can, at all age levels. And even if you're pushing 40, don't ignore MTV, Fox, and VH-1. At the other end of the spectrum, America is getting older. And older folks make great customers. Study their needs and values. Work to understand the culture you'll be selling to, whatever it is. That said, there are a number of questions a writer must ask in order to think through the direct mail effort he or she will create.

Especially if you're an outside agency or freelancer, or a staff writer but new to the company, the following questionnaire will provide valuable data. Even if you've been with the company for a long time, it will help your writing to spell out this information in your own hand, in your own words, and have them all in one place. If you're the company founder or president, it will help you to get a customer's-eye view of your product. A view, believe it or not, that you may not have.

> It has been my frequent experience that business owners and company presidents have a very proprietary view of their products and their companies.

It has been my frequent experience that business owners and company presidents have a very proprietary view of their products and their companies. Small business execs in particular. And why not? It's their baby. They likely conceived it and grew it with much hard work and pain. But that very experience tends to focus their thinking on the *product* and its *features*—what they built, not on the *customer* and the product's *benefits*.

### Your First Source of Research: Your Customer

It surprises me how often I meet with clients who have never spoken to their customers. They tend to believe they can divine their customers' views on things through the order forms and other miscellaneous types of communication that they receive. And sometimes, they feel they know what's best for their customer!

I suggest you get on the phone and call a dozen or so customers and ask them, at the very least:

a). Why they purchased the product or service (and sometimes, who bought it–it may not have been the customer-of-record).
b). How often they use it,
c). How they use it (lots of surprises there!).
d). How they might improve it.
e). What they don't like about it, and, if time permits, how they heard of you, what other media they use regularly, and what else they do that may be related.

Depending on the product or service, you'll no doubt develop special questions of your own.

If your product is a publication, such as a newsletter or magazine, you'll want to interview the editor. I've found editors' views of a publication are often much different from those of marketing people. You'll also want to read the "Letters to the Editors" file–all of them, the good, the bad, and the ugly–and in the case of a magazine, the advertising promotion people can frequently add fresh insights.

Finally, if the product is sold by salespeople, you'll want to talk to the sales manager or a top salesperson about the "hot buttons" they use and the typical points of resistance they encounter.

After you've done all that, the following questionnaire will fill in the "nuts and bolts" information you must review before you begin writing. It's designed mostly for consumer products and services. (There is a similar questionnaire for lead generation in Chapter 7.) You'll find it also relates to the Direct Mail Package Checklist in Chapter 9.

1. Description of product or service–in 50 words or fewer.
2. Purpose of the product. What does it do, how does it work, how is it used?
3. Price. How much does it cost?
4. What are the features of the product? Specs and facts about what helps it to do whatever it does. What makes it better, faster, more comfortable, more accurate, etc.?

## Get Opinions

For any product or service, there should be a "letters" file. Resolve now that you will make an effort to reach out to your customers by phone and mail, and solicit their views of your company and your products. And always include a checkbox saying, "May we quote you? ❏ yes ❏ no" so you can use the better quotes as testimonials in the future.

5. What are the benefits of the product? What will it do for me? What specific problem does it solve? How will it make me "healthy, wealthy, and wise"? (See discussion of benefits later in this chapter. For suggestions 4 and 5, it will help to make a list of features down one side of a piece of paper and list the corresponding benefit opposite each.)

6. Other key points: What will it provide that I can't get somewhere else? How and why is it new? . . . superior? . . . exclusive? What is the competition, and why should I prefer this one?

7. What is the offer? Special introductory or limited-time savings? A premium? 2-for-1 sale? Free information? Are there basic and deluxe versions? Is this a one-step sale (directly from the ad or mailing piece) or a two-step offer? (Free information now with a telephone sales or direct mail follow-up. See the Lead Generation Checklist in Chapter 7 if this is the latter.)

8. What is the method of payment? (Cash with order only? . . . Bill me? . . . Credit cards? [Which ones?] . . . Is a purchase order required [business]? Do you have an 800 number? Can they fax their orders? Order via e-mail? . . . Web site?)

9. What is the guarantee? 100% money-back anytime? 30-day no-risk trial?

10. Are there objectives other than direct sales? Image or brand building? Collecting customer information? Pass-along? Add-on or aftermarket sales?

11. Who am I mailing to; that is, what lists are being used? (You should already know this from your prequestionnaire research. It isn't "everybody," trust me. Read the List Data Sheets to determine not only who these people are, but how they got on the list. If they are mostly sweepstakes entrants, for example, that will influence your thinking.)

12. If not previously determined, What is my prospect's title and responsibility (for B-T-B), or ( for consumer)? What is his/her age, sex, marital status, economic class, etc.? You should have already determined the full spectrum of demographics and psychographics that apply to your prospect from company surveys, sales experience, customer correspondence, phone

> Read the List Data Sheets to determine not only who these people are, but how they got on the list.

calls, List Data Sheets, etc. In addition, you should have, from your own experience or that of others, insights into your prospect's day-to-day home or daily business life. In business environments, how will your product help him or her get ahead? Get the promotion and the raise? Be a more successful team leader? Be more self-confident or popular with coworkers? In home environments, how will your product help save money and/or reduce worry and hassle? How will it make the buyer a better mother? . . . father? . . . spouse? . . . friend to others? For younger people, how will it help them fit in and be popular with their peers? Will brighter teeth (feature) lead to a great relationship (benefit)?

13. What is the budget for this project? (Budgeting should be a regular part of a marketing plan, based on sales or projected sales, not "whatever it costs.") This may tell you whether you can plan an ink-jet personalized, four-color, 9" × 12" package or a two-color self-mailer, although that should be determined by other factors.

14. What is the timeline? When must the piece be mailed? Why? (Allow up to 12 weeks for detailed direct mail planning and execution from scratch. Printing and mailing will take about two weeks each. For most products, January and September are key mailing months, unless this is a seasonal product. Testing in September and rolling out in January is a viable strategy.)

15. Are there any tests planned? Copy? . . . Price? . . . Offer? (If not, why not?)

16. Are there any key copy points or phrases that must be included? . . . that must be avoided?

17. Is there any special information regarding the company and its place in the industry or stories of key people in the company that might play a role? (This should be something specific and dramatic, not a CEO bio or company history.)

> For most products, January and September are key mailing months, unless this is a seasonal product.

## All about Benefits

As students of direct marketing—as all practitioners are—we are told constantly to stress the benefits of our product or service and "turn features into benefits." So it's worthwhile, I think, to spend some time asking, "Just what is a benefit anyway?" "Why must we stress benefits rather than features?" and, "What are the differences, if any, between benefits in consumer direct marketing versus business-to-business?"

It's not as obvious as one might think. Just recently, I listened as a team of telesales trainees struggled to define the benefits of a newsletter they would soon be marketing to business executives by phone. They reminded me of a session I used to conduct as part of a full-day seminar on book marketing at the *Folio* Magazine Publishers' Conference.

As mentioned in the sidebar, "a feature becomes a benefit when it intersects the life of a human being, with favorable results." It's the favorable results we want to present to prospects as a benefit.

Dunc's Ever-Gro Seed also contained nitrogen. Since nitrogen is a fertilizer, the user needn't otherwise fertilize the lawn. Thus he or she can "Save time, save money, save work and hassle" with Dunc's Ever-Gro on the job! Those are fairly common benefits for almost any product sold by mail.

Another feature was the seed's resistance to cold. It survived at temperatures as low as 45° Fahrenheit. What does that mean to the user? That he or she will have a luscious lawn to enjoy longer than anyone else in the neighborhood—"all the way to Halloween!" (For those of us in northern latitudes).

One more feature that may be less apparent: Dunc's Seed also produced a grass plant with roots that ran 6" to 8" deeper into the ground (Hey, it's my seed!). The result is a lawn that's much sturdier than the average. The grass won't pull out as easily. Is that the benefit? Not yet. What does it mean to the lives of the people? It means "the whole family can lie on it, play on it, and your lawn will look as good on Labor Day as it did on the Fourth of July."

To repeat: **features relate to the product and are presented in the language of the seller. Benefits relate to the buyer and are presented in the language of the user.** Remember Cicero.

## Why Benefits?

So what's the big deal with benefits anyway? What's wrong with features?

Glad you asked. Depending on which study you read, you and I are bombarded by anywhere from 900 to 2,000 commercial messages every day. If we didn't have some sort of filtering mechanism for all those messages, we'd explode or maybe just go nuts before we reached our 12th birthday.

To help us stay sane, therefore, the Creator gave us the ability to filter things out based on their relevance to us. We tune into station WIFM–"What's In It For Me?" Benefits are far more significant to us than dry features that may or may not be relevant. How something improves my life, personally or professionally, is of greater interest to me than the technical nuts and bolts that drive the process. And I'm the sole judge of what's relevant and how something improves my life. You may be able to prove up one side and down the other that "it's cool to own" a Buick Regal. That it will provide me with reliable, upscale transportation at an acceptable cost, but gol-darn-it, everyone on my block drives a 10-ton sports utility vehicle, so I want one, too!

Benefits get past the mind's gatekeepers with greater reliability than do features and all the other image flotsam and message jetsam that bombard us every day.

> We tune into station WIFM—"What's In It For Me?" Benefits are far more significant to us than dry features that may or may not be relevant.

## Emotion vs. Reason

Madison Avenue's motivational gurus have long held that most purchase decisions are emotionally based, but that the justifications are rational. No one is going to admit that he or she is buying a product in order to be better than the next person. Rather, they justify the purchase with such rational benefits as saving money, saving time, saving work.

When translating these dynamics to a direct mail package, the emotional benefits are usually too subtle and complex to use up front—as an envelope teaser, for example, or the headline on a letter, or even in a brochure that is intended to show the product in use.

Those are best left to the short, rational benefits. The emotional benefits can be either carefully suggested or baldly stated in the letter, depending on the setting. This may be why the letter in a direct mail package is widely accepted as the selling document. It sells because it taps that emotional component of the purchase decision.

For the most part, rational consumer benefits are short term, while the emotional appeal is longer term. Both are based on principles of personal security and social acceptance.

Some years ago I came across psychologist Abraham Maslow's "Hierarchy of Needs and Information." (See Figure 8-1)

In his diagram, Maslow set up a progression of human needs and related each category to the type of information that best responds to that need. At the bottom are the basic biological/physiological needs of food, water, shelter, air—those elements that allow us to thrive as humans. In most cases, the "coping information" that addresses those needs is provided free in the form of editorial matter by such media as newspapers and magazines, radio and TV programs, and the like.

There are also free clinics and various kinds of medical and mental professionals that provide the coping information free or nearly free, or with third-party compensation. Not a big business here, except maybe for the HMOs.

Security needs begin to stir the revenue pot with all the products and services that provide secure shelter and physical, mental, and economic security (housing and real estate, home repair, auto repair and services, financial and insurance services, communications, education, entertainment, etc.).

The sources of this information include various professionals from real estate agents to lawyers to accountants to the cable guy. The economics run the gamut from high gross margin/low volume (almost any house in Greenwich, CT), to high volume with paper-thin margins (Windows or IBM-compatible PCs).

Figure 8-1

For the most part, we consider these the necessities of life, not luxuries, including Bill Gates' $50 million home because, as he will tell you, he "needs" that house for the business and social roles he must play in life. (That's what's relevant to him.) We buy according to our ability to pay (or charge), give or take a bit, and products and services are priced and marketed within various demographic ranges. (Mr. Gates *is* a range.) The big financial bounce is when one moves between ranges, with less dramatic profit margins within any given range.

Marketers need to remember that the basic benefit in all of this is, as Maslow tells us, *security*. You can slice it and dice it any way you like, but at bottom, your appeal should be to security, expressed in whatever terms are appropriate for the category and the market. Bill Gates may define security a little differently than you or I, but it will still be there.

Social needs mean belonging and love—simply different forms of security, really, but we think of them differently. The economics range from a Hallmark card for $1.50 (high volume, low margin) to any of those baubles Tiffany features on page 3 of the *Times* (low volume, high margin). Social needs also drive most of the stuff we buy to make our breath sweet, our bodies odorless, our teeth white, and our hair manageable.

The rational benefits here range from concepts of personal hygiene to concepts of stylishness and modernity (aka "cool"). But here again, the longer-term emotional benefits center around acceptance by others. However we position the product, we need to keep in mind that the benefits are love and belonging, and we need to work that into our presentation, in whatever configuration works best.

Ego needs are where the rubber meets the road. While it's true that ego is boosted by love and belonging as well as by social affirmation, there's a whole other world of products and services that serve ego.

As Mary Kay Ash, founder of Mary Kay Cosmetics, puts it, "Everyone has a sign hanging around his or her neck that says 'make me feel important.' If you can do that, you'll be a success not only in business, but in life as well." Maslow simply quantified it in psychological terms.

## What's In It For Me?

A few years back, a nationally known direct mail copywriter called to chat and mentioned that he had just spent some time at several corporations. "All these guys want," he had decided, "is to beat out the guy in the next cubicle." Bingo. Just like the guy with the emerald green lawn that's "the envy of the neighborhood," everyone wants to look good in front of his or her boss and colleagues, wants to get the promotion, the bonus, the kudos, the "Employee of the Month" parking spot—anything that singles him or her out above the crowd.

Note in the illustration the kind of information that feeds the ego—"empowering" information. Information that builds self-esteem and promises fulfillment and self-actualization. Those are the promises, regardless of the product!

Denny Hatch, copywriter/consultant and past editor of *Target Marketing* magazine, singles out seven benefits he feels are indispensable to any direct mail letter. "Your sales pitch must employ *at least* one of the following Seven Key Copy Drivers," he says. "And preferably all seven. If not, tear it up and start over." He lists:

1. Fear
2. Guilt
3. Flattery
4. Exclusivity
5. Greed
6. Anger
7. Salvation

## Business-to-Business Benefits

If you're selling to plant superintendents, maybe your chemical cleaner will save money, time, and work, but the final payoff is a maintenance department (and a plant superintendent) that got the job done! Draw that distinction, and you'll tap the emotional component of the decision-making process.

If you're marketing a newsletter, the subscriber is going to know more than the guy in the next office, and look better, sound better, etc., in front of his or her boss and colleagues. He or she is empowered by special knowledge to "make a more meaningful contribution" in the workplace or will enjoy "sharper, more timely, and on-target decision-making."

Maybe an individual manager or supervisor can think in terms of improving corporate or company profits, but most of us know that's pretty remote from our particular cubicle. Nonetheless, it may be the rationale for a purchase of a newsletter or a book, or to attend a seminar. Productivity is a sacred cow in America, and whatever will serve it is considered desirable.

> Maybe an individual manager or supervisor can think in terms of improving corporate or company profits, but most of us know that's pretty remote from our particular cubicle.

Also, at certain levels, reducing "time to market," another metric of productivity, is equally compelling to many CEOs. It's a strong case for improved competitiveness, which is the end purpose of productivity, after all. It then becomes a question of whose software, or which newsletter, or whatever, will do the job most cost-effectively. (Reducing time-to-market has been a prime appeal for the sale of billions of dollars of enterprise resource management [ERP] software and systems.)

Following the emotion versus reason dichotomy outlined earlier, showing how the product relates to individual productivity . . . how it keeps one ahead of the curve . . . how it boosts personal and professional performance while it saves time, saves money, improves accuracy, or whatever, is where the appeal becomes emotional even as the justifications remain rational.

This dual impact can be especially useful in lead generation. In order to get a suspect to raise his or her hand and become a prospect, we usually offer a free document of some sort—information related to the product or industry that will benefit the reader immediately by bringing him or her up to speed on some aspect of the business. The material is altruistic in nature with a value that transcends the company and the product. The prospect, in short, can take the information and run, and he or she will have something worthwhile, whether or not they ever contact you again.

A special report, a series of case studies, an industry survey, a white paper, etc. Each provides instant gratification, plus valuable "inside" information that promises to enhance personal knowledge, while the product behind the document promises various long-range competitive advantages for the team, the division, or the enterprise. The further out we get from the individual, the less emotional and more rational the benefits become.

While consumer benefits are typically short term and most often located in the social and security categories, business-to-business benefits tend to be longer term and aim straight at the ego with some self-improvement products even promising a degree of self-actualization.

## Premiums Provide Instant Gratification

In a direct mail program I've described previously, a "Guide to Software Development" promised prospects immediate knowledge on a subject of interest and value, while the software development team itself promised the software development project manager a way to a superior product out the door on time and on budget. (What a good boy is he!) That same highly successful package included a brochure with "Seven Ways to Keep Your Software Project on Time and on Budget." Instant gratification in the envelope, plus a quick burst of valuable information . . . even if the "Seven Ways" only serve to confirm what the project manager already knows. That's the emotional tug we want to employ, and that's empowerment, especially if one of the Seven really is a new idea!

### Healthy, Wealthy, and Wise

A little rhyme I have used in seminars to help dramatize key benefits is, "Early to bed and early to rise, makes one healthy, wealthy, and wise." One way or another, we all want to be *healthy* (physically, mentally, spiritually, and socially); *wealthy* (make money, save money, project wealth); and, most of all, *wise* (smarter; more productive; more professional; a better leader, mother, father, lover, bowler, etc.).

"Tell me about my lawn, not your grass seed," is about as succinct a way to remember the differences between features and benefits as I know.

There's also a well-known direct mail quatrain from our good friend Anon.:

> Tell me quick and tell me true,
> or else, dear friend, the heck with you,
> Not how this product came to be—
> But what the damn thing does for me!

## Keys to Copy Success

### Starting to Write

Each writer has his or her own method of beginning. I usually begin with the envelope teaser, because that synthesizes the major benefit and often flags the offer in a single phrase. The length and tone of the teaser (or the headline on a self-mailer) determines the look and feel of the piece from that point forward. I then rough out the headline on the letter and on the brochure, so that those key messages are coordinated to project a common theme, but not in the same words.

Then I write the first one or two paragraphs of the letter, up to the first mention of the offer, and let it all marinate for a while. If, when I get back to it, I can still stand it, I finish the letter.

It's a good idea to write the order form immediately, because that spells out, succinctly, what you'll be asking the prospect to do

> It's a good idea to write the order form immediately, because that spells out, succinctly, what you'll be asking the prospect to do.

when you've convinced him or her that he or she can't live another minute (happily and successfully) without your product.

Finally, wisdom offered by famed direct mail writer Tom Collins in a seminar I attended about 30 years ago: "Give yourself permission to write a bad first draft."

## Determining Your Package Format

Clearly, there are many different envelope sizes and shapes, large brochures and small brochures, two-page letters and four-page letters, and "much, much more." So how do you decide what combination of elements will work best for your product, your market, and your offer?

The following insights will help you get started on developing a package format. Only testing, of course, will answer the ultimate questions of which combinations of elements and which formats are best for you, but here are some guidelines for determining those first packages when the page is blank.

### 1. Self-Mailer or Envelope Package?

Many small business newcomers to direct marketing would prefer to use self-mailers simply because they're usually less costly to produce and mail. Remember, however, that if they're cheaper for you to produce, they're likely to be perceived as cheaper by your prospect or customer as well, an image you don't necessarily want to project.

The term "self-mailer" denotes any format that doesn't require an outer envelope. An oversized postcard is a self-mailer. So is a double postcard. Beyond that, self-mailers can be designed in any format that, when it's in its final folded form, is legally mailable. An 11" × 17" flat folded in half to 8 ½" × 11" is a common format. Another is to take that piece and fold it in half again to 5 ½" × 8 ½". The USPS requires self-mailers to be wafer-sealed at least once, and other specifications apply to addressing areas, etc.

Self-mailers are "look-at" pieces, not "read carefully" pieces, so if your product pitch and information is at all detailed or complex, you'll need to support it with the more robust real estate of a direct mail package.

> **Focus on the Individual**
>
> Remember, you're writing to one person, not to "markets" or to thousands. Pick out a typical customer from those you have met and keep that person in your mind's eye as you begin to write.

Also, keep in mind that direct mail works as a selling medium precisely because it is "mail!" It is essentially a letter. And it borrows from the letter all the personal attention and meaning, the business importance, and/or official significance that letters hold in our culture. (This is a U.S. and U.K. tradition. On speaking trips to South America and Asia, I found that this is not necessarily the case everywhere.)

The further away we get from the look and feel of the letter, the more we reduce the impact of the piece. Self-mailers, of course, don't have letters—except for one you might try to simulate on one of the panels. (I've also seen a single-page letter folded inside a self-mailer, but I have no idea whether that works as well as a regular letter package. Like everything else in this process, it depends on the product/offer/market mix.)

Because of their "throwaway" and impersonal look and feel, self-mailers generally have a credibility problem. You wouldn't want to use them for fund raising, for example. They can't carry the depth of feeling and sincerity that successful fund raising requires and that is achievable with a letter. Likewise financial services, which are considered too personal. All other factors being equal, a self-mailer typically pulls in the tenths-of-a-percent response, while envelope packages pull between 1 and 5 percent. The self-mailer will likely be more cost-effective, however, and naturally, there are always exceptions.

Since there is no reply envelope with a self-mailer, as noted earlier, any offer requiring payment will be significantly more difficult to achieve with a self-mailer than with an envelope package.

So what can you use self-mailers for? Lots of things. Impulse buys, like books, especially with a 30-day free trial offer, sell well with self-mailers. Seminars and conferences can be impulse buys as well, particularly for attendees, and they sell well through self-mailers. Newsletters, where a free trial issue is offered, can be marketed effectively to middle management, but not to top management. Several other factors favor self-mailers as well, including:

- Some surprisingly pricey software products have used self-mailers successfully, but mostly for lead generation (per the previous example).

> The further away we get from the look and feel of the letter, the more we reduce the impact of the piece.

- Try self-mailers for products and events where your lists are not well-targeted . . . where others in the company might be equally good prospects and might see the self-mailer around the office.
- You can also leverage the visibility of self-mailers by planning them as a campaign of three or five pieces or more. Monthly mailings, if they can be made consistently compelling, can be most effective. The repetition can offset the credibility problem I mentioned earlier.
- A self-mailer can work to a customer list, to cross-sell, upsell, or for aftermarket sales where the same offer to a cold list would bomb.
- In certain circumstances, you can also use a self-mailer to test lists cost-effectively, in advance of a more expensive direct mail campaign. The self-mailer "stalking horse" can help you get the package targeted right, especially where the list universe is large and uncertain.

### 2. One-Step or Two?

If you've decided the envelope package is the way to go, the next consideration is whether your product (including "service" as a product) will require a one-step or two-step process. Will you sell the item directly from the direct mail piece, or will you use your direct mail to obtain leads or inquiries to be followed up by phone, sales force, or more direct mail (or all three)?

If the offer is the product itself, and it's under $100, you'll want to keep it to a one-step process. Using a two-step or lead-generating process for a low-cost product simply costs too much to be profitable. Remember that, especially in lead generation, we sell the offer, not the product—so the decision to go two-step will determine the makeup of the package.

A pure product sell may dictate a "full" package: four-page letter; four-page, four-color brochure (or larger); lift letter; and order form. A business-to-business lead-generation offer may not need a brochure at all, or may be kept to two-color. Often a letter and reply form are all that's required.

## Self-Mailers Can Work Selectively

I wrote a solo self-mailer that pulled 3 percent for a professional book, primarily because it was a very selected market.

On another occasion I wrote a series of oversized double postcards (5 ½" × 8 ½") for a software system marketed to plumbers, electricians, and other service dispatch businesses. It worked extremely well because (a) it was a series of mailers, not a solo effort; (b) the folks who run this type of business tend not to sit at desks and open mail, so a sharp headline on a self-mailer is immediately visible without an envelope to open; (c) the main appeal came from other plumbers in the form of user testimonials; (d) we didn't need payment, just a phone call.

### 3. Consumer or B-T-B?

Consumer packages tend to be larger and flashier, with more "push," and therefore are more expensive than business-to-business packages. Consumer packages range from slightly oversized No. 12 and No. 13 envelopes to 6" × 9" and 9" × 12". Business-to-business packages tend to be No. 10 "business" sized or, on occasion, a 9" × 12" first class business-type envelope.

In business-to-business, your level of push will depend on what part of the food chain you're aiming at. The higher up the chain, the more conservative your look and feel should be, and usually, the less costly the package (and vice versa).

### 4. How Much Push?

Another rule of thumb I've basically followed over the years is, the greater the commitment or involvement or purchase I'm expecting from the recipient, the more "format" I have to deliver to him or her to help the person decide. A $5,000 direct purchase is going to require a series of mailings, and unless I'm basically augmenting a salesperson's efforts, I'll need to put into the package much of what a salesperson would deliver face-to-face.

I'll have to show the product with a full-color brochure, sell the product with a four-page letter, and support both with testimonials or other proofs (maybe in a lift letter). I'll need a response device and a reply envelope to make ordering easy.

But what if I am augmenting a salesperson's efforts between sales calls? Then I want him or her to do the heavy lifting (and he or she does as well). I'm going to keep my mailings quick and to the point with one-page letters, maybe no brochure at all, and at most a fax-back form or reply card in case of a response. Remember, the salesperson is doing the selling and will issue the call to action when he or she thinks the time is right.

What might I send the prospect in the case of a long sales cycle?

- A white paper (a description of a technical process)
- Updates of product data sheets

> In business-to-business, your level of push will depend on what part of the food chain you're aiming at.

- Press releases related to the product/process environment
- A related article reprint with a short note
- A reprint of the new ad campaign
- A special, limited-time price or bonus offer

These would be treated lightly with a single-page letter or note attached.

## 5. Sell the Offer

In direct mail, we sell the offer, not the product. The free trial, the no-risk 30-day preview with money-back guarantee, the free in-house consultation or survey, the limited-time 2-for-1 deal, whatever.

We support the offer basically with benefits, product information, and "reason why" persuasions urging the prospect to act now! We support that with testimonials, research, and/or test results, then wrap it all in a credible guarantee and a call for action (i.e., ASK FOR THE ORDER!).

For most products, that's going to require what we call a "full" package: outer envelope, letter, brochure, order form, perhaps a lift letter, and reply envelope. The size of each of those components will depend on how much real estate you need to get the job done. In many cases, you won't know the answer to that going in, so you should plan some tests.

- Do you need a brochure? Maybe, maybe not. Test it.
- Two-page letter or four-page letter? Test it.
- Lift letter? Test it!

But be sure you test the two key elements first: lists and offer.

If for some reason you can't test all those components, then you need to give yourself the best shot out of the gate and include all the components in your early mailings. What you don't want is to spend $x to launch a product (or to try direct mail for the first time) and end up with more questions than answers. (Would it have worked if we'd included a color brochure?)

> What you don't want is to spend $x to launch a product (or to try direct mail for the first time) and end up with more questions than answers.

### 6. Hot or Cold Lists?

Another important consideration is the list you're using. If you're mailing house lists, you may not need as much "push" as you would for cold lists. House names know you and, presumably, trust you to some degree.

I once sold a software program add-on to a house list with a two-color, four-page letter/brochure. The two-page letter was on pages 1 and 4, and brochure copy with screen illustrations was in the center spread, pages 2 and 3. I knew the recipients were already using the main product—an accounting package—and could easily understand how the add-on would enhance their capabilities.

But I'd never try that with a cold list. For a cold mailing, I'd want a separate color brochure and a four-page letter, if I'm selling it out of the package, or a two-page letter if I'm getting qualified leads. The offer in that case might be a white paper or Q&A sheet if the software is complex, and a no-risk trial.

### 7. Complex or Simple?

If your product needs to be demonstrated via photos with call-outs, etc., naturally you'll need a brochure, probably four-color. The function of the brochure is to "show the product in use," which is often essential to robust sales. If you're selling a directory—something everyone understands—you may need only show a typical listing. You still may want a brochure (8½" × 11", two folds to No. 10) to give the company some presence, and to show the listing with appropriate callouts. (A "callout" is a line drawn from a product element out from the illustration to a brief blurb describing that element. Many examples of callouts are in the margins of this book, plus the List Data Sheet illustration in Chapter 6, Figure 6-1.)

Industrial products can usually benefit from "how-it-works" or "how it's-made" illustrations. Also performance charts, test results, and maybe a case history or at least a testimonial, all of which indicate a brochure, and hopefully something more interactive than the usual deadly dull data sheet.

As you can see, there are no hard and fast rules for these decisions, just general guidelines, and lots of exceptions. Test as many

> The function of the brochure is to "show the product in use," which is often essential to robust sales.

options and variables as you can, and continue testing your package's elements going forward.

When you've tested your way to a profitable list, offer, and format, you'll have, in effect, a business-in-an-envelope. It's a business that will take care of you for as long as there's a market for your product. And remember, direct mail is a back-end business. However successful you may be, you'll be building a list of responsive customers. Be sure you have something else to sell them.

## Anatomy of a Direct Mail Letter

Direct mail letters are not correspondence, although they may borrow some of its elements, mainly the salutation and the signature. The rest of a direct mail letter is quite different, as we'll see in this brief tour of a typical letter. Not every letter will have every feature (and these apply to sales letters only—lead generation letters, especially to top management, follow some different dynamics), but you should have most of these elements if your letter is to sell, not just convey information.

### The Headline

The first thing to consider in your letter is the headline. Yes, Virginia, there is a headline. Usually. (Not always in lead generation letters.) Right away you can see that this isn't your normal business correspondence. If at all possible, the headline should pick up logically or psychologically where the teaser, if you have one, leaves off. In some cases, you may even want to repeat the teaser at the top of the letter lest it be lost as a springboard for your copy/offer strategy.

The headline focuses the reader's attention on one quick benefit or promise (or two). It gives him or her a reason to spend his or her valuable time reading this letter. It also helps close out other random thoughts and provides a context for what is about to follow.

If your company letterhead is heavily designed or attention-getting, you may want to consider putting it at the end of the letter, instead of the usual position at the top of page one. (Now you know it isn't correspondence!) That way, your logo isn't fighting for attention with the headline. You're not selling your logo.

> When you've tested your way to a profitable list, offer, and format, you'll have, in effect, a business-in-an-envelope.

I try to make a promise or allude to a key benefit, and refer in some way to the offer, perhaps in a subordinate line. The offer, remember, is what the reader will eventually act upon. Avoid negatives in copy, especially in headlines. Don't say "don't."

Try a "headline group," which consists of a headline, subhead, and one, two, or three short bulleted phrases that extend and expand on the headline message. It provides more information and takes fuller advantage of that high readership location. It promotes greater involvement than a headline alone.

### The Opening

The opening is the first sentence or first two sentences following the salutation. "I am writing to you about . . . " or "I want you to know about . . . " are not openings. The reader, frankly, doesn't care what you want. He cares about himself. Direct mail is almost universally written in the second person with "I" and "we" used as sparingly as possible.

This is a key place to say something about him or his needs, which your product will gratify. Here again, you may want to pick up on the envelope teaser and carry it forward. A documentary film on advertising titled, "The Ad and The Ego" makes the point that the purpose of all advertising is "the production of discontent" in the reader or prospect–that it seeks to "develop an inner sense of conflict" in people that the product promises to resolve. We do much the same in direct mail, but we address ourselves to one person, not multitudes. Your opening should, therefore, start with "you," and should seek out the reader's "hot button" or major problem and begin immediately to show how your product or service can solve it.

Most letters are won or lost in the first sentence. The surest way to lose is to begin talking about yourself and your organization.

### Offer Preview

After the opening, I like to make a brief reference to the offer. " . . . and you can discover it, (prove it, enjoy it) FREE, without obligation, with the certificate enclosed."

Now the reader knows I'm not going to be asking her for money. Maybe. So she can relax. And my early reference to the response device begins to set up the response behavior.

> Most letters are won or lost in the first sentence. The surest way to lose is to begin talking about yourself and your organization.

It's also helpful to "merchandise" the offer by referring to it at several points throughout the letter. "When you send for your free demo (free trial issue, 30-day no-risk trial, etc.) you'll quickly see . . . ."

### Sell Copy

From the offer preview, get right into the benefits your reader will realize when she tests, previews, examines your product. Stay in second person throughout your letter. You're talking to her (one person, not a market) about her, not you, and you're talking about yourself and your product only in terms of what it will do for her.

Remember you're selling the offer, not the product. It's much easier to sell a 30-day trial or a free examination than it is to sell the product itself. You'll discuss payment terms later.

Try to lead off sentences and phrases with benefits. "In just two short days you'll make first-hand contact with hundreds of the most active, most involved sales prospects in the industry." (For a conference.)

"As one of America's elite 'Million-Plus' pharmacies, you are in a unique position to increase sales, slash operating costs, and grow your business rapidly with xyz software tracking your inventory."

### Use Subheads to Introduce New Thoughts

You want to avoid eye-glazing, mind-numbing, wall-to-wall copy, so use subheads to introduce new thoughts and to move from one part of the letter to the next.

Write in short sentences.

Short paragraphs.

Use bullets to list:

- Benefits
- Features
- Advantages

Use words of one syllable as much as possible. Don't assume that the person you're writing to is as literate as you are. Even if he is, he's distracted, and he's trying to quickly extract the key information he needs, often by just scanning your letter.

Which is another good reason to use subheads . . . bulleted lists . . . and . . . ellipses.

> Lead off sentences and phrases with benefits.

Be ruthless in editing out unnecessary words and phrases and "write like you talk," assuming you can talk like a successful salesperson. In direct mail, clarity is more important than literary merit, and the ability to sell is more important than the ability to write.

### The Offer

When you've fully described the many ways your product will benefit the reader, show how he or she can acquire this fabulous program/product/service. Or, rather, how he/she can realize these benefits right now.

Spell out your offer in detail. What the reader gets. If you're offering a premium, this is the place to sell that a bit, too. You may also feature it in the brochure if you have one, or better yet, in a separate premium flyer.

If at all possible, and if appropriate, date your offer. An expiration date helps to keep your package from going up between the lamp and the tape dispenser for further consideration. Remember, agreement with your proposition doesn't do it. Only acting on that agreement *right now* results in sales. Six to eight weeks from arrival of the package is a good deadline window. Just be sure you meet your mail date. If you're late in the mail and you run up against your deadline, response will drop like a stone.

### The Guarantee

No one wants to make a mistake. Not an expensive mistake. Especially not a highly visible, expensive mistake. Relieve that fear with your guarantee. Mitigating risk is an essential function of successful direct mail. By law you must refund legitimate requests up to 30 days anyway, so why not make it a virtue? Some worry that a guarantee might somehow shed doubt on the product. The guarantee speaks not to your product, but to you as an honest and fair businessperson your prospects can trust.

But try to avoid the rather abrupt "Money Back Guarantee" or "Full Refund If Not Satisfied" kind of thing. That's negative. A Free (or Risk-Free or No-Risk) 30-day Trial is the same thing, expressed in positive terms. "Examine it, try it, use it for a full 30 days without risk." That's an invitation, not a warning. (Note that under FTC rules governing the use of the word "free," an offer is not "free" if the

> No one wants to make a mistake. Not an expensive mistake. Especially not a highly visible, expensive mistake.

prospect must pay something to receive it. Then it may be called "risk-free" if you guarantee a refund.)

If you can extend the guarantee to 60 or even 90 days, so much the better. Longer trial periods allow prospects to become acclimated to the product. They also get inertia working for you, instead of against you. People forget.

### The Call to Action

Even after all that, you can't assume the reader will do what you want her to do, right now. But that's what she must do. So spell it out. Ask for the order! Does she detach and complete a reply card, call a toll-free number, complete a questionnaire, check a box, punch out a token? Is there a postpaid or self-addressed reply envelope to use? Ask her to do all that right now because that expiration date will be here before she knows it. Because she really wants to try this, but if she lets it go till "later," she'll forget.

## Additional Keys to Copy Success

### Ten Copy Dos and Don'ts

**Don't** "introduce" yourself or your company. Begin immediately writing about the reader and her problem, and how your product will benefit her.

**Don't** expound on the state of the industry/world, etc. It may come across as preaching, especially to the converted. (If he doesn't already know what you're telling him, he may be too removed from the process to be a good prospect.)

**Don't** use puns. They rarely translate to the reader's context.

**Don't** ask questions in teasers and headlines that can be answered yes or no (especially no). That gives control of the communication to your reader.

**Don't** use your product name as a headline by itself (clever as it may be), without appending benefit or offer copy to it.

**Do** build your teaser/headline around a major benefit.

**Do** "preview" the offer up front and "merchandise" it throughout your letter.

**Do** test teasers to target your market.

**Do** use the product name in the corner card and letterhead rather than the company name (IBM, AT&T, and such excepted).

**Do** quantify claims as much as possible. Percentages of performance, number of dollars saved or earned, minutes and seconds of time, etc., lend credibility, and odd numbers are more credible than even numbers.

**Sales Letter Copy Tips:**
1. Tease, don't "tell it all" in lead-generation letters (leave out critical information so the prospect has something to ask for). Tell it all, don't "tease" in the fulfillment or follow-up package.
2. Sell the *offer*, not the *product*.
3. Talk the *buyer's* language (benefits), not the *seller's* (features).
4. Back up claims with proof: survey, reports, case studies, test results, testimonials.
5. Always guarantee your offer, and express it positively: "Examine it for 30 days without obligation" is more positive than "Money back if not satisfied."
6. Keep words short and simple. Seventy-five percent of your document should be words of one syllable.
7. Use Courier or equivalent serif typeface for letters.
8. Use subheads to flag new ideas. Use ellipses . . . to set off phrases . . . and underlines for emphasis.
9. Tell the reader in clear terms what you want him/her to do upon reading the letter (call to action) and ASK FOR THE ORDER.
10. P.S. Always use a P.S. to repeat a key point, offer, or benefit with a secondary call to action.

### The P.S.

Punctuate the call to action with the signature, then add a P.S. After the headline and first sentence, the P.S. commands the highest readership in the letter. Use that important space to repeat a key benefit, or add a twist or an another idea to something you've already said. Also repeat your call to action here, in slightly different words.

The mnemonic for the basic function of all direct marketing, but especially for letters, is AIDA. Get Attention. Arouse Interest. Stimulate Desire. Prompt Action.

## Interactive Copy

In direct mail we want to use words that invite the prospect into our scenario. Words that help her imagine herself using the product or that project the results of using the product in her business or personal life. Ultimately, we want her to act in some way on our offer, so we use words that help set up an action.

- **Learn, discover, try, explore, test, find.** These are words that invite the reader into our proposition and set the stage for action.
- **In addition . . . furthermore . . . what's more.** These are phrases, sometimes called the "bucket brigade," that help move the reader smoothly from paragraph to paragraph to order form.

## Power Words

These are words that relate to action, that communicate newness and promote urgency.

**YOU**—All direct mail is written in second person—"you"—with the pronouns "I" and "we" kept to an absolute minimum. Why? Because your prospects and readers are interested primarily in themselves, not in you. Surprising as it may seem, converting "I" and "me" copy written by clients to "you" copy has been one of the primary missions of my 30-plus-years copywriting career.

**FREE**–Maybe some people want something for nothing, but I believe "FREE" is one of the most powerful words in direct marketing because it minimizes risk. Whatever the case, "Free" is where it's at. Use it liberally.

**NOW**–connotes immediacy. You want your prospect to read your package right *now*, and respond, right *now*. So using the word "now" throughout your letter and brochure helps to focus the reader's attention and sets up an atmosphere for action . . . now.

**NEW**–Why is every product in the supermarket "new and improved?" Because people always want to be in on the newest of everything.

**ANNOUNCING**–is a variation on the "new" theme. It's a way of alerting the reader that something new is coming.

**INTRODUCING**–Same as Announcing.

**EASY**–Making life's processes easy is one of the primary benefits of any product. Easy to use, easy to order, easy to try.

**SUCCESS**–Success on the job, success in life and love, financial success, social success, successful children, and more are among the pinnacles of life. Use the word "success" to communicate success.

**PROVEN**–Proven techniques, proven methods, and yes, proven success all add credibility to your proposition.

**GUARANTEE(D)**–You absolutely must guarantee your offer. Note I said "offer," not product, although it may amount to the same thing. The point is, you are not diminishing your product's credibility in any way by offering a guarantee. You are, rather, adding credibility to yourself, your company, and the manner in which you do business by offering a guarantee. And don't just offer it, flaunt it in big type, surrounded by certificate borders (in the brochure), on the order form, several times in the letter, etc. As mentioned previously, you are required by law to refund any product you sell by mail or phone within 30 days.

**AT LAST!**–Also alerts the reader to something new. "At last, what?" the mind wonders. The inference is that here–at last–is THE ANSWER!

**POWER(FUL)**–Everyone wants power in their lives. Power over illness and death, power over failure, power to exert his or her will over life's situations. So give it to them, in your copy. Show how your product has the power to satisfy the reader's wants and needs.

## Focusing Exercise

A helpful exercise is to write the words "Now you can _____" on a piece of paper and then fill in the blank with a concise description of what the prospect can do now with your product or service.

**HOW TO**—Mail order has always had strong appeal to people who want to learn techniques and strategies across any spectrum of activities you care to mention. Self-empowerment (there's that word again!) and self-improvement, from better sex to better relations with God to building a deck onto the house, have been the stuff of direct mail since its inception. You can leverage that appeal by proving that your product shows the prospect "how-to" speak better, look better, be better informed, and/or work and live better in one way or another.

A neat little book that can help with finding the right words is *Words That Sell* by Richard Bayan (Caddylak Publishing, Westbury, New York). For direct mail writing, it's better than Strunk and White.

## Writing for the Web

As mentioned in the Introduction, learning the dynamics of direct mail is the best training for success on the Internet. You'll be pleased to know that most of the principles we espouse for effective direct mail also apply to writing on the Web.

People don't read online, they scan. Sound familiar? Direct mail writers tailor their writing specifically to scanners. Headlines, subheads, short bursts of copy, key words, bulleted lists—they all work well on the Web. Then add navigation. Make sure every page links forward and backward with its adjacent pages. Avoid the doublespeak, avoid the fluff, cut to the chase, anticipate questions and answer them—all old stuff to DM writers.

For more on writing for the Web:

*www.useit.com/papers/webwriting*

*www.contentious.com*

*www.cluetrain.com*

*http://edvl.com/Internet/Writing*

> You'll be pleased to know that most of the principles we espouse for effective direct mail also apply to writing on the Web.

---

For more information on this topic, visit our Web site at www.businesstown.com

---

# The Direct Mail
# Package

## A Comprehensive Checklist

> The sales letter is the primary document. Everything else— brochure, sales sheet or slick, order form, etc.— is in support of it.)

"How much do you charge to write a letter?" the voice on the phone asked. I quoted a price. "That's a pretty good price, George. Tell me, how long does it take you to write a letter like that?"

"Seventeen years," I replied. (This was some years ago. It takes 30 years now.)

Unfortunately, "writing a letter" is how many small business owners and DM newcomers think of direct mail. (Many also insist on calling a sales letter a "cover" letter–as though it were an added appendage to something more important. It isn't. If anything, it's the other way around. The sales letter is the primary document. Everything else–brochure, sales sheet or slick, order form, etc.–is in support of it.)

In any case, if you've been around more than a month or so, you've no doubt learned that there's more to direct mail than writing a letter. There's the envelope you're going to put it in, for example. How large? No. 10? 9" × 12"? What's the difference, other than cost? What form of postage should you use . . . a bulk rate stamp? . . . printed indicia? . . . metered third class? First class?

Clearly, there are dozens of decisions to be made about any direct mail package, each having an impact, large or small, on the eventual results.

The following checklist is designed to help you think your way through your next direct mail campaign, anticipate needs, and make the necessary decisions for timely production and mailing.

The commentary that follows is keyed to the list and provides detailed "how-to" suggestions for the various elements in a typical direct mail package. Not every point applies to every kind of letter, and, for the most part, exceptions are noted where appropriate.

# I. OUTER ENVELOPE

1. Format
    a). No. 10 business envelope
    b). 9" × 12" business envelope
    c). Oversized No. 12 or No. 13 envelope
    d). 6" × 9" "booklet" envelope
    e). Monarch "personal" envelope
    f). Square "invitation" envelope
    g). Poly and other novelty envelopes
    h). Closed face vs. window
    i). Literature code

2. Postage
    a). "Live" stamp (first class or precancelled third class)
    b). Meter
    c). Printed indicia

3. Mail Classification
    a). First class
    b). Third class bulk
    c). Special (certified, express, FedEx, etc.)

4. Corner card
    a). Company name and address vs. none
    b). Writer's name (handwritten or "typed" above company name)
    c). Product name vs. company name
    d). Logo conflict

5. Addressing
    a). Direct computer-addressed
    b). Cheshire label
    c). Hand-addressed
    d). Personalization vs. none

6. Teaser
    a). Teaser vs. none
    b). Offer teaser
    c). Benefit teaser
    d). Curiosity or "hook" teaser
    e). Ancillary notations

7. Envelope "look and feel"
    a). Straight business (white wove)
    b). Official or monetary value (brown or gray kraft)
    c). Big Event (four-color, display type, illustrations, etc.)
    d). Invitation/upscale
    e). Others

## II. LETTER

1. Look and Feel
    a). Length
    b). Correspondence style vs. illustrated
    c). Letter/brochure
    d). Stock (white wove vs. ivory vellum, etc.)
    e). Personalization
    f). Headline vs. none
    g). Company letterhead vs. product vs. personal; top of letter vs. end of letter
    h). Single sheets vs. 11" × 17" folded
    i). Typeface(s)
    j). Handwritten notations
    k). P.S.
    l). Literature code

## III. BROCHURE

1. Test with and without
2. Look and Feel
    a). Size and folds
    b). Four-color vs. two-color

c). Stock (matte/gloss/semi- or dull-gloss)

d). Illustrations (drawings vs. photos)

e). Second order form

f). Testimonials

g). Offer

h). Guarantee

i). Call to action

j). Company I.D. and contact information

k). Literature code

## IV. REPLY DEVICE

1. Look and Feel

a). Certificate/check design

b). Four-color vs. two-color

c). Illustrations vs. none

d). Offer boilerplate copy ("Yes! . . .")

e). Qualification questions (lead generation)

f). Signature/phone number

g). Detachable stub

h). Action device

i). Gift amount checkoff (fund raising)

j). BRC vs. BRE

2. Billing

a). Payment enclosed (hard offer)

b). Credit cards

c). Toll-free number/fax

d). P.O. number

e). Deadline date

f). Name correction

g). Key and literature codes

## V. LIFT LETTER

1. Test with and without

2. Look and feel

a). Size

b). Stock
c). Letter vs. memo vs. other
d). Offer
e). Signature

## VI. PREMIUM INSERT
1. Test with and without
2. Look and feel
a).   Buckslip vs. folded
b).   Attached to reply device vs. loose

## VII. ALTERNATIVES
1. Sweepstakes
2. Proprietary "Telegram" package
3. Proprietary "Express" package
4. Proprietary ink jet/personalized web press package
5. Self-mailer
6. Others

## Open This Envelope . . . Now!

Getting the envelope opened is probably the most difficult job in direct marketing.

For one thing, you have about three seconds in which to do it. Three seconds—while your prospect is ritually scanning the day's mail and dropping it into the round file at the post office or next to his/her desk—in which to get the reader's attention sufficient to put your package in the "A" pile: read first. Maybe there's a "B" pile: read later; maybe not. Maybe there's only the AAAaaaarrgh! pile as your pricey package sails wastefully into the trash.

So how do you make it to the "A" pile? Let's take a look at envelopes, the first category in our Direct Mail Checklist.

The very first thing you must do is send your package to the right prospect. I'll say again: junk mail is an offer sent to the wrong person. But that's list work, which we discussed in Chapter 6. We'll assume for now that your lists are on-target.

## Format and Look and Feel

I like to think of direct mail as "theater in print." Each package a little drama, complete with costumes (package design, paper stock, and illustrations), dialog (copy), and staging (layout and the natural flow from one component to the next, or from fold to fold of a brochure).

The drama can big and brassy (a Publisher's Clearing House sweepstakes promising TEN MILLION DOLLARS! or the Time-Life *History of the Universe* in 20 volumes), or it can be quietly elegant (a square invitation in ivory vellum with a light gray "RSVP" in the corner). It can be *** VERY OFFICIAL *** (a 9" × 12" brown kraft envelope), or a bit of a mystery (a three-dimensional Jiffy envelope or package the recipient has to sign for). To business executives, I've had good success with the standard first class 9" × 12" envelope with the border of green triangles.

## Size Matters

Whatever drama you decide to play out, size and shape will play a role. Big, 9" × 12" envelopes (or a 10" × 13" I once used to mail "limited edition" prints) carry some added importance just by virtue of their size. Hard to toss them out without at least a peek. Of course, they cost more . . . naturally.

Booklet envelopes (6" × 9") may seem common to those of us in the business, but in fact, they're fairly rare in the average person's mailbox. Therefore, they tend to stand out—get attention—in the day's delivery. (I like to think of that white mail truck as it comes down the street as an ice cream truck. I keep listening for the bells.)

The good old No. 10 business envelope, of course, means business. Best used for personalized messages to top management and folks like that. Number 10s don't stand out, particularly, but the business executive expects to be addressed with either a No. 10, or a 9" × 12" business type envelope. Closed-face and personalized is the way to go. We'll get to addressing in a bit.

### The Envelope Is Your Salesperson's Clothing

As if to underscore these points, an ad currently running for Dupont Tyvek® envelopes carries the headline, "The right envelope can help you say, 'Dear Sir' even before he reads your letter."

The body text reads, "Actions do speak louder than words. And usually sooner. So when you want a mailing to convey the proper respect, start right away. By sending it in a Tyvek®. A unique blend of silkiness and ruggedness, it reflects the importance of the contents and the receiver."

Some marketers are having success with larger versions of the standard business envelope: a No. 11, No. 12, or No. 14, which does stand out in the mail stack, projects the business envelope look and feel, and affords a bit more real estate on which to create a message. An oversized brown kraft can be especially effective, assuming the super-important projection is appropriate for the contents. (Brown kraft carries a strong association with checks and other documents of special importance.)

Another way to get attention is to go smaller than a No. 10. A No. 7 or Monarch envelope measures $3\,^{7}/_{8}" \times 7\,^{1}/_{2}"$ and has a strong personal look and feel. A simulated script address might be most effective here. I mentioned an invitation above. A custom square envelope or a No. 5 Baronial says "special event" under most circumstances. Reinforce that with an "RSVP" teaser.

A transparent poly envelope can be very effective, mostly for consumer applications. It affords a strong "peek-a-boo" curiosity factor that makes people want to get inside. Just don't tip off the contents too much, or they won't have to open it before they chuck it. Some envelope providers also have cello-envelopes, which are $9" \times 12"$ with a large $8" \times 10"$ clear plastic window in which you can show the front of your brochure.

There are a variety of web press mailers that are produced with the envelope, letter, and reply device printed in line, then cut and folded into a direct mail package (see "The Alternatives" later in this chapter). Some suppliers utilize ink-jet personalization and upscale paper stocks to create very interesting packages, while the less costly NCR type packages are best left to institutional mailers like the IRS and Motor Vehicle Bureau—unless, of course, that's the very impression you want to make.

A common testing practice for large consumer mailers is to introduce a new product with a $9" \times 12"$ envelope, then test smaller sizes to see if they can reduce costs without eroding the response rate.

As you can see, envelope design is a form of impression management or "theater in print," as I said earlier. Even before you consider copy teasers, your envelope can go a long way toward setting up the prospect, emotionally and psychologically, for the message inside. "Verisimilitude" is the operative word. Think your envelopes through in terms of your offer, product, and market, and more of them will get opened.

> A common testing practice for large consumer mailers is to introduce a new product with a 9" × 12" envelope, then test smaller sizes to see if they can reduce costs without eroding the response rate.

## Postage & Classification

With regard to postage, a "live" (precancelled) stamp can help make third class mail (now called Standard Mail A™) look like first class, unless you plan to have illustrations and teasers all over the envelope. In that case, I usually opt for the printed indicia and save the added cost of affixing stamps that won't have much impact.

For first class, a stamp is advisable so long as the rest of the envelope is clean. Also, if you're using first class mail, it's wise to imprint "First Class Mail" on the envelope so your prospect doesn't miss it. A Standard A™ meter can also give an impression of first class mail, since few folks pay much attention to the metered amount.

## The Corner Card

The corner card is the return address area in the upper left corner of the addressed side of an envelope. When planning your teaser, remember that the corner card can be a teaser, too, or can work with your teaser to produce a larger effect. A plain white envelope with "The White House" in the upper left corner, for example, doesn't need any further teaser except, perhaps, "RSVP."

One question to ask about the corner card is, should it reflect the company (Acme Products)? Or the product you're selling (McWidgets)? If you're Bertha's Kitty Boutique, your individual fame may supersede that of your new electronic litter box. But if you're Shazam Publishing with a dozen or more magazines and newsletters, your new *Internet Marketing* newsletter title in the corner card may mean more to a list of Web site owners than your company name.

A common technique used to enhance the personal impression of a package is to show the sender's name "typed" in black ink above the company name and address in the corner card. This also works best on a clean, first class mail, stamped envelope.

If the corporate logo is an elaborate piece of work, it's best to use some simpler version on the envelope so it won't conflict with and draw attention away from the teaser or other message. The same holds true for the letterhead vis-à-vis any headline or Johnson box that may be used at the top of the letter. (The Johnson box is described later in this chapter.)

> If the corporate logo is an elaborate piece of work, it's best to use some simpler version on the envelope so it won't conflict with and draw attention away from the teaser or other message.

I sometimes move the company logo or letterhead to the end of the letter, where it won't distract from the headline message. Presumably, you're not selling your logo.

### Addressing

A colleague of mine with a successful direct marketing agency in New York refuses to take a client if they insist on using labels on their mail. She figures anything she might do is doomed to failure with that "advertising mail!" pennant screaming across the front of the envelope.

By far the best choice is laser or ink-jet addressing, either directly onto an order form showing through a window, or onto a closed face envelope. Personalized letters are also best for most purposes because beyond this sale or inquiry, you want to build a relationship. Addressing a person by name is a darn sight more personal than "Dear Middle Manager—or current occupant."

## Do Teasers Work? More About Envelopes

Now for the question above, "Do teasers work?" The right ones do.

That's not an evasion. If you examine the direct mail you receive each day, you'll find many envelopes with teasers that are designed only for the trash bin. "20% off!" *Off what?* "Open now!" *Why?*

I probably discard more than half my mail based on the corner card alone. A lot depends on the accuracy of the list work. If you've effectively targeted your prospect (for cold mail), you're unlikely to turn him or her off with your teaser . . . assuming it speaks immediately to his need or problem and/or your solution.

One of the more successful direct mail writers of my generation is Bill Jayme, who has specialized in subscription packages for many of the nation's leading magazine publishers.

> "What works for us," he has said, "And always works for us, is the outer envelope . . . that instantly waylays the prospect, captures his attention, engages

> If you've effectively targeted your prospect (for cold mail), you're unlikely to turn him or her off with your teaser . . . assuming it speaks immediately to his need or problem and/or your solution.

him, intrigues him, grabs his curiosity. The outer envelope that wastes not a moment in commencing to make the sale. The outer envelope that orients the prospect immediately to the product, and very often to the offer, even before he gets inside."

But while you're waylaying, capturing, engaging, etc., remember that people respond to an appeal based on who *they* are, not according to who *you* are. Also, Bill was speaking mainly of magazine packages: a free trial issue of a $25 product, not business-to-business lead generation.

As to the issue of teaser or no teaser, consider that if a recipient of your package reads your teaser—then proceeds to open the envelope—he or she has already accepted a portion of your proposition. You have him/her saying "yes" to some degree even before you've made your pitch! That's a very valuable edge to take into the selling environment.

## Three Types of Teasers

As I see them, envelope teasers can be divided into three categories: offer teasers, benefit teasers, and curiosity teasers.

A separate category is the "ancillary notation," which might be a "second notice" stamp or a simulated instruction to the "Postmaster," an "Urgent" stamp, or one of the many express mail look-alikes with their various officialese notations like "Audited Delivery," "Dated Material Enclosed," "Return Within 30 Days of Receipt," and others.

### Offer Teasers

An offer teaser is just that: an offer. "Take the Next Issue of *Widget World*, FREE with the Certificate enclosed!" is a typical offer teaser. The offer can also be inside the envelope, rather than on it: "Breakthrough Upgrade Offer Enclosed" worked well for a software upgrade package. "Good through July 31st" added a touch of urgency that also helped. (But of course, that was mailed to committed users of the base product.)

---

### Target, Target, Target!

Like me, you've no doubt been told by numerous friends and associates, "I never read junk mail—I throw it all away unopened." Maybe. Or maybe they're more like an associate of mine who told me she never read "junk" mail and one morning brought in a 6" × 9" envelope from American Girl Publishing. It was opened, and the order form was gone. "How come?" I queried my non-direct-mail-reading friend. She showed me the envelope: the teaser on one side said, "Help *your* daughter grow up to be as strong and self-confident as she *deserves* to be." And on the other side: "Finally. A newsletter written *just* for parents of girls 10 to 16." Turns out, my friend is a mother of a 14-year-old girl. Case closed. "Junk" mail is an offer sent to the wrong person. *Direct* mail is an offer sent to the right one. And notice the use of italics as a means of expression.

## Combine Your Offer With a Benefit

A business-to-business offer teaser that worked especially well for me was on a package I've described elsewhere for a software development team: "Inside: Seven Proven Tips for keeping software development projects on time and on budget. PLUS exclusive 'Guide to Software Product Development, FREE!' Note how it combines an offer with a benefit.

Some other offer teasers I've noticed (but didn't write): "Business Builder Enclosed. Test it now and get ready to receive 6 Sensational FREE GIFTS!" This one adds a touch of the curiosity teaser around the otherwise undescribed "business builder." And a computer service bureau offers, "Find Out About a Complimentary File Analysis!"

Dynamically, the offer teaser is best used when you're sure of your market. You have to know that the recipient is a prospect for the offer based on your list (like the upgrade offer mentioned previously). Otherwise, the offer won't mean much; for instance, the "complimentary file analysis" in the previous example was wasted on me.

### Benefit Teasers

The benefit teaser delivers a promise or benefit to the reader, sufficient to get him or her to open the envelope. A successful benefit teaser for *OS/2* magazine: "Release the power of OS/2 for all the work you do–and get it right the first time with *OS/2* magazine!"

For a PC troubleshooting guide: "Maximize your PC–and your PC skills–with the first PC Guide that grows along with you!" For an AT&T small business service: "Now every AT&T long distance call can lower your cost of business . . . in ways you never thought of." (The last phrase was a pickup of a national campaign theme.)

One from the swipe file: "Inside: Double your PC storage and triple its speed . . . without spending thousands on hardware upgrades."

The benefit teaser is best used when you're less sure of your market and you need to start selling right away. Again, your benefit has to be on target, or forget it. You must know what's important to these people and nail it, the first time.

I like to try a combination of these two teaser types like this one for a Novell Networking binder product: "The Five Keys to LAN Success: [list of five benefits] Plus: Yours Free! 12 Powerful Programs To Help You Manage Your Novell Netware Network . . . See inside . . . "And then elsewhere on the envelope, "Dated Offer, Open Now!" That covered all the bases on a No. 12 envelope.

### The Curiosity Teaser

Perhaps one of the most celebrated curiosity teasers was penned by Bill Jayme for *Psychology Today*: "Do you close the bathroom door when no one else is home?"

As you can see, the curiosity teaser is an oblique reference designed to appeal to the type of person who is likely to be interested in the product. In my view, this is the riskiest of the three types, since it's difficult to tap into someone else's imagination for the exact hot button that will turn him or her on. In the *Psychology Today* example, only those with a psychological bent would find that teaser compelling enough to act—a good way to improve the quality of the respondents as well as improve both payup and renewal rates.

One I wrote for *3D Design* magazine: "The Splines! The Nurbs! The Blobs! Now you can bring them all together with *3D Design* magazine." That's less of a curiosity if you're a 3D designer since you'll know what those critters are, but it's a fun way to get a techie's attention.

A perennial curiosity teaser that still works when used appropriately: "R.S.V.P." It begs the response.

As you can see, curiosity teasers can be fun, but watch it: unless you're very, very sure of yourself, the offer and benefit teasers are a safer bet.

So, should you use a teaser on your packages? I don't know. But you should test them.

## The Letter

### Look and Feel.

A letter should look like a typed letter, not a quasi-brochure. I see many so-called letters in my mail each week that do not meet that requirement. They use various display typefaces, often quirky stuff that calls too much attention to itself and gets in the way of the message.

Tiresome as it may be for some of our more imaginative designers, Courier is the typeface of choice. Why? As we pointed out in Chapter 3, tests consistently show it is the most readable and that it

> A letter should look like a typed letter, not a quasi-brochure.

affords the highest levels of content retention. Times Roman, Bodoni, Garamond, and other serif typefaces are OK too, of course, but they're less "typewriter-ish" than Courier. The point is the serif, not the typeface itself.

### Length.

A simple suggestion often given is that a letter should be as long as it takes to get the message across. How do you know what that is? Write it, and see. Chances are, if you can't say it in four pages, you can't say it. Find someone who can.

Some say no one reads letters of more than one page. How silly! Millions of dollars of goods and services are being sold every day through direct mail—much of it with four-page letters. True, no one will read a boring, meaningless, poorly written—or worse, mistargeted—letter beyond the first paragraph. But when you're addressing someone's true needs, he or she will read what you have to say about it, if you make it vital and interesting. As a colleague once put it, "People don't read short letters or long letters. They read what interests them."

That said, and all other things being equal, a general rule of thumb is to keep business-to-business letters to two pages (to avoid the appearance of a time-consuming document), and consumer letters to four pages (to demonstrate that there's a heck of a lot to be said about this wonderful widget). Just remember that no one's going to have a stroke if an interesting letter runs beyond those boundaries. The prospect's level of qualification is in him, not you, and no letter is going to change that. Magazine renewals and fund-raising letters have their own dynamics but are usually brief—one to two pages.

### Correspondence vs. Illustrated; Letter/Brochure.

Sometimes, usually in consumer environments, you may wish to reduce package costs or have other reasons to combine the letter with graphic elements into an illustrated letter or letter/brochure.

### Stock.

Stock should be compatible with the envelope. Standard stock is 20-pound white wove, but if you've reached for an ivory or vellum look on the envelope, don't blow it with the letter. Have your supplier give you letter-stock options as well.

> All other things being equal, a general rule of thumb is to keep business-to-business letters to two pages and consumer letters to four pages.

### Personalization.

Personalization is the heart of the relationship you want to build with your customer/prospect. Customers especially should always be addressed by name. Whatever added costs you incur will be repaid over time by a higher lifetime customer value.

### Headline vs. None.

A headline at the top of your letter carries similar dynamics to the teaser on the envelope. It synthesizes the core message and gives the reader a reason to spend his or her time with the letter. For executive mailings, however, you want to at least test a headline before you roll out with it.

A popular headline technique is the so-called "Johnson box" created by copywriter Frank Johnson when he was at American Heritage. He placed an offer statement inside a rectangle or "box" made of asterisks and found significant increases in response. It was probably due more to the offer than to the box, but the technique marches on, nevertheless, and today most anything at the top of a letter is often referred to as a Johnson box.

### Company Letterhead vs. Product vs. Personal.

If your company logo is an elaborate affair, you might consider placing it at the end of the letter instead of at the top, so you won't distract attention from your headline. You're not selling your logo, after all. As with the corner card, you might focus attention more compellingly if you use the product name rather than the company name in your letterhead. For business executive mailings, a personal letterhead (i.e., name, title) might be more acceptable.

### Single Sheets vs. 11" × 17".

The most economical solution for a four-page letter is an 11"× 17" sheet folded to make four 8½" × 11" (front and back) panels. It's also the most manageable for the reader and helps avoid confusion over which page follows which. Some marketers have found success in business-to-business mailings with two to three individual sheets printed "executive" style on one side only.

## Connections Count

A woman showed me a package from *The Harvard Business Review*. It was a No. 10 package with a four-page letter and several inserts. "Who's going to take the time to read all this?" she exclaimed. "Harvard Business School graduates will," I told her. In fact, I knew that package had been *HBR*'s highly successful control package for about two years. I even knew who wrote it!

**Typefaces.**

As discussed earlier, Courier is the most readable typeface for letters, affording the highest levels of retention. That's physics, not opinion.

**Handwritten Notations.**

Used in moderation, a handwritten notation or two can help draw attention to a key point in a letter. It's a technique usually confined to consumer mail, but there are always exceptions.

**P.S.**

Studies show that normal eye movement goes from the (1) headline and addressee to (2) the salutation to (3) the signature block to (4) the P.S. to (5) the first paragraph of the letter. Make that P.S. count with a key benefit or other important statement. A blue ink signature aids credibility.

**Literature Code.**

To help the lettershop get the right components into the right envelopes, a literature code somewhere on the visible outside of the letter (and on all other pieces) can ensure accuracy.

See "Anatomy of a Direct Mail Letter" in Chapter 8 for help in pulling some of these factors together.

> The first thing to understand about the brochure is that you may not need one.

## The Brochure

### Test With and Without.

The first thing to understand about the brochure is that you may not need one. That's the upside. The downside is that about the only way to be sure is to test your package with it and without it, so you'll likely have to produce one in any case.

In my view, one of the main reasons brochures depress response is that they're not done right. The main function of the brochure (most of the time—there are exceptions) is to show the product in use. Many brochures I receive in the mail are little more than a repeat of the points made in the letter SET IN LARGE TYPE, or an overly detailed, long copy diatribe on the product that ends up distracting from the basic sales message.

Brochures that fail to add meaningful information to the message become a burden on the package and on the reader's time, not a help. The brochure should be a support piece to the letter. It "proves" many of the claims made in the letter by demonstrating those points with pictures, graphs, testimonials, etc.

In each case, the brochure shows the reader how the product plays out in his or her life.

## Look and Feel.

If the letter is the "sell" piece in the package, the brochure is the "show" piece. It's the salesman's sample case. The demonstration of the all-purpose juicer or the Ginsu knife . . . the computer screens that show how a software package delivers data . . . the real-as-a-roar color photo of the cheetah in a nature library; the lush look of a lemon soufflé in a cookbook; the stark beauty of the Pyramids in a historical continuity series.

### Size and Folds.

Sizes range from a simple 8½"× 11" page to a full-sized 15"× 25" "bedsheet" brochure. Some purists insist that an 8½" × 11" sheet is a "flier," and you may encounter some confusion in terminology about that with printers, mailers, etc. Fold it in half to fit a 6" × 9" package and it's more clearly a four-panel brochure. Likewise if you fold it in thirds to fit a No. 10 business envelope. Only now it has six panels. Another favorite of mine is the 11" × 15" brochure, which folds in half twice to fit a No. 10 package and yields eight panels.

As mentioned in the section on letters, the letter-brochure or so-called illustrated letter combines, on an 11" × 17" sheet, a letter on pages one and four with illustrations, usually two-color, in the center spread, pages two and three. In this case, your piece is primarily a letter and should be on letter stock. You'd have to go to a fairly heavy stock, like 60-pound cover, to avoid show-through if you used four-color art in the center.

> Brochures that fail to add meaningful information to the message become a burden on the package and on the reader's time, not a help.

You can get all the real estate you need for most projects with an 11" × 17" sheet folded in half to 8½" × 11" then folded again, either in thirds for a No. 10 envelope or in half for a 6" × 9".

The "bedsheet" brochure is usually reserved for those big, 9" × 12" packages, such as the ones Time-Life Books puts out, and for similar book-continuity programs. The extra space is needed for the dramatic photography that sells the books, mammoth headlines, and bold illustrations of the books themselves.

Whichever size you choose, be sensitive to the natural divisions the folds provide and use them to "unfold" your message a bit at a time. This allows you to control your presentation and direct the reader's attention to each point in the order you wish. You can use each panel separately, or combine two or more to create larger panels for larger illustrations.

Also be careful of elaborate brochure designs that require complicated folding, and of brochures that are stapled or saddle stitched. The former can lead to confusion on the part of the reader and the latter are often set aside for reading "later," which seldom comes. Remember, the brochure is intended to *support* the letter, not replace it. We want our reader to move through the package to the order form, not get hung up on any one part of it.

### Four-color vs. Two-color.

If you're selling food, artwork, four-color books, or almost anything to kids, you'll likely want to use four-color art. In general, consumer brochures do best in four colors, while business-to-business brochures can be effective in two colors, especially for information products and for most BTB services. Information doesn't have a color. Three colors will cost about the same as four, so you may as well go for four.

### Stock.

Beware of high-gloss stock. It can reflect too much light in an unpredictable way and make the copy and illustrations hard to read. You'll want some degree of coating if you're using photos, so look for a semi-gloss or dull coat in an 80-pound text. Beyond that, let your designer advise you. Business-to-business brochures can be effective in uncoated or matte finishes, especially in smaller sizes using two colors.

> Remember, the brochure is intended to support the letter, not replace it. We want our reader to move through the package to the order form, not get hung up on any one part of it.

### Illustrations.

Photographs and drawings are both illustrations. Photos provide greater credibility, but sometimes illustrations are the only way to get the image you want. Choose one or the other, however, not a combination. Exceptions would include an illustrated diagram that's related to a particular photo image and, of course, charts and graphs.

Every photo should be accompanied by a caption explaining what's in the photo. The pictures may be self-evident to you, but I assure you, they aren't to the reader.

Often, you can enhance the visual impact of a piece with images purchased from stock photo houses. With the large quantity and wide range of stock images available on the Internet today (see *www.photodisk.com*, among others), you should be able to find photos that will work in almost any environment.

You'll have to do your own product-in-use shots, and you could end up with some disparity in quality between your own photos and professional images. Your designer should be aware of this and should have sources for images that will enhance your material.

### Second Order Form.

It's a good idea to provide a second order form in a brochure in case the first one gets misplaced, or your reader wishes to pass the package on to a friend or colleague.

Include copy to the effect of "may be photocopied for convenience" so the reader doesn't have to cut up the brochure to use the form. Don't rely on the brochure for the only order form, however, assuming it will save money. You'll lose much more in orders than you save, trust me.

### Testimonials.

While I frequently use a testimonial or two in a letter, the brochure is the place to present a selection of testimonial statements. Give them a heading like, "Here's what your colleagues are saying about ABC widgets . . . " and include full names, titles, companies, or addresses whenever possible to reinforce credibility. You'll need peoples' permission to use them, so collect them as they come to you rather than trying to track people down six months or a year later when you're under the deadline pressures of a promotion.

> It's a good idea to provide a second order form in a brochure in case the first one gets misplaced, or your reader wishes to pass the package on to a friend or colleague.

### Offer, Guarantee, Call to Action, Company I.D.

The brochure should include all the essentials your reader needs to make a purchase decision in the event he or she loses the letter. That means repeat the offer in the brochure, feature the guarantee prominently, include a call to action, and be sure the company address and other ordering/contact information is easy to find.

### Literature Code.

Help keep the printer/mailer from going nuts and making a mistake by including a literature code in a prominent outside corner of the document.

## The Reply Device

### Look and Feel.

I refer to this document as a "reply device," because it isn't always an "order form." Sometimes it's a donor or gift form, as in fund raising. Sometimes it's an information request, as in lead generation.

Look-and-feel issues for a fund-raising reply form are much the same as they are for the rest of the package. Don't look too fancy . . . or too rich. (The exception might be a political fund campaign that carries congressional or other high-ranking governmental association.) We'll get back to fund-raising packages in a bit.

In lead generation, the reply form will include several qualifying questions and should offer space for alternative names and even addresses, in the event the package was forwarded to a more appropriate recipient.

Otherwise, order forms need to project a lot of chutzpah. They need to summarize and synthesize the offer and benefits, and sell them at the same time. Most of all, they need to GET THE ORDER.

This is the document in your package that brings home the bacon. It's a form of contract that the customer makes with you, albeit non-binding. It represents a commitment on the part of the prospect/customer to accept your free trial or other offer on the terms you've suggested, so it should look and feel authoritative, if not exactly legal. (Too much of a "legal" look might cause doubt and hesitation.)

> Repeat the offer in the brochure, feature the guarantee prominently, include a call to action, and be sure the company address and other ordering/contact information is easy to find.

Most important, the order card should be as clear and unambiguous as you can make it. Any doubt about price or terms or guarantee and your prospect may balk. Allow sufficient room for any information you request. In look and feel, the order form should be consistent with the overall look and feel of the package. If it's a fun look, you can carry that to the order card, but lightly. The order card should always instill confidence in the prospect. Here are just a few options you may wish to consider.

### Certificate/Check Design.

You've received them, lots of them. The telcos have been living off them. On what? Order forms that not only look like checks, but are checks . . . sort of. They are checks because you can cash them, but that automatically switches your long-distance service to that company. In any case, many companies use check-like documents very successfully. Not so much because people think they are checks, but because the check-like verisimilitude projects value.

Tests of bind-in and blow-in cards in magazines often result in the certificate-type card winning in head-to-head tests with other designs— perhaps because the value design is a strong counterpoint to the slicker, four-color editorial illustrations and advertisements in the book.

There's a tendency among some to reject techniques like certificates as "hype" or "junk mail" tactics. But as I've said elsewhere in these pages, we all have a professional responsibility to do what works best, not what we like or don't like. Checks and certificates work often enough that you should at least test them.

Another variation on this theme of value and importance in order forms is the personalized temporary membership card. The American Automobile Association (AAA) has used this technique forever, and many other associations and membership organizations—including some that can "borrow" the membership metaphor, like a record or video club—use a membership card as an order form.

The danger here is in making the card too real or valuable-looking so that the recipient is reluctant to send it back. A card that must be returned needs to be designed into the paper or made into a low-cost cardboard or very thin plastic stick-on. It should be clearly marked "temporary" or some such. Heavier plastic could look and feel too valuable to send back. A plastic membership card used in conjunction with an order form can be very effective, however.

Most important, the order card should be as clear and unambiguous as you can make it. Any doubt about price or terms or guarantee and your prospect may balk.

### Four-color vs. Two-color.

Magazine publishers—who do more direct mail testing than any other category I can think of—have found that four-color on an order card, often in the form of a cover photo, can increase response. It has been said that if your budget permits four-color in only one place in a direct mail package, use it on the order form. If that's the only color in the package, OK. But if you have a color brochure and other color components, make sure the order card doesn't blend in and become "lost" in the overall package design. In that case, it might be better to keep the order card to two-color, as with the blow-in/bind-in example mentioned previously.

For business-to-business lead generation (and fund raising), I'd keep the reply device to two colors. Business-to-business lead generation is usually an information transfer, and information has no color, so why pay for it? Also, the two-color look is more intellectual, generally, than four-color, which better complements the lead-generation environment. You're going to need open white space for your qualifying questions, in any case.

### Illustrations vs. None.

Most of what we've said about color applies to illustrations as well. Remember that the order card is a "contract" of sorts, so you want to keep it important-looking. Illustrations might reduce that look and feel. Except for a magazine cover on publishing order forms, I'd stay away from illustrations.

### Offer Boilerplate Copy.

The "boilerplate" copy—everything that comes after the "YES" checkbox—is written first person, as though being spoken by the recipient, now turned customer.

Don't put words in your prospect's mouth that he or she would never say: "Yes! I'd like to become a master of the universe and, with your wonderful software program, crush into powder everyone who ever crossed me . . . ."

The copy needs to spell out the offer in its entirety. If you're offering a free premium, mention that first. "Yes, send my FREE

> If your budget permits four-color in only one place in a direct mail package, use it on the order form.

report, 'The Masters of the Universe Guide to Picking Up Chicks,' and send my copy of your Masters of the Universe software package at $55 plus $3.75 shipping and handling. I may try the program for 30 days without obligation. If not satisfied, I will return the software for a full refund. The Report is mine to keep."

Note that if you ask for payment up front, you may refer to the offer as "Risk Free," instead of "Free," since it isn't technically "Free" if they have to pay to get it. That's an FTC rule. Also, under FTC regs, if you use "Free," and there's a catch, like it's free with a subscription, you are obliged to make that clear: "YOURS FREE with no-risk subscription."

You'll want to be sure to spell out all the payment options:

❐ Payment enclosed  ❐ Please bill me  ❐ Please bill my credit card and, in some cases,  ❐ Bill company (P.O.#____).

Visually, make those check boxes pop, and make the credit card line long enough to enter a 16-digit number without crunching.

If you have a deadline—and you should always have a deadline—be sure it's featured prominently on the order form, maybe in a corner slash, and in the boilerplate copy as well.

Spell out all the contact options as well: company mailing address, fax number, e-mail address if appropriate, and Web site URL, especially if there's an alternate reply form online.

### Qualification Questions.

In lead-generation packages, you'll likely want to include several questions for the prospect to answer, both to obtain certain types of information and to help "qualify" the prospect in terms of the lengths he or she will go to in order to respond to your offer.

Chapters 2 and 7 describe the "Quantity/Quality Ratio"—the fact that you can't have it both ways: higher response rate usually means lower quality of respondent, and vice versa. So decide how difficult you want to make the response process. The harder you make it, the higher the quality of the prospect will be.

A client who owns a PC network training school put his course's $6,900 pricetag on his Web site. That will surely weed out

## It's Hard to Top Value

During a stint at Ziff-Davis Publishing, most of the publications employed a dollars-off check-like certificate (with a patented, raised red portion showing the dollar amount). Nothing we "creatives" tried seemed able to beat them.

Likewise with certificates. Some years ago, I created a series of "professional courtesy vouchers" that significantly increased response for a stable of medical publications marketed to nurses, and they were used successfully for many years thereafter. My theory was that educated nurses might be turned off by simulated "checks" but "professional courtesy vouchers" compliment their sense of professionalism.

When you know the media is working for you, you can afford to ease up on the other qualification tricks and techniques.

the "tire kickers," but it also gives some good prospects the information they need on price without having to contact the school. Some of those prospects may get lost to inertia, to other schools, etc.

It's usually better to have the opportunity to speak to even a moderately good prospect, if you have the ability to sell those folks. In this particular case, however, the school's salespeople were being buried by low-quality prospects, so the owner decided to separate the wheat from the chaff by putting the price up front.

Sometimes the media itself will help qualify the prospect. A so-called "bingo card" lead, for example, may not be as well qualified as one that comes from a Web site dedicated to your topic area, or your own direct mail, assuming your lists are on target. When you know the media is working for you, you can afford to ease up on the other qualification tricks and techniques.

Questions may address the type of business the company is in (which you really should know going in), prospect's title, budget, type of competing products he/she may be using, how soon his or her next purchase or review may be planned, and other related information, usually carefully worded to be "soft" (i.e. not an in-your-face type of inquisition).

### Signature/Phone Number.

Asking for a signature tends to make people uneasy. They get the feeling they may be committing themselves to something—even if you've said they're not. In some environments, it can make or break a lead-generation scheme, so use it judiciously.

With regard to phone numbers, most people expect to be asked for that, so there may be no problem unless you say something like, "Requests without phone numbers cannot be processed." That's tantamount to saying "we're going to call you." Again, consider the impact on your quality/quantity ratio.

### Detachable Stub.

When selling subscriptions and many other categories, it's sometimes helpful to have a detachable stub on the order form. It also helps with formatting, since you can use the stub to bridge the gap from a No. 10 outer envelope with the address showing through a window to a No. 6 BRE for the return portion.

Most of all, however, it gives the customer documented "proof" of his or her purchase. I usually include spaces for dollar amount, date, and check/charge number. A brief reprise of the guarantee doesn't hurt here, either. By its nature, the stub is an "action device." That is, the customer has to do something—detach the stub—as part of the purchase process.

### Action Device.

I've always associated tokens and peel-off labels on order forms ("YES!" . . . "Yes–No–Maybe" . . . "Free!" etc.) with the pen a salesperson hands you when you've agreed to buy the insurance or the encyclopedia for the kids. It's closure to the deal. An action that signifies agreement with the proposal. A way to say, "yes." Do they work? Of course they work, or you wouldn't see any. Do they always work? Of course not. That's why direct mail is a testing medium.

What's always interested me, in response to those who say tokens aren't for business-to-business marketing (too junky, you know), is that magazines like *Fortune* and *Inc.* and *Business Week*–publications that target top management—have used these techniques successfully forever. Action devices do seem to run in packs, especially in magazine subscription marketing. That may be because magazine promotion folks watch each other's packages carefully and if a particular technique shows up twice, the others take that as a winning technique and jump on board. All that said, you will want to employ these and other direct mail "bells and whistles" carefully in business mail. Test, test, test.

### Gift Amount Checkoff (fundraising).

Most successful fundraising reply forms give the donor several gift amount options, usually with the highest amount in the first position, and often with the target gift amount circled or marked in some way. The target amount comes from the database as a step-up from the donor's last gift amount. The form itself is simply designed and personalized.

> By its nature, the stub is an "action device." That is, the customer has to do something—detach the stub—as part of the purchase process.

### BRC vs. BRE.

It may be tempting from a cost basis to want to use a Business Reply Card rather than a Business Reply Envelope—and the choice may be a good one. If you're not anticipating payment (cash, check, or money order), and if the information on the card is not confidential in any way (like a credit card number), a BRC may do the trick. Lead-generation reply cards just asking for information can often be BRCs. Even there, though, there could be some diminution of image. Judge your market, the image you want to project, and especially the relationship you hope to build when deciding which corners to cut, not only on order forms, but on every component of your package. Cheap begets cheap; quality begets quality.

## The Lift Letter

Whenever I speak to groups new to direct marketing and mention the lift letter in passing, I often get blank stares and the inevitable question, "What's a lift letter?"

The lift letter is a second "letter" or note in a direct mail package that performs a number of functions. It's called the "lift" letter because it often lifts response. In magazine promotion, it's often called the "Publisher's Letter" because it's usually signed by the publisher. One version you may be familiar with is the note that says, "Read this only if you've decided NOT to take us up on our offer." Of course, most people who have gotten that far into the package will read it in any case. But there are other ways to use a lift letter.

### Test with and without.

The first thing to know about the lift letter is that, like the brochure, you should test your package with it and without it. It may work more often than not, but it's wiser to test.

### Look and Feel.

The next thing to know about the lift letter is that it isn't really a letter. It's more like a note. Or a memo.

> The lift letter is a second "letter" or note in a direct mail package that performs a number of functions. It's called the "lift" letter because it often lifts response.

## Size.

The lift letter or lift note is usually smaller than the standard 8½" × 11" letter. It can be a 7" × 10" Monarch-sized letter, folded in half or in thirds, or any other size that will fit into the package and can be safely inserted.

## Stock.

The paper stock for the lift note should be a different color from the sales letter, and from other pieces in the package, so it stands out. It may also be printed on a better–or lesser–quality stock, depending on its nature.

## Letter vs. Memo vs. Other.

As indicated above, the lift letter can take many guises. Its primary purpose, however, is to reinforce the offer and guarantee, over the signature of someone other than–and usually senior to–the person who signed the sales letter. One way other another, the message is, "Yes, we really mean what we say." The reader can get a free issue or a 30-day trial demo or whatever, cancel and owe nothing, or get a full refund.

If for some reason that's not deemed appropriate, the lift letter can be an extension of the sales letter. It can, for example, present several testimonials with an outside teaser to the effect of, "Here's what your colleagues are saying about xyz widgets!"

It can offer other information that might have been awkward to fit into the logic and tempo of the sales letter.

The lift letter is essentially an involvement device. It's another opportunity to sell the offer and guarantee, and perhaps to present an additional point or two in the process. It holds the reader into your message a little longer, which improves your odds of a sale or response.

> The paper stock for the lift note should be a different color from the sales letter, and from other pieces in the package, so it stands out.

## The Premium Insert

### Test with and without.

This is a variable worth an A/B test.

### Look and Feel.

A premium insert should be at least as prominent in color and stock as the rest of the package, if not a bit more so. It's usually in color. Like the lift letter, it's another involvement device. Its purpose is to dramatize a hot premium—where the premium is deemed strong enough to drive a response decision.

### Buckslip vs. Folded.

A "buckslip" is a flat sheet, so-called because in a No. 10 envelope, it is roughly the size and shape of a dollar bill. In my view, the buckslip format is a little less compelling than a folded piece, because everything is right there as the recipient removes it from the envelope. It's a "glance-at" piece. Better, I believe, is taking an 8" × 7" sheet, folding it in half horizontally to 8" × 3½" and putting a teaser on the outside with the full story inside.

### Attached to Reply Device vs. Loose.

You can also place premium copy on a panel that folds down from the order form so the whole sales story is on a single piece of paper.

## The Alternatives

The alternative to designing your own direct mail package "from scratch," as the recipe writers like to say, is to utilize one of the many "pre-fab" direct mail packages available from web printers and publishers.

A web press contains a continuous roll of paper that is two- or four-color printed, computer addressed, and personalized in one or more locations, then cut and folded into a direct mail package, ready

---

**Lift Notes Can Increase Involvement**

For a package mailed to teachers, Io nce created a lift note that looked and felt like something scribbled by a young student on a scrap of yellow pad paper. Another time, it was lasered on a piece of pricey, upscale stationery presumably "From the desk of" the company president.

to mail. Ink-jet personalization is its strong suit; it can often be strategically placed in several locations within the package, such as the salutation in the letter, the order form, and perhaps a lift letter, invitation piece, or small brochure.

## Sweepstakes: You may have already blown it.

Recently, the national press was vibrating with stories about the allegedly misleading use of ink-jet announcements in sweepstakes packages promising millions to people who "have already won," but for one reason or another, fail to read the smaller print that contains the disheartening "if" phrase (IF you return the enclosed numbers and IF your number is drawn for the first prize, etc.).

That's one problem with sweepstakes, if you choose to go that route. Another is the complexity of FTC and state sweepstakes laws, which you must know and follow if you're mailing nationally. Still another is the cost, especially if you're going to put up a few million. Under FTC rules, all prizes must be awarded.

An alternative to doing your own sweepstakes is to buy into one produced by a sweepstakes provider. One company that has pretty much pioneered the turnkey co-op sweepstakes and developed a variety of custom promotions is Ventura Associates. They charge a fee to participate in a big-time sweepstakes that you can present as your own. They do all the heavy lifting; you just add your own product information and mail it. Ventura is in New York at 212-302-8277.

Another major player in co-op sweepstakes is Don Jagoda Associates, Inc., at 516-454-1800.

Finally, the late great circulation consultant Dick Benson regularly cautioned clients, and anyone else who would listen, that sweepstakes often attract opportunity seekers. They're less interested in your product than in the prize money or car or whatever, at the expense of more qualified customers who might buy more frequently and/or spend more for your product or service. Further, customers who come onto your file as the result of a sweepstakes offer, frequently require similar inducements to stay there.

### Web Tip

Ventura also provides turn-key sweepstakes you can add to your Web site.

### Proprietary Telegram Package.

Yes, the real kind from Western Union. Well, not "telegram," exactly. Western Union has a series of mailers available to marketers bearing the unmistakable logo and look of the Western Union telegram. They include the Mailgram, Priority Letter, and Custom Letter. The company's research shows opening rates of up to 93%.

One thousand half-page Mailgrams will run about $5.00 each with nominal added charges for enclosures and business reply envelope. The one-page Custom Letter was recently quoted at 63¢, but check with Western Union for the most current rates. Complete details are available at 1-800-MAILGRAM.

You can always try to fake it yourself with a "gram" mailing on yellow stock, but for the difference in cost, you're probably better off with the real fake.

### Proprietary "Express" Package.

Like the telegram verisimilitude, some companies are marketing various takes on the USPS's Express Mail/Priority Mail packages. Lots of serious eagles.

Two companies that specialize in these packages are Mega Direct (1-800-826-2869) and Response Mail Express (1-800-795-2773). Each has more than a dozen flavors of "high impact," personalized, 9" × 12" and No. 10 packages designed to project the importance and immediacy of "express" mail.

As I pointed out recently in response to a survey from one of these printers, I'd feel better about them if I ever received one from a mailer other than the company that makes them. And keep an eye out for the Feds. There's been some buzz in Congress about outlawing these look-alike packages.

> The advent of computerized ink-jet imprinting and web press technologies has made possible a variety of direct mail formats that feature personalized closed face envelopes with innovative personalization.

### Proprietary "Pre-Fab" Packages.

The advent of computerized ink-jet imprinting and web press technologies has made possible a variety of direct mail formats that feature personalized closed face envelopes with innovative personalization throughout and upscale paper stocks and colors that often make for effective packages at reasonable cost, especially at quantities of 50,000 and more.

One such printer is The Kurt H. Volk Company, who pioneered their patented Letter-Lope®. Letter-Lopes come in a wide selection of sizes and formats and can accommodate laser or ink-jet personalization at several places in the package, starting with a closed face envelope.

Letter-Lopes feature such niceties as four-color process, patterned envelope interior to prevent show-through, die cutting, embossing, personalized plastic card affixing, compatible color and/or matching stock on letter and envelope, spot-gumming, and numbering. The packages are used with success by magazines, credit card marketers, political fund raisers, retail promotions, insurance, and more.

Volk provides mailers with a template for the format they have chosen. The mailer provides the company with copy and art according to the template, together with their list on computer tape, and Volk prints and mails the package.

Kurt Volk is available on the Web at *www.kurtvolk.com* or in Connecticut at 203-878-6381.

## Self-Mailer Formats.

A self-mailer with a postcard reply device is not usually a problem for most designers and printers to create. But when you need to include a reply envelope, it can get tricky, and you may need to contact a specialty printer.

There are many of these throughout the country (see the Appendix). One such is B&W Press in Danvers, Massachusetts (978-774-2200), who boasts "more than 2,500 customers" and production of more than 8 million order/form envelopes per day on eight web presses. With that kind of schedule, however, you'd need to give yourself—and them—plenty of time to get the job done.

The packet of samples I received from B&W were all printed on uncoated stock, so you may need to search further if you're planning to use a glossy, multi-page self-mailer.

> A self-mailer with a postcard reply device is not usually a problem for most designers and printers to create. But when you need to include a reply envelope, it can get tricky, and you may need to contact a specialty printer.

**Note:** There are many other sources for the kinds of mailings described here. As mentioned elsewhere in this book and in the Appendix, *Target Marketing* magazine (*www.targetonline.com*, 215-238-5300) periodically publishes a directory of specialty printers as well as many other resource directories, including telemarketing, list experts, alternative media, catalog production, software, and more.

For more information on this topic, visit our Web site at www.businesstown.com

# Chapter 10

# Writing and Designing Response Advertising

I f obtaining a sale or an inquiry with a direct mail package is challenging—and it is—accomplishing the same goal with a direct response advertisement is virtually impossible. An ad just sits there on a page in a magazine or newspaper, waiting for the right person to come along, see your ad, stop to read it, accept the premise, and actually respond. There's no two-page or four-page letter, and no brochure to show the product or describe the service in detail, to offer proofs and testimonials, etc. There's no lift letter, order form, or reply envelope to help things along.

Direct response ads are frequently known as "long copy" ads—precisely because in writing a direct response ad, we try as best we can to replicate many of the selling aspects of direct mail package. We "design" it to include an illustration showing the product in use . . . a box containing testimonials . . . another box with bulleted benefits and more, all designed to engage the eye, create involvement, ask for the order—all the things an effective direct mail package does.

## The Headline

It doesn't take a rocket scientist to know that **the most critical element in an ad is the headline.** If the headline doesn't work, the game is over. The question is: what kind of headline? And that's the rub. I don't know. You don't know. Fact is, no one knows what headline—of all the possibilities we could write—will pull the best response.

One of the great gurus of direct response advertising was the late John Caples (*"They Laughed When I Sat Down to the Piano— But When I Started to Play!"*). Part of what made Caples a guru was the fact that he knew he didn't know what headline would pull best, so he tested headlines! He tested offers, too, as has been suggested in these pages from time to time.

Thanks to John Caples, Claude Hopkins, Max Sackheim, and the others who pioneered effective copywriting when space advertising was almost the only response media there was, we have some guidelines to follow when writing ad headlines.

> The most critical element in an ad is the headline.

First, a few "don'ts" when writing headlines:

- **Don't use negatives.** OK, OK. But the fact is, most people read negatives as positives. Seems we try so hard to avoid bad news, we just automatically drop the negative "don't" or "no" word out of the copy. Also, it's to your advantage to approach your product from a positive viewpoint, not a negative one.
- **Don't ask a question** in a headline, especially one that can be answered "no." It tempts readers to mentally say "no" and turn the page.
- **Don't try to be "clever" by being obscure.** The headline should not be a "teaser" for the body copy, but should be a complete statement in itself. The more obvious the better. Headlines are not a place for subtlety
- **Don't exaggerate or make extravagant claims.** Sometimes, even if the claims are true, they may beggar credibility. Be careful how you word them. If your product doesn't measure up to your promises, you're going to get back most of what you sell, and lose future business as well.

Following are eight suggestions for writing effective headlines, keeping in mind that no one really knows what will work best for your product, in your media, with your production values, etc. Testing is the name of the game.

> Your headline should isolate the single most important benefit your product can provide the user, and synthesize it in a few, well-chosen words.

1. Offer a benefit. Your headline should isolate the single most important benefit your product can provide the user, and synthesize it in a few, well-chosen words.
2. Try a "how-to" approach. One of the most famous headlines in history is "How to Win Friends and Influence People." It was the headline on the ad, as well as the title of the book, and it launched an empire.
3. As presented elsewhere in these pages, many of the "power words" of direct response work especially well in headlines. These include "now," "new," "announcing," "at last," and, of course, "FREE!" which is still a universal attention-getter.

4. As with lead generation and qualification, putting the price in the headline will increase the quality of the respondents (but, unless it's a no-brainer, may reduce gross response). Another problem with price-off offers is that it's you who set the price to begin with. So how do I know that 30% off is the deal you say it is?

5. Verbs are still our most powerful action words. Use them. (Find, discover, enjoy.)

6. Offering a test can be provocative, and draws the reader into the body copy. Another historically great headline was, "Do You Make These Mistakes in English?" "Can You Pass This Family Health Test?" should be followed in the body copy by a short test that reinforces the practical guidance of the *Family Health Encyclopedia* (for example).

7. A testimonial can make a powerful headline if it's short and addresses specific benefits of your product, and if the source is well known to your reader.

8. Using your company or product name in a headline in conjunction with a benefit or promise helps with branding, since most readers will at least read the headline.

## The Headline Group

In fact, the headline is so critical to the success of your ad that you might consider expanding that vital space with what I call "the Headline Group." This consists of three parts: an eyebrow, a headline, and an extension.

The eyebrow targets the market for the product. The headline presents the primary benefit. And the extension quickly expands on that benefit with a subhead or one or two bullets.

For example:

Small business owners . . .
**Triple your profits with ad headlines that bring in the orders!**

- Learn proven techniques for getting attention and holding it.
- Discover the "power words" that boost response!

> The eyebrow targets the market for the product. The headline presents the primary benefit. And the extension quickly expands on that benefit with a subhead or one or two bullets.

As you can see, the Headline Group does double or triple duty in that highly visible and critically important space over a headline by itself. It works best in a full-page ad where you have the room to create it, but there's no reason the concept can't be applied even to display classified ads. Instead of one single idea to engage the reader, it offers several, in both the head and the extension. Often, the extension or subhead or bullet alludes to the offer: "Try it without risk for 30 days."

## Use Subheads Throughout

Subheads are the signposts that help readers through the ad. They summarize the principal point or benefit of the paragraph to follow and provide a sort of stepping stone from the headline to the call for action, the coupon, or phone number. In a world of quick-take browsers, subheads may be all your reader ever sees, so make them all he or she needs to read.

## Use "Brochure" Elements in Your Ad

As mentioned previously, you can replicate some of the elements of a direct mail package in your ad.

- Three to five testimonials (select short ones) in a box will attract the eye and increase the involvement factor as they add credibility to your proposition.
- A summary of six or seven key benefits/features in another box will help to synthesize the story for the quick readers and add more involvement.
- As with a direct mail package, make your call to action stand out with type and/or color, and make the response element visible from two or three feet away. Make coupons look like coupons (you may want to test your ad with and without a coupon), with bold borders. Punch up the 800 number in as large a point size as is consistent with your overall design (exaggerate it, if that's still too small).

Subheads are the signposts that help readers through the ad.

## Copypoints

> Specifics are more credible than generalities.
> Percent of growth, actual dollar amounts, number of days, weeks, or months. And odd numbers—3, 5, 7, and 9—are more credible than even numbers.

- Make sure you write in second person ("you") throughout, and write in terms of your reader's interests, not your own or your product's. Keep your company out of it, however wonderful you may think you are.
- Focus on one primary benefit, not the kitchen sink. Present that benefit from several angles. You can include a secondary point or perhaps two, but work them in carefully. Try being all things to all people, and you'll end up being nothing to no one.
- In lead generation, focus heavily on the offer—the white paper or other information-based document you're providing. Keep the copy light.
- For order generation—selling something directly off the page—go for long copy and flog your principal points until you're blue.
- As with all response copy, specifics are more credible than generalities. Percent of growth, actual dollar amounts, number of days, weeks, or months. And odd numbers—3, 5, 7, and 9—are more credible than even numbers.
- Use a burst to set off a bonus, or a special price, or a time-limited offer.
- ASK FOR THE ORDER! Be sure you include a call to action. "Send for your no-risk trial today. Call us at 800-555-5555 with your credit card or complete the coupon below and fax it to 555-5555 or mail it to the address shown."

## John Caples' 29 Formulas for Writing Successful Headlines

As noted, John Caples was best known for testing headlines. Following are his "29 Formulas," some of which we've touched on above. Others may seem dated today, but you'll get the idea.

1. Begin your headline with the word "Announcing."
2. Use words that have an announcement quality.

3. Begin your headline with the word "New."
4. Begin your headline with the word "Now."
5. Begin your headline with the words "At last."
6. Put a date into your headline.
7. Write your headline in news style.
8. Feature the price in your headline.
9. Feature a reduced price.
10. Feature a special merchandising offer.
11. Feature an easy payment plan.
12. Feature a free offer.
13. Offer information of value.
14. Tell a story.
15. Begin your headline with the words "How to."
16. Begin your headline with the word "How."
17. Begin your headline with the word "Why."
18. Begin your headline with the word "Which."
19. Begin your headline with the words "Who else."
20. Begin your headline with the word "Wanted."
21. Begin your headline with the word "This."
22. Begin your headline with the word "Advice."
23. Use a testimonial-style headline.
24. Offer the reader a test.
25. Use a one-word headline.
26. Use a two-word headline.
27. Warn the reader to delay buying.
28. Let the advertiser speak directly to the reader.
29. Address your headline to a specific person or group.

As Mr. Caples liked to say, "Times change, people don't." I think you'll find most of these ideas as valid today as they were 50 years ago when he wrote them.

For more information on this topic, visit our Web site at www.businesstown.com

# The Supporting Cast

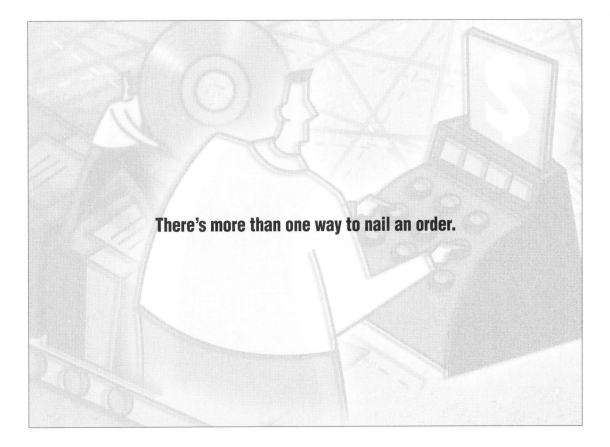

There's more than one way to nail an order.

# Chapter 11

# Alternative Print Media: A Low-Cost Prospecting Tool

R ising printing and paper costs, increased postage, skyrocketing list rental rates. Is there any way around these constantly increasing costs?

For business-to-business lead generating and even consumer prospecting, the answer increasingly is "alternative print media," one of direct marketing's surprising little secrets. Alternative print media consists mostly of package inserts and card decks, but it also includes ride-alongs, co-op mailings, statement stuffers, sampling, catalog bind-ins/blow-ins, and a few others.

These media are especially useful for start-ups with limited marketing budgets. I have seen some of them used almost exclusively by magazines, manufacturers, distributors, and others, usually in cases where the marketing niche is hard to reach through more traditional media.

## A Specialized Media Group

Because this is such a specialized media grouping, with its own unique dynamics and requirements, I called upon the champion of alternative print media, Leon Henry, for help in understanding the variety of opportunities available today.

In the last 30 years, the number of insert programs has risen dramatically, along with the variety of options being offered to mailers.

### Package Inserts

These are freestanding promotional pieces delivered to a mail order customer via a company's fulfillment package (i.e., the insert is delivered to you in a box containing a shirt you ordered from a catalog).

Naturally, the product shipment types vary dramatically: catalog generated versus space generated, continuity or club oriented, business-to-business versus consumer. Correspondingly, the responses to the outside insert will also vary.

With more than 1,000 package insert programs (PIPs) to choose from, the universe approaches half a billion and includes distributors like Hanover House and Fingerhut. There are also scores of distributors and specialty companies.

> Alternative print media consists mostly of package inserts and card decks, but it also includes ride-alongs, co-op mailings, statement stuffers, sampling, catalog bind-ins/blow-ins, and a few others.

### Card Decks

This vehicle usually consists of 20 or more 3½" × 5½" business reply cards delivered in poly packs. Rate card prices average from $25/M to $30/M and include printing from film. Mostly business-to-business, more consumer card decks have come onto the market in recent months.

Currently, some 750 decks are available in approximate circulations of 100M to 1MM each. Most decks will accept preprinted inserts at a higher cost per thousand. Many are also mailing in a larger format, 5½" × 7½", which is more pre-print friendly.

### Ride-Alongs

In this instance a company mails a catalog, circular, or announcement to its customer base and allows outside advertising to ride along. An advertiser can count on this method of distribution since the company doing the mailing has a vested interest in getting out their own promotional pieces.

Companies like music marketers Columbia House and BMG dominate this category and offer regular mailings in blocks of 2MM to 6MM to their club members. Advertisers' responses from this category are strong—comparable to those of package inserts. Average prices range from $40/M to $60/M. Outside inserts are from four to six per mailing. Response curves are similar to those for direct mail.

### Co-Op Mailings

This category, by definition, presents a group of noncompetitive advertisers mailing to a common market.

Carol Wright is typical, including both mail order and direct response offers along with packaged goods participants (coupons on brand items). Co-ops represent large numbers (up to 40MM) in a single drop, can usually provide demographic selectivity, and often provide demographic selections. Although responses are not as high as those generally received from packages, co-ops are priced more competitively, at an average of $15/M.

Other types of co-ops include mail order and direct response offers, but instead of the packaged goods coupons, local coupons are

> Currently, some 750 decks are available in approximate circulations of 100M to 1MM each.

included. These programs are usually sold on a local level by neighborhood franchises. Good examples include Val Pak and Money Mailer. Most of them are available in a No. 10 envelope format, but some mail in a 6" × 9" envelope. Circulation exceeds 50MM/quarter.

### Statement Stuffers

These mailings include invoices and statements generated by cable TV companies, utilities, credit cards, magazines, clubs, continuity programs, retailers, businesses, and so on. They are usually distributed in small envelopes, so your insert needs to be no larger than 3½" × 6½" to fit. Outside inserts are generally limited to three, since statements get mailed first class (high percentage of deliverability), and additional outside advertising would bump them into the next postal class. Response tends to be strong. The average price runs about $45/M.

### Sampling

This method of insertion offers a variety of "goody bags" distributed free to specific markets (i.e. college students, new mothers, and other special interest groups). Inserts accompany product samples and coupons. Packages are usually given out "free" in high traffic situations. Pricing ranges from $25/M to $40/M. Shelf life can be difficult to pinpoint.

### Catalog Bind-Ins/Blow-Ins

This distribution has been used in big numbers for years by the horticultural set (i.e., a magazine subscription offer or a lead generator for a lawn tool product is bound into a catalog). Many catalogs are now beginning to offer blow-in space, traditional advertising space, and business reply card (printed three-up to make a page) space in their catalogs to further serve the direct response advertiser. Blow-ins can run as little as half the price of package inserts to the same customers.

### Other Alternatives

Inserts have been included in newspapers and supermarket take-one racks, have ridden along with Pennysavers, order acknowl-

> Many catalogs are now beginning to offer blow-in space, traditional advertising space, and business reply card (printed three-up to make a page) space in their catalogs to further serve the direct response advertiser.

edgments, and FSIs (Free-Standing Inserts: overruns of Sunday Supplements), and the list goes on.

As direct marketers look for increasingly creative methods to better their bottom line and find less expensive ways to develop new customers and generate qualified inquiries, more will be developed. An experienced broker can help lead you through the maze and find the best alternatives for you.

## More about Package Inserts

The going rate for package inserts is an average of $50/M. The number of outside inserts varies from four to eight. Generally only noncompetitive pieces are included together.

If one goes heavily into a club or continuity-oriented program, the rate of duplication needs to be monitored. The response rates also vary significantly, depending on a number of other variables:

- Whether the insert is generating a lead or producing an order
- The average ticket price of the items being sold
- The size of the insert

A large-ticket item may be satisfied with two responses per thousand (.002), whereas lead-generating devices having a strong affinity between the insert and the products being delivered would require and will produce responses from 2 to 5 percent. According to Henry, average acceptable response rates for package inserts overall vary from 0.5 percent to 4 percent.

Additional advantages include the fact that you're paying only for the distribution and not for the postage. Since your insert is arriving with the customer's purchase, you're getting strictly mail order buyers and the very hottest of the "hotline" lists (most recent 30- to 90-day names). This method of distribution also has the effect of granting the advertiser a certain degree of credibility and approval from the sponsoring mailer.

Markets for inserts are highly targetable, and you can quickly achieve a large volume of impressions. As mentioned above, your

> An experienced broker can help lead you through the maze and find the best alternatives for you.

insert is guaranteed exclusive in your category, so you don't have any competitors to contend with. As with lists, you'll want to test at least 10 companies at about 10,000 to 15,000 pieces each in order to achieve statistical reliability.

In business-to-business markets especially, alternative media may be a cost-effective way to drive traffic to a Web site. Self-mailers are being used to do this now, at considerably greater expense.

Creative can be kept simple, and should run less than $30 per thousand. The piece must weigh under a quarter of an ounce.

## Getting Started in Package Inserts

For the uninitiated, package inserts—and alternative print media in general—can be a jungle. To help newcomers get headed in the right direction, broker Leon Henry offers the following 10 suggestions:

1. **Use a Broker.** Don't do it yourself. That's time-consuming and unnecessary. Brokers know all the answers. They've been there with over a billion inserts for nearly every conceivable company and industry, and they'll tell you what's good for your product, and what you should avoid.
2. **Test.** But test smart. Some mailers "test for test's sake," which unfortunately means that when they are through they don't know what and why they tested. Because of the varied nature of the insert market, it is axiomatic that you test.

   But testing smart means testing with a proven insert wherever possible. Test statistically reliable numbers relative to your offer. Test with no more than two copy approaches. Test as many programs initially as your budget allows. Remember that the batter who comes to the plate once is a hero only if he hits a home run. Test smart by coming to bat as often as possible. One strikeout won't look so bad among the homers.
3. **Test New Programs.** Along with such standbys as Hanover House, Newfield, Ambassador, Carol Wright, and Fingerhut, you want to test new ones, such as Viking Office Products and Global Computer Supplies.

> The uninitiated, package inserts—and alternative print media in general—can be a jungle.

4. **Use One Insert.** Look at all the smart mailers, and you will see that they have been going out with one insert format for years. Why one? Because you want to test the medium and not the message. If you are confident with your message, then each test of the media (the various package-insert programs you go into) will be clear in its results.

5. **Ask Lots of Questions.** Don't be afraid to ask your broker every silly question that you can think of about the source of the program that he or she is presenting to you. Just as you would ask other media salespeople, you should inquire about the source of the customers, number of years in business, other marketers that have used and continued with the program, the time that it takes for your inserts to be distributed, and so on. The more you ask, the better informed you will be. The better informed you are, the more likely you are to be successful.

6. **Be Sure to "Key" by Program.** You'd be surprised how many sophisticated mailers forget to key in such a way that when the distribution takes too long, they can't research how and when their inserts were distributed. For example, if the distribution will take three months, it makes sense to key your inserts in such a way that you can tell when the first month is completed and so forth. The small extra expense with the printer can save you headaches and cut your aspirin bill.

7. **Use the Right Sources.** Just as you should be using a knowledgeable broker, you should have the right printer, direct-mail consultant, and, where necessary, the correct mailing house working for you. Ask for competitive bids from everyone that you use. Your printer, sad to say, may not be right for the insert market even though he or she is an expert with your catalog.

   Your artist should know that inserts must be machine insertable, which means that when the finished product is delivered to the company inserting them, they must be able to place them on their inserting machine and collate your insert with the others going into the package.

> Don't be afraid to ask your broker every silly question that you can think of about the source of the program that he or she is presenting to you.

8. **Ask for Proof of Receipt and Proof of Delivery.** For decks, that means U.S Postage Receipt #3602 plus two sealed samples. These days you can be reasonably assured that the inserts you send to be distributed will be used. Why? Because too many companies are making too much money from the service to mess around. But it always pays to be cautious.

   Your broker should obtain an insert sample upon receipt and upon completion and have it in his or her file. Your printer should have receipt of delivery. Your inserts should be boxed professionally and clearly marked. The insides of some of the warehouses dwarf the imagination, and your insert can get lost.

9. **Pay the Right Price.** Because of the variety of insert programs, you want to pick the best for your offer and then decide on the right ones based on the top price you are willing to pay. After you've received the test results, there's plenty of time to negotiate for price reduction. As with other media, prices change with volume and frequency. After all, the worst your broker can report is "the rate card or nothing." It pays to ask.

10. **Expect Less, Get More.** This is a medium that is still being developed. For all the success stories, the package insert field is just like the other forms of direct response. It is a numbers game. If you watch the cost of printing and the cost of distribution, your response should be sufficient to provide you with a satisfactory cost per inquiry or cost per order.

> If you expect a miracle, this is not the medium. But for steady production of orders at reasonable and competitive costs, this medium is hard to beat.

If you expect a miracle, this is not the medium. But for steady production of orders at reasonable and competitive costs, this medium is hard to beat. And for ease of entry, low visibility, and low cost, what could be better?

## More about Card Decks

Most of what is true of package inserts applies equally to card decks. However, card decks offer even less real estate in which to get across a message. Despite that apparent shortcoming, however, marketers in every category—and business-to-business marketers especially—are finding card decks a cost-effective addition to their marketing arsenal. At an average of 2¢ to 3¢ per contact, they're certainly worth testing.

Indeed, as mentioned earlier, some use card decks exclusively to get leads, then follow up aggressively with additional direct mail and/or telemarketing efforts both to requalify respondents and to convert. In recent years I've worked with two such marketers, a magazine publisher and an electronics manufacturer.

For a quick snapshot of how a card deck media plan might look, following are actual recommendations ("recos" in list speak) for a client selling Network Certification software (prices will have changed by the time you read this).

| NAME OF DECK (CIRC) | 1x | 3x | +2ND COLOR |
|---|---|---|---|
| Computerworld | | | |
| (147,000) | $3744 | $3494 | +$435 |
| Computer Network Professional | | | |
| (100,000) | 3900 | – | +395 |
| Hi-Tech Times | | | |
| (120,000) | 3900 | 3700 | +150 |
| Internet Week | | | |
| (130,000) | 3250 | 2990 | +245 |
| Windows | | | |
| (120,000) | 3900 | 3700 | +150 |
| Windows NT | | | |
| (100,000) | 3200 | 2800 | +250 |

The most effective test of any one deck would consist of a minimum of three insertions, which puts the cost of a test in this category into the $12,000 range. As with space advertising, there is a cumulative effect to being in a card deck with some consistency. Ask your broker who the regular repeaters are in any deck and examine their offers for a fairly reliable indication of what's working in that deck.

Many trade magazine publishers also have card decks that may represent the circulation of one publication or an unduplicated list of

> Some use card decks exclusively to get leads, then follow up aggressively with additional direct mail and/or telemarketing efforts both to requalify respondents and to convert.

subscribers to several titles. And while card decks have long been a creature of business-to-business markets, more consumer-oriented companies are starting to get into decks as well. Leon Henry, VentureDirect, and Millard Group are among the companies offering consumer-related decks.

## The Downside: Quality/Quantity Balance

Somewhat like the so-called "bingo" or reader service cards in magazines, one of the problems with card decks is that it is often too easy to respond to them. Flipping through a deck of cards and pulling out anything that looks interesting at the moment makes this medium a tire-kicker's delight. Some decks even include preprinted labels so the recipient needn't write his or her name on the card, but just affix a label.

As outlined in Chapters 2 and 7, marketers need to be careful of the "Quantity/Quality Ratio." Attractive free offers with quick-and-easy response mechanisms invite abuse by less qualified respondents. It is advisable, therefore, to place a few hurdles in the road that only the more interested—and therefore better qualified—prospect will work to overcome.

These can be as simple as requiring the prospect to affix a stamp to the card, rather than using the more common postage-paid business reply mail. Another is to require a phone number and per-haps include a "best time to call" slot to make it clear that the respondent can expect a phone call. Generally, the more information you request on the card, the higher the level of qualification.

Another strategy, especially if the fulfillment material is costly, is to requalify card deck prospects through a follow-up mailing or even a phone call if the financials permit.

Finally, be sure you know how each list is compiled. Sometimes the list itself can offer substantial qualification—or not, depending. Always ask.

> Flipping through a deck of cards and pulling out anything that looks interesting at the moment makes this medium a tire-kicker's delight.

## More about Co-Ops

The competitive environment in a co-op envelope is significantly more intense than with some other alternatives. Four-color images are virtually mandatory. Graphics should be bold, but limited, with eye-catching logos.

Fine-tune your offer to match the co-op's various markets, testing several if necessary. Offers should be "no-brainers": simple, quick to read, and easy to understand. This is not a place to innovate. Make your piece as large as the envelope will permit.

Pricing for co-ops is usually negotiable, so ask questions.

## Back-End Analysis Is Critical

The primary keys to success with any form of alternative media is to carefully key each insert or card for each list and medium used and analyze the conversion rate based on your criteria for a "qualified" lead. Cost per qualified lead, not response rate, is the critical metric in alternative print media.

> Offers should be "no-brainers": simple, quick to read, and easy to understand. This is not a place to innovate.

## Alternative Print Media Sources:

Not every list broker handles alternative print media, so you'll need to shop around. Following are several sources.

Leon Henry Inc., 914-723-3176 (*www.leonhenryinc.com*)
FSdm (Fred Singer), 914-472-7100
VentureDirect Worldwide, 212-684-4800
Fred E. Allen Inc., 903-572-1701
List Services Corp. 203-743-2600
Millard A/M Group Inc., 603-924-9262

For more information on this topic, visit our Web site at www.businesstown.com

# Telemarketing: Reach Out and Touch Profits!

One of the most important ways to boost response rates is to support your direct mail (or even replace it!) with telemarketing. While it adds to your cost, the often dramatic increases in response—up to 300% and more—make telemarketing well worth testing.

In truth, there are many instances where telephone support is a necessity. Mail order catalogs, of course, couldn't exist today without inbound telesales. Most business-to-business lead-generation programs require telephone identification of the decision maker you need to address with your message. It likely won't be the name on your mail piece. That and other factors in the lead-qualification process mandate telephone support.

Companies that sell products through seminars often find telephone follow-up essential. And usually more than one call is needed. Why? Because it takes a ton of persuasion to get busy people to override their schedules and physically go from point A to point B. Most of us don't have enough control over our daily lives to know what we'll be doing on a given day two weeks from now. Indeed, any time you want people to alter behavior (and have people "do" something other than send for a free trial), you'll need to provide lots of push.

Companies that develop a customer base using direct mail and telephone often find it highly profitable to cross-sell related products, make aftermarket and repeat sales, and more by phone. Telephone sales representatives (TSRs) can develop great rapport with customers, and, when properly trained, compensated, and incentivised, they can be a virtual money machine, as many are for companies in a wide range of categories.

There are two basic types of telemarketing or telesales: inbound and outbound.

> Telephone sales representatives (TSRs) can develop great rapport with customers, and, when properly trained, compensated, and incentivised, they can be a virtual money machine.

## Inbound Telemarketing

If you've ever ordered a product by phone from a catalog, you have a good idea of how inbound telemarketing or telesales works.

The TSR gets a key number from the customer (if possible) that, when entered into the computer, calls up the customer's I.D.

information. In some systems, the ZIP code is enough. The TSR takes the call, enters the credit card number, maybe offers a special deal on some item, verifies the order, and thanks the caller.

Calls coming from 800 numbers in ads, direct mail pieces, and other media may not be so easy to manage. One way or another, the TSR must capture name, source code, address, and credit card data, and, if the product is at all technical or complex, he or she should be prepared to answer questions, or hand off the call to a technical rep. Then add complaints, customer or dealer support, changes of address, billing calls, and more, and you begin to see the problem.

## Feeding the Database

Actually, these seeming problems can be valuable opportunities to collect additional data about your customers and prospects. In Chapter 7 we saw how data flows into the lead-generation/database system. One of the prime sources of that data is your telemarketing program. Telemarketing provides the kind of two-way communication that creates rich personal information rather than flat demographic data, since trained TSRs can direct a conversation well beyond the basic requirements of whatever transaction they're involved in.

While taking an order, changing an address, handling a complaint, or any of a dozen other simple tasks, a TSR can add to customer profiles, determine buying cycles, identify product preferences, research media effectiveness, and much more.

But an amazing amount of infrastructure must be in place for that to happen, from obtaining a toll-free number and long-distance carrier to putting together the right combination of telecommunications hardware and software, personnel, training, and fulfillment.

## In-House or Outsource?

Your first decision will be whether to build your own in-house system or outsource the work to an experienced call center. The following rundown of key points is suggested by Cliff Lattin, Manager of Sales and Marketing for New England 800 Company, Waldoboro, Maine (207-832-0800).

While taking an order, changing an address, handling a complaint, or any of a dozen other simple tasks, a TSR can add to customer profiles, determine buying cycles, identify product preferences, research media effectiveness, and much more.

**Toll-Free Numbers.** For example, there are many alternatives to the 800 number today. Should you have an 800 number, or an 888, 877, 866, or 855 number? You'll want to explore the options. How about a "vanity" number (1-800-Yourname)?

**Long-Distance Provider.** You'll need to meet with the various carriers to determine the deal that's best for you. Some long-distance resellers offer better terms than the carriers. Will you operate 24-hours in-house, or hand-off overnight and weekends to an outside vendor?

> Some long-distance resellers offer better terms than the carriers.

**Phone System.** With Plain Old Telephone Service (or POTS), you purchase however many lines you need and have an operator assigned to each line with calls coming in serially. A single T-1.5 connection allows you to take up to 20 calls simultaneously. Automatic Call Distribution (ACD) distributes the calls, lets the supervisor monitor calls, and provides statistics and reports.

**Interactive Voice Response.** Interactive voice response, or IVR, is the term for those automated systems you encounter at banks, insurance companies, and more and more corporations where you "press one for sales, two for customer service," etc.

Costs for a call on an IVR system can be as low as 25¢ to 40¢ so long as the caller stays in the automated channel. But if he or she gets frustrated or worse, angry, and decides to "opt-out" to a "real person" by punching the "0" for an operator, your costs for that call skyrocket to $4 or more—and you've probably created a dissatisfied customer. (One major financial services company estimates its cost for rep-handled calls at more than $7 each, and it is working to totally automate its system.)

**Computer-Based System.** Issues involved in a computer-driven system include choosing between a Client/Server or Terminal/Host system, the processor speed, memory, storage methods, fault-tolerance and redundancy, and data backup.

For more sophisticated systems, you'll also want to be able to share the data between departments, maintain a relational database to slice and dice the data, and import/export data from other sources. (I mentioned that two weeks before my last birthday I received a birthday card from Radio Shack with a $10 "gift" coupon attached. That kind of database.)

Then there's the problem of staffing and training and keeping TSRs motivated—no easy task, as anyone who has run a call center will tell you. Even if you plan to build and staff your own call center eventually, it might be wise to outsource the process initially, until you've worked out all the kinks and learned the ropes yourself.

## Upselling and Cross-Selling: Primary Points of Contact

The opportunity telemarketing provides for upselling and cross-selling products can often make the added cost and hassle well worth it, if not a prime source of profit. Every inbound caller is a prospect, after all. But be careful. If you think your inbound TSRs can simply add an upsell pitch to their current process and you'll magically reap new profits, you're in for a nasty surprise.

The TSR, inbound or outbound, is a key point of contact with your customer, and a major player in your company's customer relationship management (CRM) process. He or she must be knowledgeable about the benefits and technical aspects of any products they will be selling. TSRs must have a pleasant voice and manner. They are the "personality" of your company—in some cases, the only identity for your company some customers will ever have. When you're dealing with high-end products and business-to-business lead qualification, TSR requirements are significantly more demanding. Ask yourself: What kind of personality should that be? And, not incidentally, how much should such a person be paid? Possibly more than you originally had in mind.

One major difficulty in this scenario is that inbound TSRs just don't consider upselling as part of their job. Oh, they'll go through the motions if you tell them to. But in most cases, you'll find their hearts and minds aren't in it. In a 1998 survey, 36% of phone-intensive catalogers queried by the Direct Marketing

> One major difficulty in this scenario is that inbound TSRs just don't consider upselling as part of their job.

Association used telemarketing to upsell—but it was *outbound* telemarketing, not inbound. Some 50% of respondents also used outbound TSRs to reactivate dormant accounts. Good idea, especially when you consider it costs five times more to get a customer than to keep one. For sales, customer reactivation, and much more, clearly the action is on the outbound side.

> It costs five times more to get a customer than to keep one.

## Outbound Telemarketing

The infrastructure for outbound telemarketing is about the same as for inbound—which may account for the tendency to assume that if you can manage the inbound calls, you can add the outbound fairly easily. Wrong.

Aside from the equipment, there's also the people, the purpose, and the psychology of outbound, not to mention the supervision and measurement of results, all of which are also quite different from inbound.

First, let's look at some of the applications of outbound telemarketing:

- Upselling current customers and reactivating dormant customers, as mentioned above
- Rapid sell-off of excess inventory
- Expand markets to other targets:
  - Geographic areas not efficiently covered by sales force
  - Consumer to commercial
  - Sell to affinity groups
  - Introduce new product line
- Thank-you calls for new orders
- Lead generation and qualification (business-to-business)
- Add demographics, buying cycles, etc., to the database
- Invitation to Web site and/or seminars
- Research
  What do your customers think of your products?
  (Get testimonials!)
  What kinds of products and services does the market want?
  What changes are taking place in your markets?

## Six Pitfalls to Avoid

Small business owners are especially vulnerable to error in applying various marketing technologies, partly because they often find it difficult in niche markets to establish the economies of scale that make many types of marketing pay off for larger marketers.

Another reason is that, as entrepreneurs, they are accustomed to "bootstrapping" their businesses: starting out on a shoestring and growing it into a successful business model. But there are areas of marketing, notably direct mail and telemarketing, where certain thresholds of quality and effort must be achieved, both for credibility and for results.

In most cases a "half-measure" doesn't produce a half-result; it produces zero, at least in the long run, even if there might be a short-term blip on the marketing screen. Put another way, don't send a postcard to do a personalized package's job, and don't expect a spit-and-bailing-wire telemarketing operation to grow your business. It isn't going to happen.

To help make the point, I called on Linda J. Neff, president of Marketing Connections Corporation, a national award-winning call center located in Bedford, New Hampshire, to bring her 20-plus years of experience to the table and help us understand some of the pitfalls that await the unwary marketer in the jungles of telemarketing. She identified six such "pitfalls," cleverly disguised as quick and low-cost strategies. However, a closer look will help you avoid these costly mistakes and show you how to put the pieces in place for a successful telemarketing program.

> In most cases a "half-measure" doesn't produce a half-result; it produces zero.

### Pitfall #1: Assigning current staff to telemarketing tasks.

Too many companies, says Linda, still consider telemarketing a clerical-level job that can be performed by almost anyone. Staff people who have shown to be capable at a variety of company tasks are often shoved into the breach and told to start selling. These are usually people with little or no sales skills, and almost no training.

However, as we pointed out earlier, the telephone is a primary point of contact with your customer. And in this era of "one-to-one" marketing, every customer contact is critical. Whatever the TSR says, and how he or she says it, will determine the "personality" of your company, at least so far as the customers you call are concerned. This is your company image and it's not something you want to play with.

Telemarketing requires carefully developed skills that combine:

- Confident tone and competent projection.
- Mature verbal and grammatical skills, uncluttered with slang.
- Effective questioning and listening skills to uncover customer needs and interests.
- Professional sales techniques, as well as the demonstrated ability to deliver an effective sales message.
- Persistence that overcomes customers' objections and convinces them of the value of your offer.
- The ability to rebound from rejection and remain enthusiastic throughout each and every call.

> Telemarketing requires the same degree of strategizing and planning that all other marketing channels do.

## Pitfall #2: Making a few calls, "just to get started."

"Fail to plan and you plan to fail," the old sales saying goes, and nowhere is it more true than in putting together an in-house telemarketing operation. Telemarketing, Linda points out, requires the same degree of strategizing and planning that all other marketing channels do—maybe more so, because on the phone, you're in direct contact with your customer . . . the "front line," so to speak. Not the place you want to mess up.

For example, have you determined your call objectives? Have you determined how you'll measure success? Do you have an effective calling message? Or, just as the right lists are the most important single element of a direct mail campaign, have you identified the right people to call in your target markets? Equally important, how can you forecast the impact of your telemarketing results on other departments in the company?

If your telemarketing is intended to generate leads, for example, will your salespeople have the time they need to follow up on them? Indeed, have you involved your salespeople in the planning process so you know what kinds of information they want? (You'll also want to get your sales force to "buy in" to the process, or all that telemarketing activity could go right down the drain. Salespeople seldom trust marketers to begin with, since they interpret most marketing programs as wastes of time solely designed to burden them with meaningless work and lousy leads.)

If your telesales effort produces a spike in sales (I know, you should have such a problem), are your manufacturing and fulfillment operations up to the task of delivering additional products quickly?

In developing your strategy, you'll want to review each of the channels you're using to reach your market. Identify the role each is playing in your total sales process and measure the cost of each channel relative to the ROI for that part of the sales cycle. Then determine how and where telemarketing can best be employed.

Check the messages being sent by each channel to your prospect and customer bases and be sure they add up to an integrated sales presentation. Ad copy, direct mail benefits/offers, and telemarketing scripts should all convey the same tone and image.

By now you should recognize that a few telemarketing calls won't prove or project your ultimate results. For any new program there's a learning curve on the part of telemarketers; before you can accurately predict bottom-line results, they must be allowed adequate time to gain confidence in—and experience with—your telemarketing message. Also, every script and sales approach needs fine-tuning; you must allow time for weak areas to surface, and for new approaches to be tried and measured.

Finally, you'll need to make calls into enough of your target market to confidently declare that all potential idiosyncrasies of geography, competitive saturation, product acceptability, and list quality have been identified and corrective actions taken.

## Pitfall #3: Assigning the telemarketing program to your sales manager or some other manager because he/she "has the time."

"A sure road to disaster," warns Linda Neff, "is to put the management of a telemarketing program into the hands of someone who doesn't understand the unique qualities and challenges of this key medium."

> **Use Personal Experience**
>
> You've no doubt received poorly handled calls yourself and wondered what the company was thinking of to put such a person on the telephone. Think that experience through and apply it to your own company.

> Telemarketing managers must be motivators, cheerleaders, inspirational trainers, and skilled evaluators.

Telemarketing is an anomaly; it's both a sales/marketing and production function. Companies essentially utilize telemarketing in two ways: to get more work (sales, research, etc.) done in a given time frame than can be accomplished in other, more traditional ways; and to make salespeople more productive and cost effective through delivery of qualified leads. A telemarketing manager has the dual challenge of managing a tightly controlled production environment while also managing a highly creative sales and marketing function. These opposing functions can be at war with each other in the workplace.

The required people skills alone can be daunting. Telemarketing managers must be motivators, cheerleaders, inspirational trainers, and skilled evaluators. They must have control over the performance of their staff and must carefully measure and report results in a way that justifies the program's expense. What's more, they must be available to monitor calls and provide feedback to improve performance. With the typical TSR workload, a significant amount of misinformation can be transmitted if the manager fails to notice the error in real time and correct it. In addition, managers need to appreciate the repetitive nature of the work and continually find ways to refresh their staffs.

Clearly, all these factors virtually mandate a trained, experienced, and dedicated telemarketing manager.

## Pitfall #4: Allowing salespeople to generate their own leads.

As alluded to earlier, salespeople and marketing types don't always see eye-to-eye. So asking your salespeople to take on what is essentially a marketing task—cold calling—may be problematic. Attitudes aside, the fact is, salespeople don't like to cold-call under any circumstances. As a result, they don't do it well. And when they do make calls, they invariably spring out of the office at the first opportunity, and they're gone when some of those calls are returned. Bottom line is, it doesn't work. And shouldn't your salespeople be out making sales calls in the first place? Selling is what they do best, so let them.

With trained TSRs to make the calls, qualify the prospects, and hand them off to your sales force, you have the best of both worlds working for you. Your telemarketers are maintaining regular contact with customers and prospects so when the salespeople do call, they're not quite so foreign.

## Pitfall #5: Expecting low-cost results.

In the matter of costs, telemarketing can be less costly than a $200 sales call, no question. But it can also be more costly than a $1 catalog. Perhaps the best way to determine costs is to forget costs entirely and focus on *value*. If an experienced TSR can coax another $75 out of a catalog buyer . . . convince a commercial customer he really needs a training package with that software program he just bought . . . come up with a reason why your latest, greatest product isn't setting new sales records . . . what would it be worth to you?

There are significant up-front costs involved, whether you do it yourself or outsource the work. But it should be clear from the above that tapping a staffer on the shoulder and seating him or her in front of a phone isn't going to cut it. Yet, that's just what a lot of small business owners do.

We've talked in the beginning of this book about the dangers of trying to do direct mail on the cheap. That you must reach a certain threshold of credibility, or you'll end up wasting whatever you do spend on your program. Same is true for telemarketing, only more so, because through the telephone, you're in direct contact with your customers and prospects. Even a short-term test program—which you should certainly consider before you go big time—has to meet credibility and quality criteria, or it will fail. Like so many small business owners, you'll find yourself saying, "we tried telemarketing; it didn't work," when what you really tried was tele*phoning*.

If you're going to try it, give it your best shot. And to help you identify the necessary steps, use the following checklist, courtesy of Linda and Glenn Neff of Marketing Connections Corporation.

### What's the Cost per Sale?

For a business-to-business lead generation program designed to sell an enterprise resource planning (ERP) application into IBM AS/400 computer locations, initial test costs were estimated at $10,000 for 500 outbound calls with fulfillment of information and management reports. That's $20 per contact, but in this case it represented less than .001 of gross margin per sale.

# A Telemarketing Checklist

## I. Planning Your Strategy

- Develop telemarketing business plan
  - Define prime function (i.e., lead generation, sales, customer service, research, etc.)
- Set program objectives
  - Use specifics: X% increase in sales volume, Y% fewer sales calls
- Develop budget
  - Manager and staff
  - Training
  - Telemarketing consulting services
  - Telecommunications equipment
  - Tracking software
  - Fulfillment items/supplies
  - Space/furnishings
  - Increased demand for product/service
- Establish criteria to evaluate ROI
- Define pilot program parameters
- Define management information requirements
- Determine how the program relates to your marketing and sales channels
- Identify the value of the telemarketing program to other departments:
  - Product development
  - Advertising/Public Relations
  - Order Processing
  - Manufacturing
  - Long-range planning
- Determine implementation strategy
  - Inbound, outbound, or both
  - Implement in-house or outsource

## II. Implementing Your Plan

- Define operational plan and procedures
- Create job descriptions

- Develop compensation plans
- Recruit, interview, and hire staff
- Select site
  - Design work environment
  - Select furnishings/workstations
- Develop specifications for telecommunications
  - Equipment
  - Service
- Develop specifications for management information systems (manual or automated)
  - Resources to support calls
  - Measurement and tracking requirements
- Evaluate and select vendors
- Train managers and staff
- Create an effective calling message
- Develop motivation and incentive programs
- Design performance analysis reports

## III. Evaluating Your Plan

Dynamic marketing programs require constant assessment. Here are some of the issues you'll need to address:

- Is the primary objective still clear?
- Are program results meeting my ROI?
- Can I get more for my investment?
- Is the advertising/direct mail generating all of the calls it can?
  - Is the offer clear and inviting?
  - Is the 800 number properly displayed?
  - Is the targeted market responding?
- Am I getting maximum performance from my people?
- What training will improve performance?
- Are my compensation and incentive programs continuing to motivate my personnel?
- Am I using optimum telecommunications systems?
- Is it time to automate?
  - What functions do I require in an automated system?

–How do I evaluate and select the right software
and hardware?
* How do I get an objective evaluation of my current operations and future plans?
* What additional applications for telemarketing exist in my company?

## IV. Expansion Potential

Consider these other telephone base applications for your company:

* Setting appointments
* Complaint handling
* Order taking
* Full account management
* Selling service contracts
* Collecting accounts receivable
* Special promotions
* Fund raising
* Consumer response
* New product announcements
* Stockholder relations
* Reservations
* Tele-recruiting/personnel screening
* Renewal service
* Marginal account development
* Market research
* Technical support

©1999, 2000 Marketing Connections Corporation, used with permission.

### Case Study

Seattle-based Uniglobe.com services about 1 million travel customers each month. Their previous benchmark for responding to telephone inquiries was 24 hours, which they discovered was too long in today's world of airfare wars and fast-changing travel plans. Callers, most of whom had just one phone line, still prefer to speak directly with an agent but had to wait until they were finished browsing the site to make the call. Uniglobe added a text "chat" capability to the Web site which allows customers and prospects to provide quick details online. For inquiries on a cruise trip, for example, the comment box invites users to provide date and length of the cruise they are interested in, destination and cruise line, names and number of people traveling, city of origin (for possible air connections), plus contact information including e-mail address. With the help of Lucent Technologies' Centre Vu Internet Solutions, incoming inquiries are routed automatically through the company database to the agent with the most knowledge of that option. Thus callers are able to interact by phone and text simultaneously, even if they have only one phone line (*www.uniglobe.com*).

### Convergence in the Call Center

Today more and more call centers are integrating inbound calls with their company's Web site in order to better serve online customers. The technology allows a customer to view products on the Web and simultaneously discuss/order them through a phone connection with a TSR.

## A Sample Cold-Calling Script

To give you an idea of how a cold calling script might be structured, I developed the following script for a client who runs a computer network engineering training school.

The ultimate purpose of this project was to determine the accuracy of a list the client had access to. Lists of qualified prospects in this sector are rare, and if the list proved out, it would be most valuable. You can see that, although it's a script, the TSR needs to be flexible and prepared to depart from the script whenever an answer (or an unexpected question) doesn't fit.

### (Cold-Calling Script, PC Age)

Hello, this is _____(name)_____ calling from PC Age vocational training school. Is this Mr./Ms. _____(name)_____?

[ if "no"]: Can you tell me when would be a good time to call back? Thank you very much.

[if "yes"]: Mr./Ms. _____(name)_____, have you heard about the serious shortage of qualified workers in the computer networking field?

[if "no"]: There are currently more than 350,000 jobs open in computer networking.

[if "yes"]: PC Age is looking for people who might be interested in becoming certified network engineers. Certified network engineers can usually earn a starting salary anywhere from $31,000 to as high as $55,000 depending on experience. Would a career like that interest you?

[if "no"]: Well, thank you very much for your time; I'm sorry if I interrupted your evening. (hang up)

[if "yes"]: Would you be able to attend classes for either six months full-time or nine months part-time evenings or weekends?

[if "no"]: Well, thank you very much for your time; I'm sorry if I interrupted your evening. (hang up)

[if "yes"]: [For high qualification]: Would you be prepared to invest $9,000 in a network engineering career where you could earn as much as $70,000 in five years?

[if "no"]: Well, thank you very much for your time; I'm sorry if I interrupted your evening. (hang up)

[if "yes"]: May I make an appointment for an interview at PC Age, where we can give you all the details? There's no obligation, of course.

[if "yes," make the appointment]

[if "no" or some other decline statement]:

May I send you our Free Computer Career Kit with details about network engineering and certification training at PC Age?

> The TSR needs to be flexible and prepared to depart from the script whenever an answer (or an unexpected question) doesn't fit.

[if "no"]: Well, thank you very much for your time; I'm sorry if I interrupted your evening. (hang up)

[if "yes"]: That's great! Let me just verify your name and address: (Read name and address or ask prospect his/her name and address, verify and close.) Thank you very much for your time—you should receive your kit within 48 (24?) hours.

Other possible questions and suggested answers:

**Q:** I don't have any computer experience. How can I qualify for network engineer?

**A:** Right now PC Age is training more than 400 students with little or no previous computer experience to become certified network engineers. The PC Age course assumes no prior computer experience.

(If you eliminate the tuition statement and want to increase inquiries with lower qualification.)

**Q:** How much does it cost?

**A:** I can't discuss tuition on the phone—but all the details are in our Free Computer Career Kit that I'd like to send you without obligation of any kind. May I verify your name and address?

**Q:** Do you guarantee a job?

**A:** Based on a 1998 survey, 94% of PC Age graduates passed their certification tests the first time—and we place almost all of our certified graduates in good jobs.

**Q:** Are you anything like Chubb?

**A:** PC Age is a state-approved, vocational training school, much like Chubb, except our network engineering course is all-inclusive. We start you with A+, go from there to CNA, and then on to MCSE certification, all for a single tuition.

For more information on this topic, visit our Web site at www.businesstown.com

# Chapter 13

# Catalogs

A s a business category, catalogs started by entrepreneurial
individuals and families are extremely idiosyncratic in terms
of how they get born and how their owners grow them in
response to customers, market forces, and especially their own interests and strengths.

Often enough there seems to be some element of chance that
helps to shape their success. While some may ascribe the following
successful case study to "being in the right place at the right time,"
it may be more accurate to see Spencer Newman's success as *placing
himself* in the right place at the right time. Luck? Some, but luck
that he helped to make.

> Catalogs are extremely
> idiosyncratic in terms of
> how they get born and how
> their owners grow them.

## A "Clicks and Mortar" Start-Up: How the Adventurous Traveler Bookstore Became AdventurousTraveler.com

Following graduation from Tufts University in 1990, Spencer
Newman took a job at an outdoors accessories wholesaler in
Burlington, Vermont, where he had moved in order to avail himself
of the area's abundant skiing and hiking trails. Part of Spencer's job
at Peregrine Outfitters was to purchase travel books from publishers
and resell them to bookstores around the country. He soon noticed
that while there was a ton of adventure-travel books out there, there
were not enough outdoor enthusiasts in any given geographical area
to power a retail operation in that particular niche.

Driven at least in part by his own interests in the outdoors, in
1994 Spencer decided to whip up a catalog of these highly specialized books. With Peregrine as a prime supplier, he set up "The
Adventurous Traveler Bookstore" (ATB) in a spare bedroom of his
home, selected about 300 items from various publishers, and
launched his first catalog. His only competitors at that time were a
few small mail-order catalogs specializing in outdoor travel and small
book and map sections in outdoor equipment stores.

Newman's original product mix consisted of guidebooks and maps for adventure travel, hiking, biking, paddlesports, and skiing. The selection has since evolved to include climbing, sailing, family travel, outdoor how-to books, extreme sport narratives, and outdoor-related CD-ROMs, prints, and posters.

The first catalog was mailed to 5,000 prospects. It grossed $45,000 in sales and acquired 6,000 customers in the first year.

## A Call from Cyberspace

The following year, Newman got a call from someone starting a Web site called Outdoor Adventure Online, which was slated to be carried by Internet giant AOL. Would Newman be interested in putting his catalog online? Spencer thought: Why not? Sales were slow, he was still in his bedroom, etc. So he gave Outdoor Adventure Online descriptions of 500 books.

Before long, Newman began receiving a few orders a day from Web site visitors. And while they didn't exactly get him out of the bedroom, they started him pondering the possibilities of the Internet.

## A Step-Up to GORP

Later that year, Spencer got another call, this time from Diane and Bill Greer, also outdoor enthusiasts, who had moved from Wall Street to start an Internet business called Great Outdoor Recreation Pages, or GORP. (Not coincidentally, "gorp" is also the name for a mix of nuts and raisins used by hikers and climbers for quick energy.)

GORP was a significant step up for Newman from Outdoor Adventure. The Greers had invested in an interactive shopping cart, among other things. They also offered him his own Web site with content linked to theirs in return for a commission on his sales. He named the site AdventurousTraveler.com, and sales jumped to 20 to 30 per day. In 1997, sales topped $1.4 million—a 44% increase over the previous year.

By 1998, Amazon.com had reared its megabuck head on the Internet, and ATB's growth curve began to slow. Newman was convinced buyers were shopping his site, then going to Amazon.com to buy the books for less.

> Before long, Newman began receiving a few orders a day from Web site visitors. And while they didn't exactly get him out of the bedroom, they started him pondering the possibilities of the Internet.

## Spencer vs. Goliath

As Amazon grew, digging further into ATB's adventure-based territory, Newman decided that his niche was, in fact, his strength. Maybe Amazon could sell books for less, but they couldn't provide the rich content ATB could offer. They couldn't connect customers with other enthusiasts who had actually been to the places the books described, or to people who had read the books. ATB's customer-service people often spent hours helping clients with their travel plans and problems.

GORP at this point was getting 900,000 hits a month, and counting. Clearly, a growing market Newman wanted to stay connected to. So he decided to push his advantage further—to provide GORP and their adventurous travelers with more and even better content.

> Maybe Amazon could sell books for less, but they couldn't provide the rich content ATB could offer.

## Three Keys to Success: Content, Content, and Content

Spencer began publishing a twice-monthly online newsletter. He expanded his book offerings to include maps, guidebooks, CD-ROMs, videos, gift items, photographs, and posters. He added online reviews by staff members, authors, and knowledgeable readers. He also conducted extensive research into titles from smaller, obscure, and foreign publishers and added powerful search capabilities to the Web site. Customers could search by location and by type of activity, creating a rich shopping experience.

Indeed, Newman received the ultimate compliment from Chris MacAskill, CEO of FatBrain.com:

> "You guys provided the original inspiration for us [FatBrain]. Back when Amazon was the most ferocious competitor I had ever seen, I looked at your site and decided there was hope. When I planned a trip to Kilimanjaro, I ordered from you because I wanted maps to go with the books and Amazon didn't have them. I loved the subject classification by type of activity, by geography, and by national park. I also loved the staff recommendations."

As this is written, AdventurousTraveler.com is planning an ambitious series of detailed Digital Guides to many of the adventure-oriented destinations around the world. It will also have a searchable, customized outdoor recreation database, all integrated with the Web site.

## An Affiliate Network

Newman also sought out related Web sites and offered to link them to ATB. That worked fine until Goliath did the same and began offering commissions on sales resulting from the links as well.

At first, Newman lost many of his affiliates to Amazon, but then he took his affiliate program to the next level with software that would help him track sales from affiliate sites so he could offer commissions, too. As a result, many returned to the ATB fold.

Today, AdventurousTraveler.com's affiliate network numbers 140 specialty sites, including northeastguidebooks.com, K2news.com, and "Joe's Hiking page." Some of the earlier affiliates, like GORP.com, GreenTravel.com, PlanetOutdoors.com, and others, have become strategic partners.

While ATB clearly took a hit from Amazon.com, the company continued to grow at a healthy 15% a year. In a further effort to diversify, Newman opened a bricks-and-mortar store in downtown Burlington. He began sponsoring lectures at the store by authors and other outdoors experts, some arranged through the nearby University of Vermont, and announced them on the Web site. The store, Newman feels, gives a more solid, community-based identity to both the print catalog and the virtual store on the Web.

While the Web site represents roughly half of Newman's sales today, the print catalog (Figure 13-1), with a circulation of 1.1 million copies, still represents the other half. The company mailed 950,000 catalogs in 1998, and 878,000 in 1999.

It's notable that the percentage of outside lists in the total mix went from as high as 60% in 1998 down to just 20% in 1999 as more and more names came from the Web site. "We did a lot of list testing

Figure 13-1

in the past," says ATB marketing director Pete Wagner. "But we aren't doing as much now, as we seek more prospects via our Web site and advertisements."

It's also notable that the catalog's two biggest sellers in 1998 were nonbook items: a National Parks Monopoly game and a Mount Everest poster signed by mountaineer-filmmaker David Breashears.

From Spencer Newman's bedroom, the business has grown to a 22-person company with projected sales for 1999 of $2.3 million. Marketing is heavily database driven. The Web site runs on SQL Database and SiteServer E-commerce. Order entry for both the Web site and phone orders is on a custom Foxpro Database. Foxpro also stores product information and outputs it into PageMaker for catalog production and printing. Newman is projecting there will be more than 1 million customers in the database by 2004.

## The Takeaways

AdventurousTraveler.com's marketing plan includes strong customer service and one-to-one strategies, including:

- Initiating conversation
- Asking customers what they would like
- Continuing conversation at each interaction
- Remembering customer preferences
- Using transaction information
- Individually targeted offers
- Personalization software

> Note that none of these strategies is exclusive to the Internet. They can all be employed in a direct mail/telemarketing environment.

Note that none of these strategies is exclusive to the Internet. They can all be employed in a direct mail/telemarketing environment. Other marketing methods employed by Newman include brand building, use of affiliates, aggressive PR and traditional advertising, banner ads and sponsorships, and, underlying it all, creation of a rich shopping experience.

To build traffic on his Web site, Newman initially relied on basic strategies, many of which are outlined in Chapter 15: an e-mail newsletter, unique content, an affiliate program paying prompt commissions, and most of all, a passion for the work that pushes him the extra mile he must travel for his customers.

Perhaps the biggest takeaway from the story of Spencer Newman's success is that one needn't be knocked out of the box by a bigger competitor, no matter how much money they have. Working the niche and providing superior service can often outflank the Amazon.coms of the world.

From Spencer Newman's start-up to Carole Ziter's long-established Sweet Energy catalog, many of the lessons remain the same: close personal attention to customers, careful testing, and documentation of results. A strong entrepreneurial bent, at least in the beginning, doesn't hurt, either.

## Sweet Marketing: How to Grow A Catalog

Call Carole Ziter a cataloger, and she'll quickly set you straight. She's a direct marketer, not a cataloger. So please keep that in mind as we follow her journey from mom of three to entrepreneur to direct marketer to highly successful c——r.

It was the blizzard of '78. Carole and her husband Tom were at a trade show in Harrisburg, Pennsylvania, for Garden Way, manufacturer and marketer of Rototillers and other large garden and home equipment. The booth next to them was selling dried fruit—banana chips, pineapple slices, peaches, pears, and big, sweet, gorgeous apricots. By the time the show was over, Tom was sick to his stomach and Carole was hooked.

Back at Garden Way, entrepreneurial Carole suggested that perhaps dried fruit would work well in their catalog as an extension to the food dehydrator the company was already selling. They said they'd give it a shot. Next thing Carole knows, she's in her spare bedroom (about the same size as Spencer Newman's spare bedroom), weighing out dried fruit. Garden Way set her up with suppliers and gave her a credit line, and she was in business. As a mother of three, she even had her own baby scale. The products themselves are imaginatively merchandised and artfully packaged groupings of dried fruits, including the very finest Turkish apricots, prunes, raisins, and figs.

> The lessons remain the same: close personal attention to customers, careful testing, and documentation of results.

The following year, Carole decided to see what she could do on her own. With a mailing list of 995 names collected on sign-up sheets at trade shows, she mailed a one-page sales flyer with a coupon selling apricots, and Sweet Energy was born. Total cost: $259. Gross sales: $561. Allowing for a 50% cost of goods, she broke even—if you don't count her labor and overhead.

In the spring of 1979, Carole placed her first 2" ad in *Yankee* magazine. It cost $456. Three months later, she had grossed $1,900, showing a slight profit. (She didn't learn until later that the ad was a fluke. It would be years before she would achieve that kind of return again.) Sweet Energy ended 1979 with gross sales of $30,000 and a customer base of 2,500.

### Test, Test, Test

With some help from her marketing consultant husband Tom, and with Garden Way's direct marketing machine as a model, Carole launched a testing program featuring eight sales flyers mailed to a 7,000-name customer file by the end of 1982. She tested a variety of offers in space ads in 12 to 15 publications. She also tested numerous outside lists. By now the business had expanded to five part-time employees and had moved to a basement laundry room with an adjacent garage. In 1981 the company acquired its first computer, a Commodore. Gross sales were doubling each year, to $206,000 in 1982.

Thanks to extensive testing, Carole's ads and direct mail were firing on all cylinders. By 1984, she rented a 2300SF warehouse and employed 28 people part time. That year also saw Sweet Energy's first four-color, 24-page catalog. The catalog had evolved from the original one-page flyer, to a four-page newsletter, to a 12-page newsletter, to a two-color booklet. Coming five years into the company's history, the catalog marked an important milestone, both for Christmas sales and for added credibility in the gift markets. Gross sales topped $912,000 that year with a customer base of 35,000.

> Thanks to extensive testing, Carole's ads and direct mail were firing on all cylinders.

## Sweets Turn Sour

In 1985, Sweet Energy hit the wall. Like many fast-growing businesses, the company reached the point where sales were outrunning their capacity to handle them. Following a very successful Christmas season in 1985 (half of all Sweet Energy's annual sales come in the ten weeks prior to Christmas), a prospecting mailing in January '86 broke a record for 661 orders in a single day. Sweet Energy was out of room and out of computer capacity. This time, Carole built her own 5,000SF facility and equipped it with a new, $30,000 computer system.

Suddenly, on top of all that, ad results were off. Direct mail response tanked. Christmas orders were late, the credit line was over-extended, payables loomed large. Carole's response—and this is why she insists she's a direct marketer, not a cataloger—was to go back to basics. Back to the fundamentals of direct marketing. Advertising was cut back. Lists were carefully segmented and mailings limited to only the very best customers. By the end of the year, the ship had righted itself. Payables were under control, the credit line was paid off, and Sweet Energy entered 1987 with little or no debt.

> Like many fast-growing businesses, the company reached the point where sales were outrunning their capacity to handle them.

## A Mature and Thriving Business

"After 21 years of growing pains, battles won and lost, and countless lessons learned, Sweet Energy is finally enjoying a mature lifestyle," says Carole Ziter. Although they burst at the seams each holiday season, Carole has drawn the line on further expansions. She controls her marketing activities to bring in just what she can handle, and to show a reasonable profit. Growth is no longer a priority. From her $259 outlay in 1978, Sweet Energy today grosses close to $2 million a year and 100,000 loyal customers.

## The Real Product: Carole Ziter

We mentioned the product description above: "Imaginatively merchandised and artfully packaged groupings of dried fruits, including the very finest Turkish apricots, prunes, raisins, and figs." But that's just the beginning of the story. In the long run, Sweet Energy's real product is Carole's own sweet energy, communicated through her merchandising decisions and her numerous personalized contacts with her customers throughout the year.

Just as Spencer Newman's own passion for outdoor adventure drives his demand for excellence in the products and service he delivers to his customers, so does Carole Ziter's personal warmth and natural friendliness shine through the gift packages she delivers to her special niche customers, whom she describes as "female apricot lovers over 50 who are mail order buyers." Put another way, older women who recognize and appreciate someone who takes the time and trouble to show they care.

"The secret to success in this business—as in most others," says Carole, "is getting your customer to buy again and again. When we spend 15% to 20% of our sales getting a customer in the door, we can't afford to let her leave after just one purchase. So we talk to her—more than 15 times a year—each time giving her a reason to buy our products."

To accomplish this, Carole sends each customer eight issues of the *Sweet Energy Gazette* (Figure 13-2) throughout the year, plus two 48-page, four-color holiday gift catalogs before Christmas (Figure 13-2). She sends a dividend check every January to thank the customer for her purchases the year before, and she sends her a greeting card with a gift certificate on her birthday. When the customer orders, she talks to her again, in the personalized letter she includes with every order. What does Carole say in these letters? Like any family, she tells the customer about family adventures—a family trip, the kids' graduation, a new pet ferret. And at the bottom of the letter is a coupon with a discount toward the next purchase. So what's the product? It's Carole. And Carole's kids. And Tom, her husband, and the warmth of the life they live together. It's family.

**Figure 13-2**

## Data Analysis Doesn't Cost, It Pays

Does she do all this just because it's nice to do? Forget that. Sweet Energy diligently tracks the results of every mailing they send out, runs P&L's on every newsletter and catalog, and perform square inch analysis* of every product on every page. If a product doesn't pull its weight, it's gone. Response rates range anywhere from 6% for an off-season sale to 25% for the Apricot Sale, which carries the dividend check. Of course, they don't mail to all 100,000 customers 15 times a year. Mailings are carefully planned, and lists are painstakingly segmented for each offering based on RFM** data in the database.

If you assume all these mailings and all this constant contact with the customer builds loyalty, you're right, as Carole herself learned in a pleasant surprise. For her 50th birthday, her husband Tom sneaked a note into 10,000 mailings without Carole's knowledge. He tipped customers to Carole's upcoming "big 5-0" and asked them to send her a card. A few months later, Carole received 2,000 birthday cards, all individually selected, written, and mailed by her Sweet Energy "family." That's what's known as a customer relationship.

Stories about catalogs like Adventurous Traveler and Sweet Energy can give you a feel for the challenge you face in starting a catalog, and point you in helpful directions. But the simple fact is, your catalog experience will be shaped by many factors, most of them unpredictable: the dynamics of your market, the availability of your customer and of lists, the creative requirements of the merchandise and methods of presentation, your buyer's views, your own merchandising skills, and much more.

As you can see, there are numerous factors to consider in starting a catalog from scratch. It's very costly, which is why most catalogs grow more or less naturally out of personal experiences like Spencer's and Carole's. Full-fledged launches are usually only undertaken by

**Figure 13-3**

---

* Square inch analysis is just what it sounds like. Total catalog costs are divided by the number of pages and each page assigned its share of the total. The page is then divided into one-square-inch boxes and the revenue from each square inch is calculated to determine its contribution to the total. Pages can be then redesigned, and the merchandising revised to maximize profits per square inch.

**Recency, Frequency, and Monetary.

## Words vs. Pictures

I wrote the inaugural catalogs for Boston Proper, an upscale clothing and accessories book for "the working woman." For the first few editions, I wrote long copy blurbs, romancing each item with a clever lead-in headline followed by five to eight lines of text, which is a lot for a catalog blurb (especially at 2 a.m.!). The book survived the first few editions when a new art director came in who didn't believe in long copy blurbs, but rather felt (surprise!) that the photo did the selling. Copy was cut to the bone and I moved on. That's what I meant by "idiosyncratic" earlier. This buyer believes in one approach, that one another, and the art director a third.

companies that already publish one or more catalogs and have the resources to bring to the effort, and have identified a likely market, often a spinoff of one of their existing books.

As far as "creative" is concerned, there are as many copy and design approaches as there are catalogs, and only testing will ultimately reveal which approach is best. Sometimes the creative approach is a function of the owner, the buyer, the art director, or whomever.

More appropriately, the creative approach is dictated by the product category and the information needs of the buyer.

The Direct Marketing Association conducts extensive catalog seminars around the country for would-be start-ups, and in my opinion, anyone planning a catalog is nuts not to attend them. Check the DMA Web site at *www.the-dma.org*.

## Checklists for Better Catalogs

For the specific "how-to's" to help you get your catalog out of the spare bedroom, the following checklists will guide you through some of the practical steps you need to consider along the way.

### Checklist #1: The front cover

The cover of your catalog needs to persuade your customer to pick up the catalog excited about (or at least interested in) its contents. It needs to create desire and motivate the customer to read more. Above all, it needs to attract attention from the right customers—the ones who will buy your products.

- Establish theme.
- Determine approach.
- Select merchandise.
- Select special message.
- Design cover.

Always:

1. Put company name on cover.
2. Show continuity of theme.
3. Indicate seasonality.
4. Motivate the customer, both visually and verbally, to look inside.

Strongly Consider:

1. Charge card availability.
2. Toll-free number.
3. Credibility factors, such as company longevity, customer testimonials, or guarantees.
4. Ordering incentives, such as sales, free gift, discount, or sweepstakes.

## Checklist #2: The back cover

Products both pictured and referenced from the back cover will enjoy more sales than those simply referenced. Specific categories whose inside page numbers are referenced will also sell better.

- Determine method of front cover theme carryover, if used.
- Select direct-sale merchandise.
- Select referral-sale merchandise.
- Determine size of address panel.
- Determine address correction message.
- Design back cover.

Always:

1. Put company name and address on back cover.
2. Put toll-free or regular telephone number.
3. Show charge card acceptance visually.
4. Refer customer inside the catalog in some way.

### Tell the Story

In writing a catalog of training films for CRM Films, the copy had to project the learning benefits each film or video brought to the viewer. Each blurb had to provide enough of the content for the training director to feel comfortable with the topic and general presentation and to be sure certain key points were covered. The solution was again a somewhat lengthy blurb, supplemented with three to five quick-reading bullet points.

Strongly Consider:

1. Credibility factors, such as company longevity, customer testimonials, or guarantees.
2. Special-offer announcements: sale, free gift, contests.
3. Mini-index.
4. Retail store location.
5. Phone specials.
6. Guarantee statement.
7. Customer testimonials.

## Checklist #3: The inside pages

Once your "doorway" has lured in customers, the hard work begins. The customer's interest must be carried over eagerly from the cover and held on every page throughout the catalog. Each product must call for attention independently, without overpowering other products. The catalog designer must exercise great skill in creating eye-flow while calling attention to special offers and product benefits—and never losing sight of the need for customer convenience.

- Determine best style or format.
- Review key sales areas.
- Select layout approach.
- Determine basic page design.

Always:

1. Consider customer convenience.
2. Consider individuality of product line.
3. Consider advantages of product comparison.
4. Choose the best approach for moving the customer through the catalog.
5. Understand your budget restrictions.

> Each product must call for attention independently, without overpowering other products.

Strongly Consider:

1. Trying several of the basic approaches before making a final decision.
2. Choosing a layout approach you can live with.

## Checklist #4: Product work sessions

Product work sessions are vital to the success of your catalog. This is where it all comes together: your merchandise, your market, and the creative approach that makes the sale!

Prepare Ahead:

- Acquire product sample.
- Gather competitor catalog or media art samples.
- Gather competitor catalog or media copy samples.
- Test product.
- Acquire manufacturer information.
- Have list of merchandiser or buyer comments.

Actual Meeting:

- Have merchandiser conduct meeting.
- Have all buyers responsible for product selection attend.
- Have copywriter responsible for product copy attend.

Always:

1. Present production sample.
2. Review reasons for product selection.
3. Review competitor art presentations and copy descriptions.
4. Review merchandiser's and buyer's art and headline visualization.
5. Review testing results.
6. Review manufacturer's information.

Strongly Consider:

1. Trying the product yourself to further understand it.

## Checklist #5: Front cover photography

It is the front cover that will most likely determine whether your customer rescues your catalog from the mail and sets it aside for careful reading. As you plan your front cover, consider the following checklist.

- Define approach. There are three basic approaches: the dramatic approach, the product-line identification approach, and the sales/benefit approach.
- Review clip files for ideas.
- Decide method of creative execution. You have four options: studio shooting, location shooting, stock photos, and art illustration.
- Select photographer.
- Select artist.
- Consider budget.

Always:

1. Consider your customers' tastes.
2. Consider using stock photos.
3. Consider going with an approach you can stay with and become recognized for.

Strongly Consider:

1. A separate and specialized photographer for cover shots.

## Checklist #6: Back cover photography

The back cover plays many important roles. It carries the customer's name and address, required postal indicia, and your name and address. The back cover, like the front cover, must attract the customer's attention—especially if the mail carrier has tossed the catalog on the floor face down. Once your photography approach has been determined, the layout artist can use his/her talents to bring the back cover to life.

> It is the front cover that will most likely determine whether your customer rescues your catalog from the mail and sets it aside for careful reading.

- Decide approach.
- Double-check address-panel requirements.

Always:

1. Clearly represent catalog image.
2. Use a product that is exemplary of your product line.

Strongly Consider:

1. Selling products directly on the back cover.
2. Continuing the mood of the front cover.

## Checklist #7: Product photography

Nothing is as believable to the viewer as a photograph of an item. Photos are invariably the first choice for presenting a product, mainly because they perform a function that drawing cannot: they encourage credibility. The customer is viewing the "real thing."

- Obtain actual production sample of product if possible.
- Determine mood of your catalog to be transmitted in photographs.
- Review product presentation with artist, merchandiser, and copywriter.

> Nothing is as believable to the viewer as a photograph of an item.

Always:

1. Focus on the product or resulting benefit.
2. Review background colors for visual coordination.
3. Review competitors' presentations.

Strongly Consider:

1. Utilizing insets for product detail or functional emphasis.
2. Using props to enhance visual attraction or to size product.
3. Using a natural setting in which to photograph products.
4. Artful presentation for greater definition of product or product function.

## Checklist #8: Headlines

Picture a newspaper without headlines. How would you determine what to read? Headlines are meant to call attention to a particular item. They save time for your customers. Here are a few tips for writing headlines.

1. Attract your prospects' attention. Speak directly to your customers and hold their attention.
2. Headlines should stress your strongest sales point.
3. Highlight your company's unique benefits. Tell customers about your exceptional service or unconditional guarantee through headlines.
4. Long headlines that sell your products are better than short, cute, or clever headlines that say nothing.
5. Give customers reason to order soon. Try to close the deal before customers lose attention.

- Determine thrust of product.
- Determine headline technique(s).
- Establish type standards.
- Establish style.

Always:

1. Be enthusiastic and truthful.
2. Inform the customer.
3. Edit judiciously.
4. Work with the artist.

Strongly Consider:

1. Using short words and few adjectives and adverbs.

> Give customers reason to order soon. Try to close the deal before customers lose attention.

## Checklist #9: Pricing

Wording used in your price lines can have different effects on the customer. Changing a few words can add emphasis and pizzazz to a normally straightforward merchandise action.

Regular Pricing: normal retail that reflects the cataloger's required or desired profit.

Sale Pricing: show a markdown from the regular price.

Special Purchase Pricing: results from the cataloger's receiving products at a lesser price (e.g., discontinued products).

Membership Pricing: this is self-explanatory.

Value Pricing: buying products in bulk may allow for savings from the individual item cost.

- Verify retail price with management.
- Confirm reason for pricing.
- Verify product number.
- Set price line style.

Always:

1. Use cent sign for price if less than $1.
2. Write $1.00, not $1.

Strongly Consider:

1. Putting salesmanship into the price line.
2. Separate product number from retail price for easy visual.

## Checklist #10: Guarantees

A guarantee should always be worded to sell. Keep your guarantee direct and to the point. Establish rapport and be sincere and positive. Include limitations and conditions so the customer has no surprise.

- Choose strongest guarantee possible.
- Investigate manufacturers' guarantees.
- Make sure guarantee is believable.
- Keep the "small print" out of your guarantee.

Always:

1. Display guarantee prominently.
2. Be careful in the wording and claims—be prepared to follow through with them.
3. Use guarantee as selling point.

Strongly Consider:

1. Placing your guarantee on front and/or back cover.
2. Utilizing your guarantee in headlines, copy, and punch lines.
3. Placing your guarantee on the order form.
4. Using manufacturer's guarantee as yours.

## Checklist #11: Order Forms

Order forms can make or break a sale. A complicated order form that is hard to understand may discourage a customer from placing an order. Customers do not like to wrestle with details. The easier your order form is to understand, the better your response will be.

- Gather information to include.
- Decide on position within the catalog.

> A guarantee should always be worded to sell.

Always:

1. Design with simplicity.
2. Keep customer uppermost in mind.
3. State information clearly and simply.
4. Include your company name and address.
5. Provide a phone number.
6. Allow ample room for customer to fill in information.
7. Thank the customer.

Strongly Consider:

1. Including guarantee on order form panel.
2. Taking the customer through the order steps via a numbering system.

## Checklist #12: Catalog Printing

Developing a good working relationship is a two-way street. Just as you need to know your printer's capabilities, your printer needs to know something about the way you and your company operate. Scheduling is extremely important. Set realistic deadlines and then stick to them—or you risk compromising your mailing date.

- Prepare a bid sheet.
- Define your printing needs for quality, price, and service.
- Identify early your method of addressing.

Always:

1. Ask for printing samples on the same kind of paper you intend to use.
2. Be uniform and thorough about job specifications with all printers.
3. Select paper to match your products and image.
4. Consider weight of paper.
5. Project your printing volume needs.

> Ask for printing samples on the same kind of paper you intend to use.

Strongly Consider:

1. Visiting the printer plant prior to the final decision.
2. A slightly lighter or lesser-grade paper than prime.
3. A two-color catalog, if only for an off-season or sale version.
4. Being on site as the catalog is printed.

Catalog checklists from the Maxwell Sroge book *How to Create Successful Catalogs* used with permission. Also, visit the Web site *www.catalog-news.com*.

The Direct Marketing Association also conducts several in-depth seminars on Catalog Essentials and Catalog Creative Critique throughout the year. Call 212-790-1444 for their seminar program, (*www.the-dma.org/seminars*).

Finally, a key industry conference and expo is Catalog Tech. Details on the Web at *www.catalogtechexpo.com*, 1-888-627-2630.

For more information on this topic, visit our Web site at www.businesstown.com

# Chapter 14

## Trade Shows

> Properly planned and executed, trade shows can be an excellent source of qualified leads for most small businesses.

Before there was the Internet, there was the telephone. Before the telephone, there was direct mail. And before there was much of anything, there were agricultural fairs. Fairs brought people together at harvest time—farmers to sell their produce and livestock, and the general populace to buy. As populations grew, these fairs became major events, and it wasn't long before the artisans saw them as a place to sell their wares as well. Soon the agricultural fairs evolved into craft fairs, and eventually they morphed into the trade shows we have today. The fourth direct channel, face-to-face selling, was the original direct channel.

Properly planned and executed, trade shows can be an excellent source of qualified leads for most small businesses. Studies place trade shows second only to direct sales in the marketing mix. For small businesses, smaller shows and regionals can be as profitable as the pricey extravaganzas. Poorly planned and executed, however, any trade show can also be a costly mistake. Ultimately, your success with any particular trade show will come from your own experience—from careful selection of the shows you attend to the effectiveness of your display, and, especially, your sales lead follow-up process. Some metrics to help you with the selection process include:

## The AIF and the PIF

AIF stands for *Audience Interest Factor*. It's a rough calculation of the percentage of attendees that visit 20% of the exhibits. Ask the show producer what their AIF is. Multiply the show's expected attendance by the AIF to determine the number of high-interest visitors.

PIF is the *Product Interest Factor*. This is the number of people seeking information on any one product. Again, the show management should be able to give you the show's PIF. Multiply the number of high-interest attendees by the PIF to calculate your potential audience. Using hypothetical numbers:

3,000 anticipated attendees × 40% AIF = 1,200 high-interest visitors.
1,200 × 23% PIF = 276 people as a potential audience for your product.

Both metrics are calculated for individual trade shows by Exhibit Surveys, Inc. (*www.exhibitsurveys.com*), a company that provides consulting services to companies seeking to market through trade shows. When you've identified the shows that offer the most promise for your company, check with Exhibit Surveys to see if your selections are among the shows they track.

## How Many Visitors per Hour?

This is an important metric for deciding how many staff people you will need for the show. Exhibit Surveys suggests the following formula:

Total attendees – nonbuyers × .16 = high-interest attendees
High-interest attendees × .57 = Booth traffic for show
Booth traffic for show ÷ hours the show is open = visitors per hour

Using our example above,
4,000 total attendees – 1,000 nonbuyers = 3,000 buying attendees
3,000 buying attendees × .16 = 480 high-interest attendees
480 high-interest attendees × .57 = 273 booth traffic for show
273 booth traffic for show ÷ 19 hours open = 14.3 visitors per hour

## Tracking Traffic Density

Another critical index of a show's value to an exhibitor is traffic density–the number of attendees occupying every 100 square feet of exhibit space. Exhibit Surveys, Inc., conducts detailed surveys of 100 major expositions each year. Their traffic density index remained at about 2.6 for 1996 and 1997, the last two years for which figures are available. "Shows with Traffic Density figures of less than 2 are at some risk," says the research group. At the same time, low densities are more conducive to better one-to-one contacts on the show floor. Says Exhibit Surveys:

"Trends in our exhibition research indicate that, on average, attendees continued spending over eight hours viewing exhibits (despite increased pressures

> Another critical index of a show's value to an exhibitor is traffic density—the number of attendees occupying every 100 square feet of exhibit space.

> The growth in numbers of exhibitors in recent years has also led to greater competition for the time and attention of attendees.

on their time), and the quality of attendees in terms of buying plans and buying influence levels remained very high. Traffic Density levels on the show floor have declined in the early '90s, but have leveled off over the last three years. The decline in Traffic Density is not a function of lower attendance. It is a result of a faster rate of growth in exhibit space sales relative to attendance growth."

The growth in numbers of exhibitors in recent years has also led to greater competition for the time and attention of attendees. Exhibit Surveys suggests exhibitors use more preshow promotion, set up advance appointments, and use "at-show promotion and other types of attention-getting techniques (e.g., demonstrations, presentations, theaters, etc.) to *selectively* attract prospects." They add, "Exhibitors can't just 'show up' and expect to achieve good results."

## Is the Show Vertical or Horizontal?

A vertical-seller show is one in which the exhibitors belong to an identifiable niche, with little variation. A telecommunications show would be vertical-seller.

A horizontal-seller show is one in which the exhibitors offer a wide range of products. The Consumer Electronics Show is an example.

A vertical-buyer show is one where the *buyers* are all within an identifiable niche—farmers attending a farm machinery show, for example.

A horizontal-buyer show is where the buyers are from various businesses. The Direct Marketing Association's semiannual conferences are horizontal-buyer.

It won't surprise you as a direct marketer to learn that vertical-seller/vertical-buyer shows have the highest AIF, or that horizontal-seller/vertical buyer have the lowest.

Remember, these are averages for general guidance only, not a definitive answer. For that, you'll need to conduct . . .

## Hands-On Research

Numbers notwithstanding, don't take anyone's word for how a specific trade show performs. Every business is different, and every process produces different results. Body counts mean nothing (up to a point–zero is still zero). What you must determine is *who* is attending show x and show y, not just how many. If your product or service is costly and/or complex, you'll need to qualify your leads as carefully as possible. On the other hand, just one or two sales may make the show a winner for you. If you need to sell at the show, you'll want a different kind of attendee–based on customer models. If your buyers are homogeneous, you'll likely do better at a vertical-buyer show. If they are diverse, a horizontal-buyer show may be the answer.

The best way to determine who is there is to attend the shows yourself, get the attendee rosters, eyeball the badges, and observe the activity. See which companies' booths are attracting prospects and which are essentially empty, and determine why. Decide whether it's a lead-generation show or a selling show. Check out the booth displays, the hype level, the "show-biz" quotient. The greater the glitz, the less desirable the show is from a small business perspective, in my opinion–unless you happen to be a TV program syndicator or computer game developer.

Visit your competitor's booths and see what they're offering, although they may spot you if your company name is prominent on your badge. Perhaps you can put a sticker over it and do a little covert intelligence. At least you can observe from a distance and keep track of their visitors. Try to determine whether they are genuinely interested or just picking up freebies. Take careful notes of everything you see (possibly with a small cassette recorder), including random impressions, so you can review them later. Don't trust your memory. Also, ask the show managers or salespeople how many of your competitors have attended that show and for how many years.

### Online Trade Show Info

Many trade shows today have a Web site where you can get most of the nuts-and-bolts information you need, although, of course, it will be a bit one-sided. For an example, point your browser to *www.zdshows.com/comdex* for an overview of one of the world's largest computer shows.

## The Exhibitor Kit

When you've selected one or more shows, send for each one's exhibitor kit. The kit gives you a diagram of the show floor with booth locations and numbers. Needless to say, you need to move early and quickly to get the better locations. The kit spells out the show rules and includes ordering information for on-site services. It also provides details on show hours and payment policy, shipping instructions, target dates for material arrival and removal, fire regulations, hotel and travel reservations, registration information, and inquiry collection processes.

It may also include any on-site or preshow promotion opportunities, such as ad space in the daily show bulletin and availability of the attendee roster for mailing purposes. It will include information about telephone installation and electrical connections available at your booth, booth drapery and carpet availability, show labor regulations, and extra-cost services. Trade show labor is often union labor, and clearly defined as to who does what with electrical work, carpentry, drapery, rigging, and drayage, etc. If you require an Internet connection or other network connections, you'll especially want to determine how they are accomplished.

> If you require a live Internet connection or other network connections, you'll especially want to determine how they are accomplished.

# Designing Your Booth

Once you've decided on the shows you will attend, and you've reviewed your notes on the types of booths used at those shows, you'll want to get your booth into design mode. You'll find a bunch of design companies on the Web (see the "Resources" section), but you should have a firm idea of what you want your booth to do and how you want it to look *before* you contact them.

As with everything else in direct marketing, you have just a few precious seconds to capture your prospects' attention and in the sturm and drang of most trade shows, that's no small task. The first question you must answer is whether you will have actual products at the show (with or without a "live" demonstration), a video-type demonstration, or just literature. And remember that, regardless of the dynamics of the booth itself, your purpose is to engage selected prospects in a brief conversation. That means, in most cases, you'll want them to be able to step into the booth, not just stand at the periphery. So don't put a table or worse, chairs, at the entrance to the booth.

Some companies have their booth flooring raised an inch or two above the show floor and covered with a different color carpeting. This sets up a commitment on the part of anyone "crossing the line" and "stepping up" to your booth. It also discourages casual browsers. Rather than having your demonstration video or whatever facing outward toward the passing crowd, turn it so it faces into the booth, and anyone who wants to see it must come all the way into the booth to do so.

If you can allow people to handle products, fine. If not, however, it might be better not to have them there at all. Product photo blowups might even be better in any case—might pique greater curiosity and prompt more questions than having the "real thing," giving you and your staff more opportunities for qualifying. It's a little like lead generation, where we don't want to give away everything up front but want to leave something for the prospect to inquire about.

In the same vein, if you have a pricey, comprehensive brochure, you might be wise NOT to have it at the show. Have an *offer* for it, perhaps in a smaller flier. It's bound to get short shrift in the 28 pounds of junk everyone collects at a trade show, only to be tossed out back at the hotel room.

If you have an interactive, computer-based display, let the prospect run his or her own show. Self-running demos are often deadly dull. Design the display so it takes people wherever they want to go. Make it colorful and fun, even if it's for sump pumps—not that there's anything wrong with them.

If you must have a product demonstration, make sure the booth is large enough to accommodate a group and give everyone a clear view, plus room to write down information, exchange cards, etc. If the product is large and involved, consider renting a hotel suite or meeting room for the demo and use the booth to invite people up. You'll want to take special care in qualifying folks for the hotel suite, since it will likely involve eating and drinking while they're there. Many companies use a hospitality suite in connection with their booth.

> Rather than having your demonstration video or whatever facing outward toward the passing crowd, turn it so it faces into the booth, and anyone who wants to see it must come all the way into the booth to do so.

Booth graphics should be large and bold—one strong, single image rather than multiple images. If that's a product blow up, make sure it's well lighted. (Never depend on the facility's lighting to illuminate your booth or anything in it. Make sure you bring your own.)

Also, don't assume that your logo is necessarily the BIG image. Ask yourself honestly and objectively how well known your logo is. A bold product benefit statement (in eight words or less) or a provocative question regarding the product might make a surer traffic stopper if your logo is less well known. If your product/service is new, say so with a big "NEW!" on a separate poster or banner. Red and yellow are still the most visible colors, so use them liberally, even if they make your teeth ache.

Once you've decided these issues, established traffic flow patterns, etc., you're ready to consider booth design and construction. There are exhibit distributors who deal in modular units that can be adapted to your needs, and custom builders who do it from scratch. You might be wise to start out with a lower-priced modular until you have some experience with what actually happens at your booth before you go for a more costly custom job.

For an overview of display possibilities, from custom jobs to table tops, click on *www.exhibitcenter.com*. The owners of this site are distributors for several manufacturers, and they provide links to their sites and even some pricing info online.

> Your booth should be staffed with your most experienced people—because they must be ready to respond knowledgeably to any potential customer's question.

## Preparing Booth Staff

While you may still see a few here and there, the days of decorating booths with leggy models are over. Your booth should be staffed with your most experienced people—because they must be ready to respond knowledgeably to any potential customer's question. The more technical or involved your product, the more professional and prepared your staff must be.

Train and rehearse your booth personnel on how to:

1. Identify prospects (by job, title, size of company, etc.)
2. Engage them with open-ended questions

3. Qualify them quickly as to product/solution needs and interest
4. Obtain their business card (even if you can scan their badge) and make a note of any specific comments or questions
5. Say thank you and move on to the next prospect

Make sure everyone in the booth knows the various colors or other badge distinctions that identify buyers versus press, other exhibitors, speakers, spouses, etc. Booth attendants should never sit in the booth, or eat or drink there. Each should have a price sheet in his or her pocket for ready reference and speak slowly and clearly to prospects. Trade shows are usually noisy.

Identify a special strategy for a "hot" prospect—someone who's clearly ready to buy. Turn him or her over to a "closer" (like the sales manager) and have a place specified for a longer, quieter conversation, if necessary.

## Follow Up Quickly

Absolutely critical to the success of any trade show is the immediacy of getting information to prospects who requested it. One way is to have a small mailing setup at the booth or at the hotel so you can get your fulfillment kit out before the show is over, perhaps with a personal, handwritten note, and it's on your prospect's desk when he or she gets back. You can also call or fax prospect information back to your office each evening and have prewritten form letters go out for each product in an appropriate fulfillment or information kit.

Always follow up with a telephone call to make sure your prospect received the material and to begin your normal sales cycle. As with prospects from any source, you'll want to determine his role in the decision process, his current need, and names of other "influencers" who may be involved in the decision-making process. You'll also want to know what he's currently using and what other solutions he is looking at. All this information needs to be fed into your marketing database for continuing follow-up and results measuring. It's how you'll determine the ROI of your trade show activity and whether you wish to continue your participation or even expand it.

### Instant Response

One company set up a laptop computer with all their material in computer files and e-mailed or faxed the appropriate documents to the prospect's company before he even left the booth. When he or she arrived back at the office, it was all there, waiting.

## Promote Your Attendance

Well before any show, make a hit list of prospects you'd like to see at the show and send them an invitation to stop by *for something specific*. Plan more than one mailing, starting 90 days prior to the event, then three weeks, then a fax the week before. Also check the attendees list that the show promoters will make available to you and cull out those who are your best prospects for inclusion in your mail campaign—if the names are available soon enough. If not, mail two weeks before the show and follow up with the fax a week before.

Like any good lead-generation program, your copy shouldn't tell the whole story, but rather "tease" the product and its benefits, with the more critical answers to be provided at your booth. Your offer should be something of value, available only at the booth.

If you spring for a hospitality suite at the hotel, you may wish to invite VIPs up for a nosh and a pitch. In fact, show attendees enjoy being invited to a place where they can sit for a few minutes and eat something other than rubber hot dogs, and they fully expect to be pitched. If you plan a product demo at the suite, you may need to establish "show times" and take reservations accordingly.

In any case, sending free show passes to VIPs is good idea. Many shows provide a set number of such passes for exhibitors, sometimes preimprinted with the company name. If they are not imprinted, have a stamp made and stamp each pass so recipients know where they came from.

Ads in trade publications that specifically address your show attendance, show offer, and booth number can help get your company on the "visit" lists of those in your industry who make such lists in advance of attending a show.

## Trade Show Tips and Facts

### The Seven Deadly Sins of Pre-Show Mail Campaigns

Face it: there's no end to the ways you can mess up a direct mail campaign. Throughout this book, we have highlighted the mis-

---

### Make Your Offer Value-Add

A software company I worked with was exhibiting at a college teachers' association conference and sent out a self-mailer offering a free "Teacher's Kit" designed to provide teachers with valuable help in using that category of software generally in the classrooms. The booth was mobbed.

takes that lead to certain direct mail death: don't ask for any action, mail the item too late, don't use benefits-oriented copy, and more.

Pre-show mailers are a particularly demanding breed of the direct mail species. As such, there's even more room for error. Here are seven common pre-show direct mailer errors identified by Lorraine Denham, executive vice president of Unipro Marketing Services, courtesy of *Exhibitor* magazine. Watch for them in your planning.

1. **Wrongful assumptions.** Don't assume that people know all about your company or its products. Keep your copy to one message, and keep that message simple. You can educate them on the other levels of your company and products once they are in the booth.
2. **Mailer overboard.** Giant type, multiple exclamation points, a dozen vibrant colors—ouch! Remember that pre-show mailers set the tone and spirit of your booth. You might discourage attendees from visiting your booth if your mailer is too loud.
3. **Error of excess.** Often, a pre-show mailer ends up looking like a product catalog, filled with specs and details. "You don't have to tell them how your product works," Denham says. "Just get them to see the benefit of coming to visit you."
4. **It's the message, stupid.** Sometimes, pre-show mail creators are so caught up in the "creative" side of things that they forget what they are supposed to accomplish. The goal is to bring people to the booth, not convince them this is the cutest mailer in the history of exhibiting.
5. **"We're the greatest."** The pre-show mailer is not the place to laud your company's latest accomplishments. Instead, you need to tell attendees why they should visit your booth. Think about how your product/service benefits them, and let that drive the message.
6. **Know the show limitations.** If show management will be sending the mailer for you, be sure to check their guidelines up front. One company planned to ship its comic-book-style mailer in clear-coated envelopes. They found out too late that the show management's mail house couldn't process the materials.

> Pre-show mailers are a particularly demanding breed of the direct mail species.

**7. Too many hoops.** Some mailers simply ask for too much action. "Bring the mailer to the front desk, have it stamped, fill out a form, visit three product stations . . . ." Make it easy for your recipient. Give them one simple step, such as interfacing with a sales representative or viewing a presentation, to redeem the mailer.

Used with permission from *Exhibitor* magazine, ©1999, Rochester, MN (888) 235-6155. *www.Exhibitornet.com*

We've said time and again: sell the offer, not the product. As with the math software firm mentioned previously, pitch the premium or the demo, not the company. Keep it simple, quick, and easy to read. A two-color self-mailer can often do the job.

## Six More Trade-Show Tips:

> Nothing is worse than a booth host or hostess with drooping eyes or a bored stare.

- Tie a special show discount or show-related premium into your product offers so prospects will have an added reason to keep your material after the show. With so much literature thrown away at the end of most shows, you'll want to make yours more valuable and worth holding on to.
- Make sure you have sufficient staff to allow for downtime and rest periods. Nothing is worse than a booth host or hostess with drooping eyes or a bored stare. Attendants should be smiling and alert throughout the show. They should also be immediately identifiable, by either special clothing or large, clearly marked badges, or both. Wear comfortable shoes.
- Try not to look like show security. Don't stand with arms crossed in the center of your booth. Keep your hands out of your pockets. Hold a product flier or fact sheet, and stand at the side of the booth facing oncoming traffic, at a 45-degree angle to the booth, for a more inviting appearance.
- Conduct a post-mortem at the end of each day. Note problems and get them resolved before the next morning. Identify peo-

ple you may want to follow up with the next day. Keep careful notes of anything that's working well, or anything that's causing problems. They'll help with your next show's planning.

- Don't stack literature on counters or put out baskets of giveaways that only encourage the grab-and-run crowd. Keep the literature out of sight, except for the few pieces you hold in your hand. Remember, you want to talk to people. Same with giveaways. Keep a few in your pocket and give them to folks *after* you've spoken to them.

- Use round tables, rather than rectangular. Square and rectangular tables invite an "us/them" configuration with you on one side and your prospect on the other. The table acts a barrier between you and is not conducive to easy dialog.

## Four Facts on Trade Shows from the Center for Exhibition Industry Research

"My attitude is, unequivocally: If you're in business and you don't take full advantage of trade shows, you ought to have your head examined." If you're a small company just starting out, go to the first exhibition you can afford to go to because that's the best way to get started. If you're a large company, you should go not only because exhibitions help you grow but because exhibitions give you a look at the future. A lot of small companies offer new ideas and new technologies at exhibitions. The large companies need to be there."

–Vice Chairman, major electronics firm

> Closing a sale that begins with contact at an exhibition saves you nearly half the cost of closing a sale that doesn't have the exhibition advantage.

**Fact #1:** Closing a sale that begins with contact at an exhibition saves you nearly half the cost of closing a sale that doesn't have the exhibition advantage: $550 and 1.4 sales calls compared to $997 and 3.6 sales calls.

**Fact #2:** A carefully crafted integrated exhibition marketing plan produces the best results. Successful exhibitors see increases in conversion to qualified leads attributable to pre-show preparation (+50%), at-show hospitality (+62%), and staff training (+68%).

**Fact #3:** People remember an exhibit for many reasons other than size: interest in products (33%); demonstration/presentation (27%); well-known company (11%); design of exhibit (10%); booth personnel (9%); literature (7%); and giveaways and advertising (3%).

**Fact #4:** Eighty-three percent of the decision makers who attend exhibitions say exhibitions bring them up to date on the latest trends and developments in their industries. Eighty five percent are there to save time and money by seeing many vendors at once.

## Trade-Show Worksheet

Use the following worksheet to compare the suitability of various shows for your marketing purposes. Make copies of the worksheet, and complete one for each show you're considering.

First, mark (Y) for each factor that is important to your show marketing program; mark (N) for each factor that is unimportant to you. Next, for each factor that is important to your marketing program (the "Ys"), give the show a score of +1 if the show meets the criterion or offers that item, and a rating of –1 if it does not.

Add up the rating numbers. Use this total to compare different shows you are considering. *Remember that other, harder-to-quantify factors may influence the suitability of a show for your objectives.* These other factors are listed at the end of the worksheet. Gather this information for each show, and use it along with the rating number as part of your decision-making process.

# TRADE SHOWS

NAME OF SHOW _____

DATE _____

LOCATION _____

| | FACTOR IMPORTANT TO MARKETING OBJECTIVES? | RATING (+1 OR -1) |
|---|---|---|
| **Targeting/Type of show** | | |
| International | Y ☐   N ☐ | _____ |
| National | Y ☐   N ☐ | _____ |
| Regional | Y ☐   N ☐ | _____ |
| Buyer | Y ☐   N ☐ | _____ |
| Reseller | Y ☐   N ☐ | _____ |
| Association-related | Y ☐   N ☐ | _____ |
| Niche-specific | Y ☐   N ☐ | _____ |
| Educational component (seminars, etc.) | Y ☐   N ☐ | _____ |
| | | |
| **Audience** | | |
| Attendance audited? | Y ☐   N ☐ | _____ |
| Limitations on types of attendees | Y ☐   N ☐ | _____ |
| | | |
| **Factors influencing exhibitors** | | |
| Limitations on types of exhibitors | Y ☐   N ☐ | _____ |
| Competitors planning to exhibit at show | Y ☐   N ☐ | _____ |
| Industry leaders planning to exhibit at show | Y ☐   N ☐ | _____ |
| Were objectives met at last attendance of show? | Y ☐   N ☐ | _____ |
| Ability to specify/negotiate booth size, location, etc. | Y ☐   N ☐ | _____ |
| Availability of exhibitor lounge | Y ☐   N ☐ | _____ |
| High-quality press attendance expected | Y ☐   N ☐ | _____ |
| High-quality leads obtained from previous year's show | Y ☐   N ☐ | _____ |
| | | |
| **Factors influencing visitors** | | |
| Pre-registration available? | Y ☐   N ☐ | _____ |
| Easy on-site registration | Y ☐   N ☐ | _____ |

|  | FACTOR IMPORTANT TO MARKETING OBJECTIVES? |  | RATING |
|---|---|---|---|
| Parking facilities | Y ☐ | N ☐ | _____ |
| Public transportation | Y ☐ | N ☐ | _____ |
| Air and lodging available through show management? | Y ☐ | N ☐ | _____ |
| Convenient eating facilities | Y ☐ | N ☐ | _____ |
| Hotel availability | Y ☐ | N ☐ | _____ |

**Factors influencing press attendance**

|  |  |  |  |
|---|---|---|---|
| Adequacy of press facilities | Y ☐ | N ☐ | _____ |
| Ease of registration | Y ☐ | N ☐ | _____ |
| Quality of keynote speaker | Y ☐ | N ☐ | _____ |
| Attendance by top company executives expected | Y ☐ | N ☐ | _____ |
| Press conferences/product announcements scheduled | Y ☐ | N ☐ | _____ |
| Limitations on access to events | Y ☐ | N ☐ | _____ |
| Press lounge | Y ☐ | N ☐ | _____ |
| Working press room | Y ☐ | N ☐ | _____ |

**Logistics**

|  |  |  |  |
|---|---|---|---|
| Good security | Y ☐ | N ☐ | _____ |
| Move-in/out assistance provided | Y ☐ | N ☐ | _____ |
| Move-in/out facilities adequate | Y ☐ | N ☐ | _____ |
| Availability of hospitality suites | Y ☐ | N ☐ | _____ |
| Exhibitor's lounge? | Y ☐ | N ☐ | _____ |
| Local unions at show site | Y ☐ | N ☐ | _____ |

**Show management**

|  |  |  |  |
|---|---|---|---|
| Does show management mail to press list? | Y ☐ | N ☐ | _____ |
| Promotions planned by show organizers | Y ☐ | N ☐ | _____ |
| Show management involved in exhibitor promotion | Y ☐ | N ☐ | _____ |
| Show management experienced and skilled in business | Y ☐ | N ☐ | _____ |
| Show management able to accommodate unusual requests | Y ☐ | N ☐ | _____ |
| Show management responds well to emergencies/unforeseen events | Y ☐ | N ☐ | _____ |
| Quality and availability of exhibitor's kit | Y ☐ | N ☐ | _____ |

**Total Score:** _____

**Additional factors**

| | |
|---|---|
| Projected attendance | Number: _____ |
| Attendance for last show | Number: _____ |
| Proportion of decision makers | Percentage: _____ |
| Proportion of expected attendees matching target market | Percentage: _____ |
| Proportion of expected attendees matching secondary market | Percentage: _____ |
| | |
| Cost of space per square foot | Cost: _____ |
| Cost of utilities/additional services | Cost: _____ |
| Distance from home office | Distance: _____ |
| Length of show in hours | Length: _____ |
| Duration in days | Duration: _____ |
| Show frequency | How often: _____ |
| | |
| Entrance cost | Dollars: _____ |
| Geographic location | Where: _____ |
| Time of year | When: _____ |

## 18-Month Show-Planning Timetable and Checklist

### 16–18 Months in Advance
❏ Be sure company marketing objectives are well defined.
❏ Begin considering whether trade shows will meet
   your objectives.
❏ Begin looking for shows you may want to attend.
❏ Begin preliminary discussions with affected company
   members—marketing, sales, R&D.

### 14 Months
❏ Collect information on each show you are considering.

### 13 Months
❏ Evaluate and decide on show.

## 12 Months

- ❏ Examine show guidelines for space-purchasing requirements.
- ❏ Write down specific objectives for show.
- ❏ Obtain feedback on objectives from affected company members.
- ❏ Contact and evaluate outside vendors for booth design and construction, if necessary.

## 10 Months

- ❏ Hold meeting to determine needs for graphics, packaging, printing.

## 6 Months

- ❏ Carefully review exhibitor's manual for special restrictions, etc.
- ❏ Check progress of booth construction.

## 4 Months

- ❏ Design press kits, product spec sheets, other literature.
- ❏ Decide on special events (hospitality, press conference) and book rooms.
- ❏ Review marketing objectives.
- ❏ Decide on staff for show.
- ❏ Review trade show plan with everyone involved.
- ❏ Compile target lists: customers for VIP passes, press.

## 3 Months

- ❏ Print literature.
- ❏ Order special promotional items.
- ❏ Order VIP guest passes from show management.
- ❏ Book hotels.
- ❏ Make airline reservations.
- ❏ Design pre-show promotion.
- ❏ Monitor progress of advertising plan, if any.
- ❏ Submit editorial material for show daily.
- ❏ Check all show deadlines.

**2 Months**

- ❏ Finalize staff assignments.
- ❏ Pre-register all attending staff.
- ❏ Check status of
  - ❏ booth construction
  - ❏ literature printing
  - ❏ promotional items
- ❏ Order labor contractor.
- ❏ Order lead/registration system materials.
- ❏ Authorize all services.
- ❏ Obtain mailing list for pre-show promotion.
- ❏ Make shipping arrangements.
- ❏ Design at-the-show information package for all staff.
- ❏ Make dinner reservations at area hotels for client/staff dinners.

**1 Month**

- ❏ Mail pre-show promotion to target audience.
- ❏ Mail pre-show promotion/announcement to press.
- ❏ Mail VIP tickets to valued customers.
- ❏ Produce at-the-show information package for all staff.
- ❏ Order special equipment, lighting, flowers, furniture, food, etc.
- ❏ Confirm telephone, electrical, cleaning.

**3 Weeks**

- ❏ Create final shipping checklist.
- ❏ Ship booth.
- ❏ Confirm air and hotel reservations.
- ❏ Train staff for booth duty.

**2 Weeks**

- ❏ Confirm special orders—computers, audio-visual.
- ❏ Schedule wiring, carpet, phone, other installation.

**1 Week**

- ❏ Review show goals, plans, activities with staff.

**3–4 Days**
- ❏ Fly to show location.

**1–3 Days**
- ❏ Supervise booth setup.
- ❏ Orient staff to show facility.

**Day of Show**
- ❏ Hold briefing/motivational meeting.

## 12-Month Publicity Timetable and Checklist
**12 Months in Advance**
- ❏ Begin investigating speaking possibilities.
- ❏ Write down specific objectives for publicity.
- ❏ Obtain feedback on objectives from affected Company members.

**10 Months**
- ❏ Request speaker guidelines from conference manager or speaker coordinator.
- ❏ Check all speaker deadlines.

**6 Months**
- ❏ Decide on theme for marketing communications material.
- ❏ Decide on special events (hospitality, press conference).
- ❏ Prepare preliminary outline of speaker's presentation.

**4 Months**
- ❏ Go over speaker's presentation with marketing department, others.
- ❏ Book rooms for hospitality events, press conferences.

**3 Months**
- ❏ Print press kits.
- ❏ Design promotion campaign to press.
- ❏ Identify target publications.

❏ Submit editorial material for show daily.
❏ Go over press objectives with other company members.
❏ Be sure show guide has necessary information about speaker.

## 1 Month

❏ Mail invitations to preregistered press list.
❏ Call very important press members to invite them to your booth or press conference.
❏ Finalize speaker's presentation.

## 3 Weeks

❏ Call to set up appointments with the press at the show.
❏ Train booth staff on PR objectives and how to handle press.
❏ Rehearse speaker's presentation.
❏ Make arrangements to ship press kits to show.

## 2 Weeks

❏ Confirm special audio-visual for speaker.
❏ Confirm special needs for press conference room.

## 1 Week

❏ Review show goals, plans, activities with staff.

## 3 Days

❏ Fly to show location.

## 1 Day

❏ Visit press room.
❏ Visit press conference location.
❏ Stock press room with press kits (if allowed).

## Day of Show

❏ Test audio-visual equipment for speaker, press conference.

## Budget Worksheet

Use this worksheet to track anticipated and actual costs associated with each trade show.

Show Name _____

|  | ANTICIPATED | REVISED | ACTUAL |
|---|---|---|---|
| **Space purchase** | _____ | _____ | _____ |
| **Graphic design** | _____ | _____ | _____ |
| Corporate logo/image | _____ | _____ | _____ |
| Brochures | _____ | _____ | _____ |
| Direct Mail | _____ | _____ | _____ |
| Signs | _____ | _____ | _____ |
| **Booth design** | _____ | _____ | _____ |
| **Booth construction** | _____ | _____ | _____ |
| **Booth rental** | _____ | _____ | _____ |
| **Show services** | | | |
| Equipment rental | _____ | _____ | _____ |
| Carpet rental | _____ | _____ | _____ |
| Security | _____ | _____ | _____ |
| Installation/Dismantling (floor labor) | _____ | _____ | _____ |
| Electric labor | _____ | _____ | _____ |
| Electric connection | _____ | _____ | _____ |
| Telephone connection | _____ | _____ | _____ |
| Water/Drain | _____ | _____ | _____ |
| Accessories (wastebaskets, etc.) | _____ | _____ | _____ |
| Plants | _____ | _____ | _____ |
| Registration connections | _____ | _____ | _____ |
| Audio/visual | _____ | _____ | _____ |
| **Personnel** | | | |
| Temporary booth staff | _____ | _____ | _____ |
| Actors, specialty personnel | _____ | _____ | _____ |
| Staff salaries | _____ | _____ | _____ |
| **Exhibit transportation and drayage** | | | |
| Shipping | _____ | _____ | _____ |
| Drayage | _____ | _____ | _____ |

| | ANTICIPATED | REVISED | ACTUAL |
|---|---|---|---|
| **Printing/Production** | | | |
| Literature | _____ | _____ | _____ |
| Invitations | _____ | _____ | _____ |
| Signs | _____ | _____ | _____ |
| Specialty Items | _____ | _____ | _____ |
| **Special promotions** | | | |
| Hospitality suite | _____ | _____ | _____ |
| Hospitality catering | _____ | _____ | _____ |
| Advertising | _____ | _____ | _____ |
| Giveaways | _____ | _____ | _____ |
| **Airfare and travel** | _____ | _____ | _____ |
| **Lodging** | _____ | _____ | _____ |
| **Entertainment** | _____ | _____ | _____ |
| **Miscellaneous** | _____ | _____ | _____ |
| | | | |
| **TOTAL =** | _____ | _____ | _____ |

## Resources

**Center for Exhibition Industry Research**
(Formerly the Trade Show Bureau)
*www.ceir.org*

**Cyber-Centre**
An electronic trade show venue with useful links. In particular,
you'll discover many associated organizations listed at:
*www.cyber-centre.com/assoc.htm*

**Trade Show News Network**
Searchable database of trade shows, exhibitors, and suppliers to
the industry.
*www.tsnn.com*

### Trade Show Central
Largest and most complete online directory of trade shows, with more than 10,000 events.
*www.tradeshowcentral.com*

### EXPOguide
Directory of more than 6,000 shows, conferences, and exhibitions, plus information for meeting planners and show services.
*www.expoguide.com*

### TechWeb
Guide to technology-based events. Includes the Computer Events Directory.
*www.techweb.com*

### Image4Concepts
Distributor for manufacturers of display booths.
*www.exhibitcenter.com*

### *Exhibitor* Magazine
Directory of events, facilities, and suppliers plus how-to articles and ideas. Glossary.
*www.exhibitornet.com*

### Exhibit Surveys, Inc.
Provides research and consulting to companies for their trade show activities. Also conducts post-show studies on a published list of leading events. Check the list at their Web site:
*www.exhibitsurveys.com*

### Tradeshow Week Magazine on the Web
Trade Show Directory with keyword search and buyer's guide.
*www.tradeshoweek.com*

---

**For more information on this topic, visit our Web site at www.businesstown.com**

# The Internet: Marketing's 800-Pound Electric Gorilla

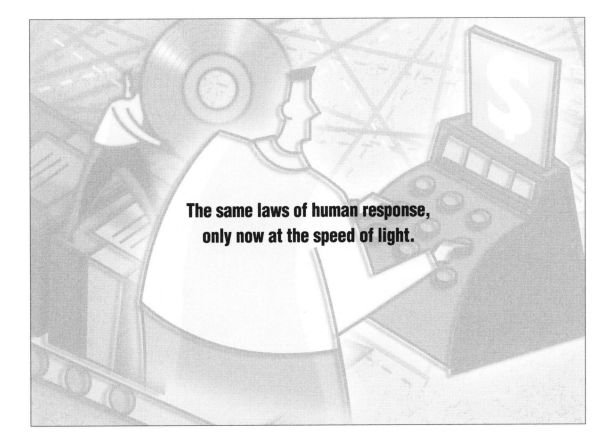

**The same laws of human response, only now at the speed of light.**

# Chapter 15

# Direct Marketing on the Internet: Bringing Your Company Into the 21st Century

## Spinning an E-Commerce Web

*The Net is the finest direct-marketing mechanism in the history of mankind. It is direct mail with free stamps.*
—SETH GODIN, VP OF DIRECT MARKETING, YAHOO!, AND FOUNDER, YOYODYNE ENTERTAINMENT

Al Gore's claim to paternity notwithstanding, direct marketers are tripping over one another in various efforts to "own" the Internet and its promise of marketing riches. As one direct marketing agency head put it during a conference panel, "The Internet is to marketing what fire was to man."

Safe to say, it is generally recognized by marketers of every stripe that the dynamics of direct response are pretty much driving today's Web wonderland and will continue to do so as marketing techniques become more clearly defined in the months and years ahead.

Should you be on the Web? Of course you should. There can be little doubt today that the Internet has become a major channel for sales and leads in both the consumer and business markets.

How major?

- The Yankee Group (*www.yankeegroup.com*) reports that half of all wired households made purchases online in 1999 and projects that two-thirds of all U.S. households will be online by 2004 (up from 33% in 1999).
- On the business-to-business side, Yankee sees it soaring from $138 billion in 1999 to $541 billion in 2003.
- Forrester Research (*www.forrester.com*) expects e-business to grow from $43 billion in 1998 to $410.3 billion in 2003, and business-to-business e-commerce to top *$1.3 trillion* by 2003.
- International Data Corporation puts Web shopping at $78.5 billion by 2003.
- Trans Union Business Information Group (*www.transunionbig.com*) places the small business sector at $270 billion by 2001.

> There can be little doubt today that the Internet has become a major channel for sales and leads in both the consumer and business markets.

- In a survey of 600 chief executive officers, 92% agreed that "the Internet will reshape the world marketplace by 2001."
- And *Fast Company* magazine reports, "If the Internet is not central to your business, the belief among the ranking chieftains is that you will soon be out of business. As Andy Grove of Intel put it: In five years, every business has to be an Internet business."

Are you going to ignore a marketing channel like that? Hardly. Especially when going online need not be a major expenditure as technology costs continue to drop. Caveat: There are as many statistics on Internet usage as there are organizations measuring it, so firm, reliable numbers from a single, universally accepted source are just not available.

## Direct Marketing on the Web

One source that's more pertinent to direct marketers than most surveys is the Electronic Media Survey, conducted by the Direct Marketing Association (*www.the-dma.org*).

- Ninety-five percent of direct marketers reported using the Internet for sales or marketing applications in 1999. That's up from 83% the previous year.
- Direct marketers with Web sites increased from 82% in 1997 to 90% in 1999.
- Primary purposes of Web sites were described as:
  - Marketing/information, 88%
  - Lead generation, 60%
  - Sales/e-commerce, 51%
- Sixty-seven percent (67%) are in the business-to-business category, 44% consumer: some do both.
- One third (33%) run banner ads on other Web sites, and 66% of those say they pay for the ads.
- Over half of the respondents use a combination of in-house and outside resources to build and maintain their sites. About one third (38%) do it all themselves, and 10% outsource it.
- Almost half of companies (47%) budget their sites as part of their marketing budget, and 26% have a separate interactive budget.

### Web Savvy

Regardless of whose numbers you choose to believe, they are big, and all trends are up. Nationally, internationally, consumer, or business-to-business, you cannot afford to ignore the Internet and the Web if you're going to stay competitive and bring your business into the 21st century.

## Stay Current With the "Streetwise" Web Site

Internet technologies and e-commerce trends are moving so rapidly that many of this chapter's specific references will be obsolete by the time you read them. To help you keep current, therefore, I have tied this chapter to a Web site where you can log on and track the latest and greatest in applying response techniques to your Web site as you go forward. Details are at the end of the chapter.

## Make a Plan

If your previous planning efforts have been somewhat spotty and "seat of the pants," now's the time to get real. You *must* know why you're going on the Web, at least after the initial novelty wears off. And since time is money, and your competition may already be well staked out on the Web, you don't want to waste any more time than necessary with novelties. Without a plan and a purpose for your Web site, you'll have no clue as to how it should be designed, what tools you need, or what kind of navigation to use (see the following checklist).

Following are the principal reasons companies and organizations establish an Internet presence. Each requirement will carry its own dynamics, its own technologies and Webware applications, and its own marketing strategies, just like in the real world.

1. To establish a presence (your competitors are there)
2. To sell (a) a single product
   (b) multiple products (catalog)
3. To obtain qualified leads for sales follow-up
4. Customer service—tech support, Frequently Asked Questions
5. To disseminate specialized information
6. To communicate with  ❑ salespeople;  ❑ distributors;  ❑ retailers;  ❑ business partners
7. Public information/PR
8. To serve your local consumer market
9. To expand internationally

## Getting on the World Wide Web

Especially in the business-to-business environment, your Web site is one of the first places prospects will look to get a handle on who you are—and, like your stationery, logo, brochure, etc., your Web site will project an image of you and your company, for good or ill. Try to avoid it by not being there, and you invite a credibility problem. It's not for everyone all the time, but if your competitors are there, you probably should be, too—even if you choose not to sell products online.

## The Great Paradigm Shift

Overused as that phrase has become in today's technology-driven culture, it really does apply to going online with your business. Perhaps the greatest single expression of the shift is that the control of communications with your market shifts from you to your customers and prospects.

You can make yourself more visible through various search-engine placement techniques, link exchanges, sponsorships, partnerships, and other strategies, and you can stimulate traffic through e-mail communications, traditional direct marketing, advertising, and public relations solutions.

Ultimately, however, the decision to visit your site, and when, and how long to stay (called "stickiness"), is not your call. In that regard, the Web is like a huge trade show, and you're vying for attention with all the other booths. Or, as one wag put it, it's like placing a Post-It Note on the bulletin board at the supermarket. Except it's a supermarket that's constantly expanding (2 million individual Web sites and counting!).

The more vertical your niche, the better your chances of attracting those who have an interest in your category and are actively seeking your information. They stand a good chance of finding you so long as you work to get your Web address out there on the search engines, promote it through the techniques outlined in this chapter, and generally "do the drill."

## Go Surfing!

To demonstrate some of these dynamics, fire up your browser and spend some time surfing the Net, if you haven't already done so. (This assumes you have at least a dial-up connection to the Internet. If not, see "Finding an ISP" below.) Start at the major portal sites and search engines, like Microsoft, Yahoo!, Excite, Lycos, HotBot, AltaVista, and Web Crawler. Enter a few keywords for your business or industry and see who turns up.

Pay particular attention to the length of time some sites take to get their graphics up and visible. Note how often you click off a site because it just took too long to load. Also note the differences

> The more vertical your niche, the better your chances of attracting those who have an interest in your category and are actively seeking your information.

## E-Commerce Benefits

In a recent nationwide poll, Chief Information Officers were asked what the greatest benefits of e-commerce were for their firms. Their replies:

Reach a broader range of prospects—37%
Value-added benefit for current customers—21%
Reduced operating costs—17%
Faster service or product delivery—3%

Source: RHI Management Resources, *www.rhimr.com*

between sites that are easy to understand and navigate and those that are confusing, often leaving you wondering where to click next. There are important lessons in these sessions, so keep a notepad handy. If you want to really do your homework, make copies of the following checklist and use it to rate other Web sites. It could save you several hundred dollars in seminar fees.

Check out the major online communities, AOL/Netscape and MSN. (AOL has always been a kiddieland to me, but it may grow up into a legitimate e-commerce environment at some point.) Go to Amazon.com and open an account. Buy some books and CDs. Shop on other sites and send for white papers and other documents offered on business-to-business sites.

Then go back and research your own business sector in depth. Become thoroughly familiar with your competitors' sites. See where they rank on each of the major search engines. Check their keywords and meta tags. Note their business partners, their lead-generation processes and offers. Subscribe to any newsletters they may have—and to the Web marketing newsletters listed at the end of this chapter. Then go find an ISP.

## Finding an ISP or Web Host

ISP stands for Internet Service Provider, and you can't get online without one. These are the folks who have phone lines connected to the Internet backbone. They provide the connection to your computer or network. Your computer must also be equipped with a modem.

Likely the quickest way to locate your local ISPs is to check the ads in the business section of your local newspaper, or ask other Web-savvy people in your area. Service quality can vary significantly from one ISP to another, so be sure to ask around and get other folks' experience. If you have a company MIS department, they'll have a valuable role to play in ISP selection and site implementation. Web hosts also advertise in the back of *Wired* magazine and several other popular computer publications.

As you might expect, there is also an online source: *http://thelist.internet.com*, which will guide you to about 7,500 ISPs listed by state. The search engine AltaVista (*www.altavista.com*) is offering free Web connections if you are willing to watch a bunch of advertising and reply to periodic surveys. Another major player in the free Web access/free e-mail game is Netzero.com.

Your ISP may very likely also be a Web host, and that may be your best choice. The ISP/host will also register your domain name–*www.yourcompany.com*. You'll want to check to see if your company name–or whatever domain name you prefer–is available. A quick way to check is to go to Network Solutions' InterNIC's registration site and their *Whois* service at *http://rs.internic.net/cgi-bin/whois*. Enter the domain name in the search box and see if it pops up. If not, it's yours. I suggest you line up at least a dozen or more domain candidates before you begin your search. You'll be surprised how many of your choices will be taken.

Keep your domain name as intuitive as possible. Avoid acronyms since most searchers won't think to use them. If your name is Acme Marine Products, for example, don't use *www.amp.com*, spell out the full name as in *www.acmemarineproducts.com* or *AcmeMarineProducts.com*. Also, if your company name is frequently misspelled, it would be wise to register the misspelled versions of your domain name as well as the correct one. Remember, you can have a .net extension as well as .com, and more extensions are becoming available, although for a while they're likely to be treated like bubonic plague by the "trendies" among us.

Network Solutions (at *www.internic.net*) was the original monopoly holder on registration of domain names, but that was recently changed, and now a number of companies share the domain booty. Alternatives to Network Solutions include Register.com, at *www.register.com*, and the Internet Domain Registrars's site, at *www.registrars.com*. As I said, your ISP or Web host service can also handle the registration for you. At this writing, Network Solutions' registration fee is $70 for two years. However, you may want to shop around for the best package of services, and to at least check your ISP's benefits and prices against industry norms.

To give you the flavor and an idea of what Web hosting components might consist of, following is a typical Web host offering that arrived in my e-mail:

> Line up at least a dozen or more domain candidates before you begin your search. You'll be surprised how many of your choices will be taken.

FREE E-COMMERCE IF YOU HOST WITH US!!

Tired of expensive e-commerce software, setup fees, and leasing contracts? Here is the deal: You host your site with us, and you get free E-Commerce, including a merchant account, real-time software, and shopping cart.

If you'd rather stay with your current hosting company, you still can get the same deal. Check it out first and make an informed decision.

- Your own merchant account with one of the lowest rates in the industry
- Accept Visa, MasterCard, American Express, and Discover
- Direct deposit within 48 hrs. into your checking account
- Shopping Cart storefront software with an easy-to-use Web based interface
- Real-Time Credit Card Processing software
- Virtual terminal for phone/fax/mail orders
- E-mail receipts
- Recurring billing feature
- Password generation for membership sites
- Automatic batch closing
- Address verification system (AVS)
- Back office to 24/7 access account history
- 50 MB (megabytes) of disk space
- 10 GB (gigabytes) of data transfer per month
- 15 POP3 E-mail accounts
- Unlimited alias E-mail addresses
- Your own E-mail server
- Live Web site statistics
- Unlimited FTP uploads (File Transfer Protocol, for placing files on your site)
- Anonymous FTP (A universal access to many FTP computer sites)
- Telnet access (UNIX) (A way to access your host server)
- CGI directory for your own scripts (An essential server program)

- Site control panel
- Installation included
- Tech support included

All this and more when you sign up for our E-Commerce Hosting plan for ONLY $69.95 per month and a one-time setup fee of $149.00.

NO LEASING, NO LONG-TERM COMMITMENT. YOU CAN CANCEL ANYTIME.

## Hire an Experienced Web Designer

For my money—and yours—this is the only way to fly. Web sites are written in a semi-programming language called HTML (Hypertext Markup Language), which is really a take on the old typesetting tags newspapers used to use. While HTML isn't all that difficult, your time is likely too valuable to be spent sitting through hours of HTML training. Then there's XML, HTML's big brother; Java, a programming language that isn't so easy; PDF files for document presentation; a variety of Web authoring tools; "back office" technologies; and more. If you do prefer to learn HTML yourself, you'll find support from the HTML Writers Guild, which has more than 100,000 members, at *www.hwg.org*.

If you're still determined to do it yourself, there are online resources you can use. One of these is Yahoo! Store (*www.store.yahoo.com*). The site claims to provide everything you need to get a Web store designed and running *in minutes*. Yahoo! charges $100 per month for putting it online, but there are no other charges. You'll also find a selection of free image files, or GIFs, at Media Builder (*www.mediabuilder.com*). The site offers tools to use for 3D banners and buttons, fonts, animated banners, and more.

Check local Web sites for particular examples you like and contact the designers who did them. Designers' contact information or live links can often be found at the very end of the Web page, or e-mail the site owner and ask who designed it. Your ISP may have designers they can refer to you. You may want to check with your

> While HTML isn't all that difficult, your time is likely too valuable to be spent sitting through hours of HTML training.

Chamber of Commerce (check *their* site) and speak with colleagues for recommendations. You should also make a list of sites you like with the features you think would be useful to your own site (see Comprehensive Web Site Checklist), both for your own understanding and as guidance for your designer. Design consultant Lynda Weinman dispenses Web wisdom on her Web site at *www.lynda.com*.

Keep in mind that designing and building the site is only half the job. Maintaining it is the other half. You'll need a trustworthy resource to keep your site updated. In-house is probably best, and if you can use the same person who designed it, all the better.

## Go Easy on the Bells and Whistles

It won't take you long to discover the wide range (which is getting wider all the time) of graphical tricks and techniques that are available, from blinking text to animated illustrations, sound and video files, and more. But go easy. Not every visitor to your site has the most advanced Web browser, and many of these trick ponies require special plug-in programs to activate them. That means asking your visitor to go to some third-party site to get the plug-in, which is B-O-R-I-N-G! If the plug-in is limited to one, you'd be well advised to make it available on your site. Adobe Acrobat is an example if you want to show PDF files, or Real Audio for sound files.

In addition, not everyone has the latest, greatest modem, and others may be far more interested in the text than the graphics and not thrilled with waiting around until the four-color shot of your factory completely downloads. Recent studies show that Web site visitors' patience is wearing thinner with time. Pages that take more than eight seconds to load are losing sales. It would be wise to have a "text-only" version of your site that will help people get what they want, pronto!

Just recently, I was looking for a particular piece of information on a Web site. It turned out to be about three or four layers down, which would have been OK if I didn't have to wait for their big, honking logo to reload on every page! You may want your name on every page for branding purposes. That's fine. But keep it small and fast-loading.

> Recent studies show that Web site visitors' patience is wearing thinner with time. Pages that take more than eight seconds to load are losing sales.

## The Seven Deadly Sins of Web Design

1. **Using frames.** While frames appear to eliminate some navigation issues by keeping more content immediately visible, they cause more problems than they solve. You can't bookmark a page with frames, they are often unprintable, and they create a very constricted feeling on the site, with areas of content confined to little windows requiring a lot of scrolling.

2. **Changing link colors.** The universally accepted scheme for links on the Web is blue for live hyperlinks that change to purple or red when they've been clicked. If you change any of those colors, you'll confuse people. As we know from direct mail, when people become confused, they back off and do nothing.

3. **Keeping outdated content on the site.** If you've ever surfed a site only to find everything dated 1997, you know you want to get out of there quick. Are these folks still in business, or is this a bit of junk floating in cyberspace? If your content will be up for more than a year, it's probably best to remove the dates, or extend the dates to the current year.

4. **Slow-loading graphics.** It's denounced in everything we read, but it still happens. Fancy graphic intros to your site that take more than 30 seconds to load only prompt visitors to click away. A resource that might help is GIF LUBE, at *www.websitegarage.com*. They claim to take some of the colors out of your graphics without substantially altering their appearance.

5. **No site map.** Especially if yours is a robust site with lots of stuff, a site map can help visitors get where they're going—and tip them off to some of the more desirable links on your site.

6. **Complicated URL.** Short names in lowercase make it easier for visitors to type in your URL, which many often have to do.

7. **Creating a Web-tech showcase.** As mentioned previously, streaming video and the latest MP3 hot rocks may seem cool to you, but they're likely a pain in the butt for the person who doesn't have all the plug-ins and other cutting-edge jazz in their browser.

> While frames appear to eliminate some navigation issues by keeping more content immediately visible, they cause more problems than they solve.

Every Web site is a constant work in progress, not something you finish and go on to other things. If your Web site is going to play a major role in your marketing plan, you'll likely need a Webmaster to keep it up and running and to update it regularly, which could mean daily or even hourly.

While the intricacies of Web site design are beyond the scope of this book, the following checklist will provide a guide to the features a well-designed site should contain. You may not be familiar with all the terms, and not every feature will be relevant to every site, but it would be wise to at least go through the list with your designer and decide how your site plan deals with each of the elements listed.

> If your Web site is going to play a major role in your marketing plan, you'll likely need a Webmaster to keep it up and running.

## Comprehensive Web Site Checklist

1. General
   A written Internet plan: purpose of the site, benchmarks, etc.
   URL: Descriptive domain name? Logical extensions?
   Loading time, first image (10 seconds, max.)
   Support multiple browsers?
   Site search test: company name; product/service category; product/service name

2. Opening Graphic and Text
   Communication of site purpose
   Quickly identifies market
   Attractive and inviting
   Minimize scrolling (800 × 600 screens)
   Heads/subheads (vs. long text)
   Critical information provided: email, phone, fax, address, contact, site URL, etc.

3. Content I (related directly to site's product/service)
   Targeted
   Quality
   Relevance
   Interactive event(s)

Content updating
Interactive device for new content notice

4. Copy
   Short bursts of text
   Comfortable line width and screen depth
   Interactivity
   Readability
   Stresses benefits
   Offers
   No errors (spelling, grammar)
   Interestingly written
   Link to separate document for printing or saving
   Printability
   Auto-responder for sending text to e-mail
   Feedback device on each page or segment
   Response to feedback
   Indicate number of pages or download time for lengthy documents

5. Graphics
   Clear and understandable
   Quick-loading (10 seconds max.)
   Relevant
   Alert reader to links to large graphics/documents
   Provide text-only alternatives
   Image map: helpful?
   Background
   Printing functionality

6. Links/buttons
   Link test
   Clearly identifiable (index)
   Navigability
   Relevance
   Distractions (off site, nonrelated links, etc.)
   Delineate clickable areas in image maps (text alternates)
   Title header on each page (accuracy?)

7. Security
    Online ordering
    Password-protected information
    Firewalls in place where needed
    Privacy policy in place

8. Netiquette
    Maintain polite good taste throughout
    Safeguard copyrighted materials and trademarks

9. Content II (related links and services)
    Targeted to market
    Unambiguous directions
    Relevance
    Controlled depth (three levels w/back and index links)
    Fun factor
    Content updating
    Interactive new-content notice

10. Direct Sales Sites
    Product info FAQs
    Appropriate products/services/price points
    "Sell" copy (hype level)
    Promises, benefits
    Proofs, testimonials
    Offer clarity
    Premiums
    Guarantee
    Call to action
    Accessible purchase engine (shopping cart)
        Clear instructions
        Easy to use
        Multiple purchase
        Secure transaction option
    Links or directions to further information
        E-mail option (update notice)

Logic of sequence
Return-visit incentives

11. Lead-Generation Sites
    Content quality
    Content quantity
    Offers:
        Primary
        Secondary
    Prospect-capture tool
    Logic of sequence
    Update notice
    Return-visit incentives
    Privacy policy

12. Customer Service Features
    New product announcements
    Technical reports/white papers
    FAQs
    Bulletin board
    Application information
    Sales and technical support contacts

13. Internet Tools
    Web-based bulletin board (newsgroup)
    Traffic monitoring (password to track visits?)
    Auto-responders
    E-mail buttons for updating
    Random picture rotation
    Audio
    Video/animation
    On-site search utility
    Mailing list applications (one-way, two-way)
    Other controlled-access applications

©The InterNauts®. Used with permission.

Navigation
Is Queen

If content is king on a Web site, navigation is queen, as the various elements listed previously might indicate. Lest you think this a matter of convenience, a survey of online buyers showed that:

90% of e-commerce sites are counter-intuitive, meaning things don't work the way users expect them to.
83 % of visitors leave e-commerce sites frustrated and empty-handed.
87 % were unable to successfully navigate most Web sites.
73 % could not find the product they were looking for.
68 % became frustrated by the number of clicks it took to find anything.
54 % just got lost.

Further findings showed that when people cannot navigate a particular site, they do not come back. Ideally, a visitor should be able to reach any destination on your site with just three clicks in a maximum of 30 seconds. And once you *get* them there, your next task is to *keep* them there!

For a comprehensive—if somewhat dated—guide to Web site planning and design, try the Sun Microsystems "cookbook" at *www.sun.com/styleguide*.

## The Four Cs of Web Design

I've maintained forever that the forerunner of today's direct marketing was the door-to-door salesman. The Electro-Lux guy would ring a doorbell and then offer to vacuum the prospect's carpets "FREE" and without obligation. Once set up inside, he took his good time vacuuming as he delivered his spiel. He knew that the longer he could stick around, the better his chances of a sale.

The same is true here, except now the "home" is a Web site, and the vacuum has morphed into a variety of online tools and techniques designed to keep visitors on a Web site as long as possible. It's called "stickiness," and the key is often referred to as the "Four Cs"—Content, Community, Communication, and Commerce. Let's look at each.

### C#1: Content

"Content is king!" has been the battle cry of the netizens ever since 1993, when Marc Andreesen fired up Mosaic, the first browser, and unleashed the graphical power of the Internet that became known as the World Wide Web. And so it is, especially for business sites. The larger consumer sites have exploded in the last few years in a paroxysm of games and quizzes, news stories, movie and TV schedules, software downloads, and free online utilities, like calendars and address books, all in an effort to keep people involved, keep them on the site longer, and bring them back.

Some of the news and utilities concepts may work for business-to-business sites, but you want to offer information more closely related to your product or service. Indeed, nothing has validated the lead-generating technique of offering valuable information free as much as have business-to-business Web sites.

White papers, special reports, articles by industry leaders, online surveys, interviews with customers—almost anything that adds value to your site and provides value to your customers and prospects is appropriate content for your Web site. Conventional wisdom says Web copy should be kept short and snappy, not requiring long reading time. A rule of thumb is to write about half the copy for a Web site that you would write in print. Pages should not exceed the depth of the computer screen in length, and they should have frequent subhead/hypertext links to break up the text. Better Web practice is to post a brief introduction or précis of an article with a link to the longer piece and give visitors the choice of whether to spend the time to read it online or download the full text.

On the other hand, for several years I have posted "how-to" articles on direct marketing on my own Web site that have met with great acceptance, judging from the e-mails I receive, and most of them are several pages long. Of course, they can be printed out and read at one's leisure. Nevertheless, I'll be shortening up my stuff going forward.

Most important, I add a new article each month. Keeping content fresh is almost as important as posting it. In fact, more so, since a moribund Web site suggests a company that may be out of business. You might be better off with no Web site rather than one that's never updated, unless it's a pure electronic billboard type of thing—which some organizations can use, so long as it's clear that's what it is. Prominent contact information with a request to call or e-mail for information would be critical in that instance.

### Online Response Forms

Whatever types of content you offer, some or all of it should require completion of an online response form to access. It may be better psychologically to allow visitors onto the site, where they can peruse material of interest as a way of establishing your bona fides, and require registration for admission to other, more valuable information. Most people have an aversion to completing a lengthy form and giving you their e-mail address before they can assess the pertinence of the site to their needs.

## Make Your Site Your Bizcentral.com

Starting with a product's FAQ (frequently asked questions), your Web site should be an accurate and reliable center of information, not only about your products, but maybe about your industry as well. Industry news, gathered from the trade publications that serve your sector (with appropriate and legal permissions and attributions), can make your site a central source of information for your prospects. A collection of links to related sites can make you a "mini-portal"—a place where visitors know they can connect with other sites that are important to them. (There are some trade-offs here in directing visitors off your site, but the increased traffic may make it worthwhile, and there are some software workarounds that can bring them back.)

The online response form is a document similar to the reply device you might include in a lead-generation direct mail package. It is designed to capture name and title, company, address, phone, e-mail address, and other pertinent points of information about anyone who wishes to receive your material. The more questions you ask, the fewer people will complete it, but those people will be better qualified (i.e., more interested in your site) than those who didn't. Be sure to include a checkbox for permission to send them your e-letter or special offers or product information, or whatever.

The material itself can be delivered several ways. You can send it instantly via e-mail with an auto-responder on the site, send the prospect a special URL where he or she can view the material and/or print it out, unlock a file that can be downloaded (a demo, for example), or send the document by conventional mail or fax. You'll also want to be able to export that prospect information to your marketing database.

### Privacy Matters

Note that if you collect information of any kind on your site, you'll need to have a privacy policy statement plainly visible. The Federal Trade Commission is cracking down on Websters who collect data and don't have a privacy statement. In Europe, too, privacy concerns are strict, so if you expect to do business with the European Union, you'll need a privacy policy. For an example of a statement that will pass muster with the FTC, point your browser to the Direct Marketing Association (DMA) site at *www.the-dma.org/policy.html* and download their policy model. Dr. Ralph Wilson also has policy samples on his voluminous Web site for marketers at *www.wilsonweb.com/webmarket/privacy.htm.*

Your customers care about privacy, too. But they are reasonable about it. They want to see your privacy statement clearly posted on your site. Beyond that, a recent study showed that 86% of online users surveyed believe that whether or not to reveal personal information should be an individual matter. Fifty three percent are willing to give marketers personal information if compensated by some form of gift or other benefit. Most (86%) believe that collecting information for marketing purposes is OK. Seventy nine percent are willing to

> Be sure to include a checkbox for permission to send them your e-letter or special offers or product information, or whatever.

trade the inconvenience of banner ads for a free product or service. Fifty nine percent think it's OK to provide e-mail addresses to reputable firms if the people are receiving freebies of some sort. Seventy five percent of Internet users surveyed (equal to 64 million adults) say they want online benefits in addition to good privacy policies.

Seth Godin calls this "Permission Marketing," which is also the title of his book (Simon & Schuster). Seth is among the latest to decry traditional advertising's uncertainty and unaccountability. He describes it all as "interruption marketing," which is precisely what he, you, and I must achieve in direct marketing to be effective. That notwithstanding, Godin recognizes the new paradigm of the Web, in which the customer is in charge of the dialog and advocates getting permission, through rewards, to market to the customer.

That, of course, is what basic lead generation has always been about—offering product/industry information of value in return for information about the prospect. But on the Web, we need to incorporate that concept into all of our points of contact, whether we're asking for very many specifics or not.

## C#2: Community
### The E-Letter
*Community* refers to any activities or devices that help people identify with your Web site and return regularly to obtain new information or interact with your company in some way. Once of the best tools for building community is the e-mail newsletter, or "e-letter." (See Chapter 16 for a discussion of e-letters.)

### Online Services and Utilities
Another way to keep visitors coming back is to offer them services while they're on your site that saves them the time and trouble of surfing elsewhere, like yellow pages and white pages directories. InfoUSA.com (*www.infoUSA.com*) offers both, FREE, plus a third database called "People Finder." When you go to Yahoo! or Microsoft's Web sites, the databases used there are from InfoUSA.com. Visitors won't even know they've left your site when they use it to search for businesses or friends and associates.

### Keep It Moving

Be careful what you date. If there is any possibility that content will not be updated in a timely manner, leave the date out. Better that new visitors not know how long it's been since material was posted than you should tell them you're asleep at the switch. Your regular visitors, alas, will know.

Other services you might consider for the convenience of visitors are an online calculator—especially if your field has special metrics—and an online or virtual desktop that provides users with an address book, to-do list, and appointment scheduler they can use from any computer with Web access.

## C#3: Communication

If "location, location, location" are the three most important factors of real estate success, "communicate, communicate, communicate" are the three most important aspects of a successful Web site. Providing ways for your customers/prospects to reach you is critical.

You can also make it possible for visitors to your site to recommend it to friends and colleagues. By registering your site with Recommend-It (*www.recommend-it.com*), your visitors click on the Recommend-It logo, fill out a quick form with an e-mail address, and click!—they've recommended your site to their friends. And it's FREE! (See Viral Marketing, Chapter 16).

Your e-mail address should be prominent on all key pages, with a live link that will call up an e-mail form for instant messaging.

### Complete Customer Service

When your competitor is just a mouse-click away, you'd be well advised to make sure customers can get the service they demand quickly and easily. Obvious as that may be, however, studies show that an amazingly high percentage of Web sites are still not providing even basic customer service.

In fact, one recent study of more than 700 e-commerce sites worldwide found that online shopping sites aren't all that customer-friendly. The study, conducted by the International Marketing Supervision Network, also found that:

- 62% of sites had no refund information.
- 75% had no privacy policy.
- 78% offered no information about submitting complaints.
- Over 50% had no security information about payments.
- 90% had no customer rights information.
- 25% had no physical contact address on the site.

> You can also make it possible for visitors to your site to recommend it to friends and colleagues.

Experienced online shoppers will use the presence or absence of these services as an indicator of the reliability of the site and the merchant. Inexperienced shoppers will look to these services for reassurance. Either way, they are as essential to online commerce success as the products themselves are. And not just the raw information about these services, but active links and quick-and-easy e-mail processes that permit the transactions.

## C#4: Commerce

*Commerce* refers to all the ways you make it easy for customers to do business with you. It includes the ability of customers to customize their order however they want. Dell is an outstanding example of that, with online sales of computers and peripherals of a breathtaking $16 million *per day*! (By now you probably know that's at *www.dell.com.*)

It means the ability of customers to track their orders online. (See FedEx.com or UPS.com for examples of great tracking.) But it also means sending customers an e-mail confirmation immediately upon purchase, perhaps with shipping details. It may mean giving your customers access to your parts inventory, detailed product information, pricing and payment terms, delivery schedules, links to business partners, an auction desk where you sell off surplus and date-sensitive merchandise, and, in today's tight job market, employment opportunities.

If you include warranty/registration cards with your products, make them available online and offer customers a premium if they go to the Web to complete them. Other e-commerce strategies include sending product and support information, product-use information, updates for the product they bought, new and related product announcements, and more.

It's always nice to say "thank you," especially in the consumer world. A "thanks for your business" e-mail can help you stand out from the crowd, and if it's accompanied by a certificate for $5 off the next purchase, it can invite another visit. Amazon.com does this with great success. E-mail can be an especially low-cost way to market low-margin products that would be too pricey to sell by phone.

### How to Interact With Visitors

On my own site, I have a "comment" box that allows visitors to ask a question or make a suggestion or any other type of comment as easily as typing it in a box. It does allow for anonymous entries since the commentator needn't include his or her name or e-mail address, but that hasn't been a problem. I also have an e-mail notifier for anyone who signs up to receive it, which sends an e-mail automatically whenever I make a change on the site. The software for this is at *www.netminder.com.*

Nothing is more aggravating to customers than expecting the immediacy of e-mail and getting the same old delays in response.

But be prudent in sending e-mails. Always include clear and prominent "unsubscribe" instructions at the top of your e-mails, and don't overdo them. Most businesspeople get a ton of e-mail for various reasons, much of it unwanted "spam," and you don't want to be tossed out with the bathwater.

You might want to coordinate with your vendors and suppliers to help refer leads, or even sales, to them. You might set up a database that signals suppliers to ship products automatically when inventories reach specified levels. And if you're a retailer, you might tie that system directly to your scanners. You might provide secure purchase orders with any of the growing crop of electronic payment options.

Whatever e-mail strategies you pursue, be sure you're set up to handle the increased traffic. Nothing is more aggravating to customers than expecting the immediacy of e-mail and getting the same old delays in response. It's a great way to lose business. Some companies are using software solutions to route inbound e-mails to their TSR/customer service reps. The reps respond to the e-mails during idle telephone time.

Product bulletins online, with or without e-mail notification; online seminars; allied software distribution; video conferencing; and customer chat or online discussion forums are some additional e-commerce options. Some of these may blur the lines between communication and commerce a bit, but if it relates directly to sales, it's commerce. The payoff for these various systems is a reduced cost of doing business that goes straight to the ROI.

### Plan It Again, Sam

Before you undertake any such e-commerce initiatives, survey your customers and meet with every department in your company to determine what your customers need and want (the answers may surprise you) how these systems will impact each department's operation, and how they can help facilitate their implementation and integration into your present plan of operations. Chances are, much of that plan will need to be revised.

### E-Commerce and E-Tailing

There are significant differences in scale between the commerce-related applications you may place on an information-oriented or lead-generation Web site and a full bore e-commerce or retail ("e-tailing" in Web parlance) Web site designed to sell products online.

The majority of e-commerce sites now on the Web are extensions of either "bricks and mortar" stores or existing print catalogs. That may change as we go forward, but for now the primary challenge is to identify, evaluate, and implement the most effective software solutions for your needs: bringing your business to the Web, showing products, communicating with customers, and providing such other customer services as handling returns. Most critical of all is the need to provide a seamless integration among the customer/prospect data that's gathered online, your offline data counterparts, and your marketing database.

Indeed, most of the labor costs cited above are incurred in the task of getting all the diverse parts of the company—marketing, IS, accounting, etc.—to work together and with the Web interface. It often means changing the way you do business.

With the Web's 24/7 availability, you may experience some new pressures in 24-hour order entry and fulfillment, as well as customer service. Also, with your competition just a mouse-click away, you may find your online customers a tad more price-sensitive than the offline variety, but those are problems you can solve fairly easily.

Other key processes include secure credit card transactions, shopping cart technology, order entry and fulfillment, inventory control, and, with the wealth of data available on Web sites, programs to analyze visitor/customer traffic patterns through your site, and a rich variety of other metrics.

Start small if you need to with one of the template or syndicated Web store/catalog suppliers on the Web and progress toward a fully customized site as you build brand-awareness online and work the kinks out of your back office and support. However you choose to start, the point is to start—and build critical mass as quickly as possible. Forrester Research projects online retail revenues of over $100 billion by 2001. You'll need to be there, if only to protect your brand from the online onslaught.

**E-Commerce Costs—Big Time!**

Forrester Research, Inc., puts development costs for a business-to-business e-commerce site at $1.5 million for what they call a "basic" site up to $15 million for top-of-the-line sites, with an additional $700,000 per year in maintenance cost for a basic site and up to $4 million a year for a high-end site. Most of those costs are for labor, Forrester says.

Two companies providing full-service support for e-tailing and online cataloging are R.R. Donnelley Online Services (*www.goselectsource.com*) and Millard Group Interactive (*www.millard.com*). A major catalog-enabling site is Catalog City, which has more than 600 catalogs at this writing, at *ww.catalogcity.com*. You may also want to visit Shop.org, an online retailing association, at *www.shop.org*.

### An ROI for the Rest of Us

To help you calculate your investment and likely return from a less lofty Web site, the following pro forma worksheet was prepared by Gary Cloutier, Regional Manager of the Small Business Development Center at Keene State College, Keene, New Hampshire. It is offered on page 271 with his permission.

### Internet, Intranet, or Extranet?

For some of these e-commerce tools, you might want to explore the construction of an Intranet or Extranet. An Intranet is typically configured for internal use only. It's much like a Web site, except access is strictly controlled by firewalls and passwords and limited to employees and selected others. An Extranet is similar, but it looks outward to include suppliers, vendors, and business partners. Your ISP/Web host, company MIS department, and Web designer can help you explore these options.

### Application Service Providers: McWebsite?

Today, a new breed of Internet provider is emerging, in the form of syndicated Web services known as Application Service Providers (ASPs) that an e-commerce site can subscribe to. If you buy into the full range of services, you can point-and-click your way from a choice of templates to a more or less customized portal all your own that combines internal information with outsourced content. In some cases, these sites can also take the place of a more costly Extranet.

"The Epicentric Portal Server product family," states the site, "allows total ownership from a hosting, branding, and design perspective. The Epicentric portal desktop provides quick, easy, and secure

> For some of these e-commerce tools, you might want to explore the construction of an Intranet or Extranet.

**ROI Model for Web Businesses**
Enter the information requested in the blocks below and
an estimate of ROI on your web investments will be made

This model is designed for an existing "bricks and mortar" business to analyze
its investment in a new web based business unit

**The goal of this worksheet is to:**
Understand the concept of true cost of doing business on line
Establish realistic goals
To determine if you are ready to proceed
Manage your business' ROI

1 Initial Cost of Site                                 $2,000

2 Your Cost of Captial                                 9.00%

3 Major (Semi Annual) Upgrade                          $1,000

4 Gross Margin on Products you're selling              40.00%
  (WAGM)  Weighted Average Gross Margin

|                                          | Qtr 1  | Qtr 2  | Qtr 3  | Qtr 4  |
|------------------------------------------|--------|--------|--------|--------|
| 5 Sales in next 4 qtrs                   | 8,000  | 17,000 | 21,000 | 24,000 |
|   due to the Internet enterprise         |        |        |        |        |
| *Gross Profit of Web Business*           | 3,200  | 6,800  | 8,400  | 9,600  |
| 6 Increased Infra-structure costs        | 2,000  | 1,000  | 1,000  | 1,000  |
| 7 Increased Operations                   | 1,000  | 1,000  | 1,000  | 1,000  |
| 8 Increased GSA                          | 1,000  | 500    | 500    | 500    |
| 9 Increased Training                     | 500    | 500    | 500    | 500    |
| 10 Site Maint Cost                       | 1,000  | 1,000  | 1,000  | 1,000  |
| 11 Increased Promotional Costs           | 1,000  | 1,000  | 1,000  | 1,000  |
| *Total Expenses due to Web Business*     | 6,500  | 5,000  | 5,000  | 5,000  |
| *Gross Profit (Loss) of Web Business*    | -3,300 | 1,800  | 3,400  | 4,600  |

**Return on Web Investment    11.61%**

Please see supplemental notes on pg. 272.

## Notes to ROI Worksheet

1.  The initial cost of the Web site includes hardware purchases, design, legal cost, programming, de-bugging the programming, re-design and any other cost associated with getting the site up and running. Don t forget the PR cost of launching the site like increased advertising and mailings, etc.

2. Your cost of capital is the cost you incurr to borrow money. For instance, if you take out a bank loan at 9% to finance your web business, your cost of capital is 9%. Even if you finance the Web site from cash, however, that does not mean your cost of capital is zero. Ask yourself, what would my money be earning if it weren t invested in the Web? Even if it was only in a savings account, that s 2% to 3% that you re not earning.

3. It is assumed that the site will need a major upgrade every 6 months or so.

4. What is the average Gross Profit Margin for your products? If you re in retail, that number is probably in the range of 40-50%.

**For Items 5 through 10, it is expected that figures are broken down for each of the next four quarters:**

5. Project the sales you think you may be able to achieve over the internet BE REALISTIC.

6. Infra-structure refers to hardware and other equipment and technology costs needed to support your Web business. This could include computers, extra shipping equipment, etc.

7. Operations cost refers to staff, increased rent for warehouse space, additional overhead, etc.

8. GSA means General, Sales, and Administrative cost. Include here the cost of promoting the Web site, increased sales staff, and other costs associated with generating and processing orders.

9. Training includes the cost of training your staff and yourself in new technology and business practices. This cost should include not just the basic cost of classes, etc., but also the time lost from work, travel and other areas.

10. Site Maintenance includes programming, design service, monthly ISP or other hosting fees, and any other recurring cost of providing the Web site.

access to the widest range of services, applications, content, and commerce available." Or so they claim. Check it out at *www.epicentric.com.*

Many ASPs are emerging in specialty areas. Bridgepath.com provides womb-to-tomb services for executive recruiters. In construction, buzzsaw.com offers "business-to-business e-commerce and collaboration services for everyone in design and construction."

Another Intranet service, perhaps for smaller companies, is HotOffice.com. Designed to help team members work collaboratively, HotOffice provides document sharing, group calendars, contact managers, bulletin boards, company chat rooms, Web-based e-mail, and more—all of which can be accessed from any computer with a modem. You pay a monthly fee and avoid a lot of MISery and cost. Staples is a major investor. They're at *www.hotoffice.com.*

And for the *really* small business or free agent, there's Comercis. Comercis offers a menu designed to get you out of yourself and join a business community with a free Web site. It includes multiple pages with special content like catalogs and service listings, the ability to post forms, documents, files, and more. Services also include "Cybermovers" who help you with move-in, management, maintenance, and relocation. You'll find these folks at *www.comercis.com/fastcompany.*

Other small business services designed to help merchants create a low-cost online store include Sitematic Express (*www.sitematic.com*), Virtual Office (*www.netopia.com/software/nvo*), Yahoo! Store (*www.store.yahoo.com*), and Bigstep.com (*www.bigstep.com*).

### Focus on the Process, Not the Place

Whatever you do with your Web site, don't forget why you're building it—to serve customers. Seth Godin, who we quoted at the beginning of this chapter, tells the story of wanting to refinance his house. He went to General Electric Company's Web site and had to click his way through 17 pages of stuff before he found the refinance page, only to be told to call the 800 number. "Corporate Web sites should be only two or three pages long," Godin says. "Companies are spending tons of money building a place rather

> Whatever you do with your Web site, don't forget why you're building it— to serve customers.

than a process. Build the process first. The place is irrelevant because there are always places that are going to be cooler, hipper, and more fun than yours." Great advice. (Quoted in *CIO Web Business*, 1/8/99)

I'm not sure I agree that place is irrelevant, even if there are places cooler than mine. I fully expect that to be the case. Content is what people go online for, and if the content is relevant and valuable, they'll come back. Of course, the process that gives them access to that content surely must come before the bells and whistles, just as copy in direct marketing takes precedence over design.

## Getting the Word Out: How to Promote Your Site

### Traditional Methods

> Starting with an announcement mailing to your house list, direct mail is an excellent way to tell people about your Web site.

While the temptation to use electronic means exclusively to promote your site with their "almost free" costs may be powerful, I believe traditional methods will have greater impact over time.

The very first traditional promotion tactic is to be sure your Web site URL is on everything you send out—your business card, stationery, brochures, e-mail signature. Anywhere your company name, address, and phone number appear should also bear your Web site address.

Starting with an announcement mailing to your house list, direct mail is an excellent way to tell people about your Web site. This could be as simple as an oversized postcard featuring the URL in some imaginative way, or it could be a personal letter from you. Indeed, a postcard a month, especially in the first year, would not be overkill by any means. Let each announce a new feature or reason to visit.

One reason traditional media can be very effective in promoting your site is due to the virtual nature of the Web itself. Let's face it, it isn't there. It isn't here, either. Where is it? Do you really know? It's "out there" in cyberspace, whatever that is. And we've all had the experience of revisiting a site after a while only to find that's it's "not found," or the links are broken, or it hasn't been touched in two years.

By sending attractive, hold-it-in-your-hand direct mail, you affirm your presence on and off the Web. You prove to people you exist, you show that you're thinking about them, and that you want them to visit—and you can tell them why they should. (As I was writing this, a self-mailer arrived from Flycast, the online media agency. It's a promotion for their advertising services and includes an engaging wheel chart I can use to determine ROI at various response rates and CPMs. Very solid, highly credible.)

## Search Engines and Directories

Search engines are an exercise in frustration, but since some 85% of first-time visitors arrive at your site via the search engines, you need to know how to get listed. The frustration comes in trying to come up in the mythic "top 10" on one or more of the major engines.

Search engines are actually robot-type programs—often called "spiders" because they crawl around the Web—that automatically catalog Web pages by saving key data to their hard drive based on the criteria they are given. Like monkeys sweeping through the treetops in a rainforest, spiders sweep through Web pages following the links. Directories, on the other hand, are built by humans. Sites are submitted, reviewed by directory staffers, and assigned a position in a particular category. AltaVista is an example of a popular search engine, while Yahoo! is the largest and best known of the directories. There are also some hybrids that combine elements of both, and so-called "metasearch" engines that provide a single point of access to several major engines. MetaCrawler, Ask Jeeves, and Dogpile are examples of metasearch engines.

To give you an idea of how the Web's growth is rapidly outpacing the ability of the search engines to keep up, following are the percentages of Web coverage the major engines track:

Northern Light, 16%

SNAP, 15.5%

AltaVista, 15.5%

### Search Engine Stats

- 85% of visitors to a Web site are referred by search engines.
- 97% of search engine searchers never go beyond the first three pages listed.
- 84% of Web pages are not listed in any major search engine.

(NEC Research Institute, 1999)

HotBot, 11%

Microsoft/MSN, 8.5%

Google, 7.6%

Yahoo!, 7.4%

Excite, 5.6%

Lycos, 2.5%

(Source: MediaMatrix)

> Search engine positioning must be an integral part of any Web site's promotion strategy.

Nevertheless, search engine positioning must be an integral part of any Web site's promotion strategy. Each search engine has its own listing form on the site, but before you submit your site, you need to do some homework.

### Keywords and Meta Tags

While each search engine has its own protocols for collecting and cataloging Web sites, one of the principal ways common to most is through the keywords that appear toward the top of each home-page and, in some instances, on all the pages on a site. Go to any Web site and click on the View/View Page or View Source button, and you'll see the keywords and meta tags on the page, normally invisible when viewing the site through the browser. You want as many relevant keywords at the top of your site as you can think of. One designer I know has clients list 250 keywords, then cut that list to 50, then to 10 to get the most descriptive, on-target words possible for the site.

Search engines rank sites through a complex formula that begins with:

- The keywords in a site's title
- The site's content
- The number of times keywords appear on the page (but too many times can trigger the engine's reject button!)

- The proximity of keywords to each other and to the top of the page
- The popularity of the site as indicated by the number of other sites that are linked to it, and other factors

Get your Webmaster or designer to help you develop your list of keywords. Visit your competitors' sites and see what keywords they are using. Be sure you include those on your site. And ask yourself: what keywords would you enter in a search engine to find yourself?

Also prepare a 100-word, 50-word, and 20-word description of your Web site. Some search engines ask for it. A site called Submit-It (*www.submit-it.com*) will provide the interface to allow you to submit your site yourself to about 400 search engines by keying in the information just once. A free service once upon a time, the site is today part of Microsoft. You can purchase a search-engine submission license, which costs $59 per year and up, depending on the levels of service you prefer. The site has a number of other services as well, plus useful "Search Engine Tips" you can access for free, and a free trial of Submit-it.

Better yet, don't do it yourself. Search-engine positioning is a time-consuming, tedious task, even to do once. Fact is, the search engines periodically dump a certain percentage of their sites in order to make room for new listings. They also change the rules frequently, so what may have worked last month doesn't work this month. It is necessary to resubmit your site several times a year to be sure you're being picked up.

> Search-engine positioning is a time-consuming, tedious task, even to do once.

## Websourcing: A New Basket of Services

I hope your time is too valuable to spend updating your search-engine registrations (like the newsletter publisher who proudly boasted to me that he had written his own subscription letter—it only took him all summer!). You'll be much better off, time-wise and head-wise, to outsource the whole search-engine dance to someone who knows the steps. Indeed, many Web-based activities, like Web hosting, software applications, customer relationship management, Web services, and online delivery are rapidly moving into a new mix of services dubbed "Websourcing," not unlike the Application Service Providers described earlier. It includes Web hosting, link exchanges, search engine updating, banner placement and monitoring, and more.

Even if you use one of the autosubmission services, back it up periodically by having your own person keep close track of the changing rules and resubmit your site by hand. The NEC report cited previously maintains that it takes an average of 186 days for a search engine to include a new Web page in its results. You'll find help with all this from the guru of search engines, Danny Sullivan, at *www.searchenginewatch.com.*

An expert search engine placement service with which I'm familiar is Web Site Publicity.com. They offer a variety of basic and customized placement plans at *www.websitepublicity.com.*

## Words Are Us: Hop aboard a Keyword

Another way to get search engines working for you is to purchase keywords on search-engine sites that call up your banner ad whenever someone enters that keyword. If you were in the pet-supply business, for example, you might purchase the keywords "cats" and "dogs" on, say, Lycos. Each time a person on the Lycos site entered either "cats" or "dogs," your special banner ad would appear, promoting your Cat Obedience School with a "click here" button as a call to action. People would click the banner and go straight to your Web site.

A few drawbacks to keyword purchases are that they are pricey and the most desirable ones are often taken. For most common keywords you may have a waiting period until the person using it drops the contract.

## Reciprocal Links

In addition to boosting your site's popularity index with the search engines, reciprocal links with other sites make good sense for many reasons. Reciprocal linking simply means "you link to my site and I'll link to yours." I've linked my site to other direct marketing-related sites, such as DirectMailQuotes.com, which provides printing quotes to direct marketers, and *ThinkDirectMarketing.com,* which pro-

> Even if you use one of the autosubmission services, back it up periodically by having your own person keep close track of the changing rules and resubmit your site by hand.

vides a large list database. I've backed off adding links just for the sake of adding links, however. (There's even a service that will link your site to 1,700 "Free For All" sites.) I'd rather maintain the quality of my site at the cost of some popularity.

Microsoft also maintains the Web site MSN Link Exchange (*www.linkexchange.com*), which offers more than 20 services and links for starting and managing a Web site from registration to search-engine positioning, banner advertising, and more. Indeed, the link exchange service is almost hidden by all the other offerings on the site. Lots of helpful stuff, nonetheless.

## Affiliate Programs

Affiliate Programs are pay-per-click arrangements you make with other sites who direct traffic to your site. If your site is funded by advertising, an affiliate program can help boost your eyeball count. If the affiliate site is closely related, you may not suffer much loss of quality. You can also pay per lead or pay per sale, depending on the types of sites and relationships you can develop. A typical pricing structure might be 25¢ per click, $5 per lead, and $20 per sale, or a percentage of the selling price.

Here's the deal, for example, for the Biztoolsplus.com Affiliate Program:

I agree to place a Biztoolsplus.com link on my Web site. That's my "private-labeled" or "co-branded version" of the Biztoolsplus content.

If my site gets 10,000 to 50,000 visitors each month (defined as visitors to the page that displays the link to Biztoolsplus.com), I get a $100 sign-up bonus and 50% of the ad revenue from my cobranded version of the Biztoolsplus banner on my site.

- 50,000 to 150,000 visitors per month earns a $200 cash bonus and 55% of ad revenues.
- 150,000 to 250,000 visitors per month earns $300 cash and 60% of revenues.
- 250,000 to 500,000 visitors per month earns $400 and 70% of revenues.
- 500,000+ qualifies for a $500 bonus and 70% of ad revenues.

> If your site is funded by advertising, an affiliate program can help boost your eyeball count.

A site that helps create and manage Affiliate Programs is LinkShare (*www.linkshare.com*). Here you'll find descriptions of Affiliate Marketing Programs, a Merchant Information Center, and more.

## Banner Ads

Banner ads are those 1" × 5" mini-billboards that grace the tops of most Web sites. Although the copy space is severely limited, they can change panels to deliver a message in quick stages or even by alternating two or three words, like "Eat/At/Mom's," and some have a small "click here." The "click here" button is as important to a banner ad as the call to action is to a direct mail piece. Giving people directions pays off in greater response. Click on the banner, and you're suddenly transported to the Web site for Mom's Diner. (That action equals one "clickthrough.")

Technically, banners are known as GIF files. As with Web sites, and with the same caveats, they can flash and blink, be animated, and include drop-down menus, sound files, and more. There are also "tile ads," two-inch squares that nestle along the sides of Web pages.

There is a lot of theory around the creation of banner ads, some of it backed by clickthrough statistics and some not. Animated ads, not surprisingly, receive higher rates of clickthroughs than static ads. As with print advertising, it's still best to lead with benefits. Mom's, for example, might lead with "Deeply Delicious, Blue Ribbon Pies" and flip to a panel featuring a pie graphic with a blue ribbon attached. Animation might have a mouthwatering wedge of pie coming up and out toward the viewer. That's more likely to get juices flowing than Mom's name. At these smaller dimensions the illustration possibilities are somewhat limited, but you can achieve interesting results nonetheless.

Despite the fact that clickthrough rates have been declining in the last few years, from well over 10% to around 2% and often less (funny how that 2% keeps popping up), there is evidence that banner advertising will continue to grow in the years ahead. No doubt that applies primarily to the large portal sites that attract millions of page views a day. However, so long as the concept of banner advertising is validated by the "bigs," smaller sites should be able to claim their

> Animated ads, not surprisingly, receive higher rates of clickthroughs than static ads.

piece of the action, especially if they can demonstrate strong niche or vertical market interest. Many site owners report a majority of their page views coming from banner ads.

A Forrester Research, Inc., study states that ad spending on the Web will triple by 2004 to more than $22 billion per year, but the emphasis will switch from cost-per-thousand pricing to cost-per-click or even cost-per-sale. That may put smaller niche marketers in an even better position relative to the MSNs and Yahoo!s if they can deliver clicks and sales through accurate targeting, just as direct marketers have done with direct mail.

There are agencies that specialize in banner ad creation, and others that do them as part of their larger creative or media services. They can blink and shout and even sell products directly. To experience the possibilities for yourself, go online and click on a few dozen banners.

If you are good with graphics programs, there are a number of programs that will allow you to create banner ads, from the paint programs that come with some word processors to Adobe Photoshop. You can get a knowledgeable view of banner advertising at *www.microscope.com*, a Z-Net (Ziff-Davis) site.

Banner ads are given to what is known as "banner fatigue," which simply means they wear out quickly. You'll want to plan not just one ad for each placement, but a series of graphics and copy approaches for any one offer or message that can be rotated on a site, so the banner always looks fresh.

If you're going to spend serious money on banner advertising, you'll want to buy the ads through a Web agency that sells and places them and provides comprehensive reports on numbers of impressions (clickthroughs) and other metrics, including those who complete an inquiry form and buy. They can also manage the banner rotation mentioned earlier.

One of the major providers of banner ad services, which grew out of the direct marketing field, is Web Connect, which bills itself as "The ad placement service of the Internet." They're at *www.webconnect.com*. Three other ad networks are FlyCast (*www.flycast.com*), BURST! Media (*www.burstmedia.com*), and

> Banner ads are given to what is known as "banner fatigue," which simply means they wear out quickly.

> By inserting a banner into your Web page, you automatically display advertisements for other members and, in return, your banners are displayed across the member network.

DoubleClick (*www.doubleclick.net*). These agencies can also represent you to other Web sites, of course, if you have the numbers to sell advertising on your site. Those numbers don't have to be huge, by the way. If you can attract specialty or niche marketers, you may be able to do very well.

## Free Banner Exchange

Just as you can exchange links with other sites, so can you exchange banner ads. Exchange-It.com seeks to use the combined advertising power of a large network of Web sites to promote your site. It's a free service designed to help sites trade banner ads with each other. By inserting a banner into your Web page, you automatically display advertisements for other members and, in return, your banners are displayed across the member network. Get full details at *www.exchange-it.com*. But be careful with this, or any "free" Web service, about what happens to your name and e-mail address after you've signed up. You may find yourself the unwitting target of all manner of advertisers as a result of giving this or that site good targeting information. (On the other hand, if it is well targeted, the information might be valuable.) Two other sites that handle banner ad exchanges are Link Exchange (mentioned earlier) and Smart Age (*www.smartage.com*). Smart Age especially is an expeditor of free banner exchanges. For example, if you sell golf balls, Smart Age will find a site selling golf clubs and arrange an exchange, meanwhile placing their own banner on both of your sites.

## Proprietary Banners

These are banners you run on your own site to promote something located on another page on your site. In addition to providing a link to a special offer, highlight the offer in a banner ad on your most popular page—probably your homepage. Offering a free newsletter? Instead of, or in addition to, a "Subscribe To Our Free Newsletter" link, a banner ad could announce "Industry news and events, FREE! Click here," perhaps with an animated GIF of a turning newspaper page. Alternate such a banner message with "Special reports and studies" and "Hot links to the latest industry Web sites!"

## Direct Marketing Banners

One reason for the decline in banner ad clickthroughs is undoubtedly the fact that clicking on a banner takes you off the site you presumably wanted to be on. Then you have to backtrack or even re-enter the URL of the original site to get back to it. Direct marketing banners don't do that. Click on a direct marketing banner, and you may get a signup form for more information, or an entry form for a sweepstakes, or a contest invitation, or *something* that prompts a response—without leaving the host site. These are new at this writing, so there are no performance stats yet.

## Mailing Lists and Newsgroups

One of the guerrilla methods of promoting your site is to join any number of mailing lists and/or newsgroups and participate in the daily dialogs. A mailing or discussion list is an e-mail-enabled community of people who message one another in response to an ongoing discussion on the mailing list's topic of interest. The list (also known as a "Listserv," named after the software that runs many of them) is usually moderated, either by a live person or by the program. Most are free, but some are fee-based. There are about 70,000 discussion lists on the Net on every topic imaginable. For a list of available lists, point your browser to *www.listz.com*. Another source of list information is at *http://net.gurus.com/lists*.

Newsgroups are similar in that they are e-mail communities that discuss matters related to a particular topic area. The technology is different, in that mailing-list messages go straight to your e-mailbox, while newsgroup messages go to your ISP's server, where they can be read by your browser's news reader. Each ISP determines which newsgroups it is going to carry. Deja News (*www.dejanews.com*) is the prime source of newsgroup listings.

In either case, you'd be best advised to tread carefully. One thing both these groups hold as anathema is the commercialization of their medium. And while things have loosened up some, you'll want to avoid coming on like a jerk interested only in promoting yourself and your site. You're likely to touch off a series of "flames"—

> One of the guerrilla methods of promoting your site is to join any number of mailing lists and/or newsgroups and participate in the daily dialogs.

nasty, nasty e-mails, maybe hundreds of them, telling you in no uncertain terms where you went wrong. You could even evoke an e-mail "bomb," which is an attack of e-mails so severe it could crash the server and your ISP would be very, very mad at you. A brief description of your company in your e-mail signature is about as much promotion as the culture will accept. Following is the signature I use on all my e-mail messages, and it constitutes the "promotion" element of any message I might post to a mailing or discussion list. You should have a similar signature for your business, even if you're not participating in discussion lists.

> Duncan Direct Associates
> —Since 1976—
> Copy, consulting, and creative support for direct mail marketing and response advertising in all formats.
> *http://www.duncandirect.com*
> Voice: 603-924-3121 Fax: 603-924-8511
> 16 Elm Street, Peterborough, NH 03458

Find the newsgroups and discussion lists that are related to your topic area and "lurk" for a while. That is, follow the conversation for a few weeks and get the flavor of the discussion before you jump in. Each has very specific rules for participation. Newsgroups carry FAQs—Frequently Asked Questions—for "newbies" to read and be cautioned thereby.

It was in the newsgroups that terms like "spam," "flame," and "mail bomb" originated, and they're all still very much alive, thank you. That said, there are some very large discussion lists out there, and if you approach them properly, you'll meet some interesting people, make worthwhile business connections, and maybe even learn a few things.

It would be a stretch, but if yours is a field for which there is no listserv, you might want to start one of your own. There are several Web sites that host mailing lists, paid for by ads on the site or by "sponsorship" messages added to the e-mails. Check out *www.listbot.com, www.onelist.com, www.egroups.com*, and *http://list-tips.com/archives/list-resources*.

> Find the newsgroups and discussion lists that are related to your topic area and "lurk" for a while. That is, follow the conversation for a few weeks and get the flavor of the discussion before you jump in.

Running your own discussion list can pay off in a number of ways. If the list is large enough, you can sell classified ads or sponsorships to help defray costs. You also spark interest in your product or service, which may lead to added sales. It's a quick way to announce new products and services and get (favorable) word-of-mouth advertising started. It can provide customer support and/or become a forum for your dealers, resellers, business partners, and others.

## Traffic Report: Counting the Eyeballs

One of the most important ways of determining where your Web site needs improvement is to analyze the traffic patterns through it. You can do this with the help of the log files maintained by your ISP or Web-hosting service at the server.

Initially, the method of determining a Web site's "circulation," if you will, was to count "hits." A hit was each and every click a visitor made on a Web page, and it was multiplied by every file, graphic or otherwise, on the page. As tracking software became more sophisticated, hits soon became irrelevant as the focus shifted to knowing not just how many visitors come to a site, but how they travel through the site, page by page.

The current method is to count "page views." A page view is registered each time an HTML page is called up from the server, but usually only the first time. For example, if I click on your homepage "A," move on to page "B," and then return to "A," my return visit may not be clocked, since my browser stored page A in a cache the first time and pulled it from there on the second visit, rather than from the server.

Nevertheless, your Web host's log files provide an illuminating road map of how people enter your site and from where, which pages they visit, how long they stay on each, and from which page they exit. As you can see, this is very useful information for reworking your pages for maximum effect. If visitors are viewing your offer but not reaching your information request form, for example, you might move the form forward to the offer page or test more compelling offers.

There are also a number of outside services on the Web that will provide software or direct service tracking of your site traffic with a

### Shoestring Tip

Included among the services listed on *www.cio.com/ resources/SiteMgte.html* is HitBOX Tracker, a free "Site Analyzer." HitBOX comes in two flavors, a basic free service that provides some 500 statistics on your site's traffic, plus an enhanced paid service. The basic service requires you to place a button on your site. The enhanced service does not.

variety of useful reports. Since these vendors change frequently, your best bet would be to query the search engines for "Web traffic tools" or something similar. One current site that provides a comprehensive list of services is *www.cio.com/resources/SiteMgte_trackers.html*. The site provides links to more than 30 sources for analysis tools, plus articles, companies and services, and site counters and trackers.

## Outsourcing Site Services

Most of the site services and chores mentioned in this chapter can be outsourced. From creating and placing banner ads, to ad and link exchanges, search-engine placement and monitoring, traffic reports, and mailing-list management, there are sites able to provide what you need. Some are free (with the list-building caveat I mentioned earlier), and some charge nominal monthly fees for each of a basket of services in the hope you'll find it easier to let them do them all rather than hassling with them yourself.

I highly recommend you seek these sites out (e.g., Smart Age) and give them serious consideration. If you're a super-techie, fine. You may be able to handle it. But if you're an average businessperson trying to run a company, you'll likely find these services far more cost-effective than doing it yourself. And if you're reading this chapter to learn about the Web, you're likely not in a position to take on all those tasks alone. Many Web marketers find they need a Webmaster.

From creating and placing banner ads, to ad and link exchanges, search-engine placement and monitoring, traffic reports, and mailing-list management, there are sites able to provide what you need.

For more information on this topic, visit our Web site at www.businesstown.com

# E-Mail Marketing: The Other Side of the Net

It should surprise no one that the e-mail channel has gotten marketers' juices flowing, especially when you consider the low cost per message and the high general usage of what has been called the "killer app" of the Internet. Little wonder, when the Electronic Messaging Association reports that 30+ million people have used e-mail in the last 24 hours.

In fact, according to the eMail Marketing Report (2/00), there will be 135 million e-mail users by the end of 2002, or 59% of U.S. adults and teens. Opt-in e-mail volume is expected to reach 240 million messages by 2003, with total e-mail marketing expenditures projected to $4.6 billion that same year. Those ain't just howdies!

As of now, however, marketing via e-mail lists has a way to go. E-mail is still considered very private, and most recipients regard any form of commercial messages or other unsolicited e-mail as an intrusion, also known as "spam." The biggest challenges to e-mail advertising are accurate "opt-in" targeting and distinguishing your message from spam, even when it's sent to people who requested it. The big advantage, of course, is the cost, especially for your own house lists. There's no postage or paper, and no folding or inserting to do; just compose and click. This gives marketers the unfortunate tendency to play it a little loose in their definitions of who they can and should send e-mail to.

> The biggest challenges to e-mail advertising are accurate "opt-in" targeting and distinguishing your message from spam, even when it's sent to people who requested it.

## Create an E-Letter

Just about anything you would put in a promotional newsletter (as described in Chapter 7) can be adapted to an e-letter. In this case, you really do want to keep articles brief and to the point, consistent with e-mail culture. Think telegram. Ideally, your newsletter should refer readers to your Web site, where readers can get the complete story or additional details. Each item can be accompanied by the URL for that page on your site. The free sharing of information is also part of Internet culture, so don't hesitate to provide links or references to items of interest on other sites.

E-letters are a particular application of the permission-marketing concepts described previously, in that we need to get the customer/prospect's permission to send it. Create a signup form on your Web site and have a sample of what they'll get (e.g., an "archive" of back issues) available for visitors to view.

If you have an e-mail address and you're *sure* the e-letter is *very* targeted to that person's interests (not just *your* interest in getting them on the file), you might try to send it unsolicited, but you'll be taking a big chance on being confused with "spam"—the evocative name for unsolicited e-mail. If you do send it unrequested, be sure to lead with a statement that makes it quick and easy for the reader to "unsubscribe," right then and there—not via a Web site or a phone number that rings only at the Arctic Circle. A brief apology in advance in case they're not interested might actually head off the cancellation.

Make it clear as well what the letter has to offer (why they should not unsubscribe), and if you can provide some form of physical bonus gift, all the better. Don't, don't, don't try to con people by telling them they're receiving this letter because they subscribed or requested info or whatever. That just insults their intelligence and makes you a liar. One thing that never pays off in response marketing is obtaining a response through any type of subterfuge. Anyone responding is not just unqualified, he or she is anti-qualified!

If you're going to be using those e-mail addresses to market products and services—the ultimate purpose of collecting them—you want those folks as warmly disposed to you as possible. In e-commerce terms, you want them to "opt-in" to receive e-mails.

"Opt-in" refers to the practice of obtaining the recipient's permission to send e-mail, thus creating a list of people who have "opted-in" to the list. The first distinction to be made here is between opt-in lists of those who have agreed to receive *any and all* e-mail and those who have agreed to receive *your* e-mail. Frankly, I have to wonder about the sanity of the first group, and I can't see myself recommending marketing to them, regardless of cost. All you know about them is they have a computer and an e-mail address. I'll assume you're not among the Multi-Level Marketing (MLM) or Networking and make-your-fortune-on-the-Internet types.

But just in case there may be a few MLM/Networking folks reading this, I'll pass on what I've shared with several inquirers in recent years who wanted to know if they could use direct mail to

> The first distinction to be made here is between opt-in lists of those who have agreed to receive any and all e-mail and those who have agreed to receive your e-mail.

increase their "down-line." In my view, MLM works, to whatever degree it does work, because it is based on personal contact. People bringing friends and acquaintances to a motivational meeting and exerting peer pressure with lots of bonhomie and stories of untold riches (they bought this guy *a house*, for heaven's sake!), are the dynamics that drive MLM. Move away from the personal touch into direct mail, and you're just another cold-prospect mailer with gross response rates under 1% and net rates near zero. E-mail may cost less than print mail, but the results will be pretty much the same.

## Viral Marketing

Come back! It's not a disease! In chapter 7 we saw how we develop a "Suspect" into an "Advocate," or someone who likes our product or company so much, they help do our marketing for us by recommending us to friends, etc. On the Internet, that's called viral marketing and it simply means "word of mouth," or in this case, maybe word of mouse.

You can help generate the viral effect by placing a "Recommend-It" button on your Web site or in your e-letter. By clicking on the Recommend-It button, a reader can instantly pass your Web or e-letter information on to a friend. And, of course, it's a snap to forward an e-mail letter to one person or a hundred.

"You tell one friend and he tells two friends . . . " You remember how the popular commercial went. Perhaps viral marketing is so dubbed because it multiplies your information like a virus from one person to two, to four, to eight, to sixteen, etc. Next thing you know it's in the millions.

Ralph Wilson, editor of *Web Marketing Today* and other excellent newsletters (*www.wilsonweb.com*) offers six elements of a viral strategy, none of which will be foreign to an experience direct marketer:

1. Give away a product or service (free!).
2. Provide for quick-and-easy transfer to others (like Member-Get-A-Member).
3. Make it easily scaleable from small to large (be able to add mail servers quickly).

> Perhaps viral marketing is so dubbed because it multiplies your information like a virus from one person to two, to four, to eight, to sixteen, etc. Next thing you know it's in the millions.

4. Exploit common interests and motives (desire to be cool).
5. Use existing communication networks (newsgroups, opt-in e-mail lists).
6. Use others' resources (news releases, articles on other Web sites, affiliate programs, etc.).

Wilson gives as an example his newest e-mail newsletter, Doctor Ebiz (*http://doctorebiz.com*) which he inserts into *Web Marketing Today* (and which I have now inserted into this book).

He urges readers to go to the Doctor Ebiz Web site and click on the Recommend-It button and report back to him how effective they think it is. He also gives permission for readers to reproduce the complete Viral Marketing article on their Web sites. (My apologies, Doctor, for not reproducing your article exactly as you requested. I did put it on my Web site.)

## E-List Rental

The number of companies getting into the e-mail list rental business is growing rapidly, and it promises to take off in the next year or so, as we all become more familiar with e-mail marketing generally— and, let's face it, a bit worn down by the spammers. Especially when we find a gem or two in that mountain of spam!

No doubt because the transmitting cost is so low, brokers are charging $200 per thousand and up for lists. Not cheap. Among the first of the serious e-brokers was Net Creations, Inc., at *www.postmasterdirect.com*. Company founder Rosalind Resnick urges users to verify that any list described as opt-in really is. One way to check out a broker is to go to their Web site and register. If you're not presented with an opt-in/opt-out choice, be careful. And be sure to determine how the list was built. What was the opt-in proposition? How was it worded? Is it in any way misleading or ambiguous? You may also find that although people have opted-in to a particular category of mail or to a particular company, unlike our opportunity seekers mentioned above, they're not up for *any* mail from just *anyone*.

Many of the e-lists available today have been "harvested" from e-mails to companies or their Web sites using software programs that

One way to check out a broker is to go to their Web site and register. If you're not presented with an opt-in/opt-out choice, be careful.

extract the e-mail addresses from the messages. Or they've been compiled from rosters or membership lists, or collected from sweepstakes. You've probably received unsolicited ads for CD-ROMs packed with such e-mail addresses. There's little in the way of demographics or psychographics or purchase behavior to go on. And when it comes to predicting response rates, forget it. E-mail lists are even more unpredictable than postal mail lists, mainly because they deteriorate even faster. You're likely to get as many leads with a general e-mail list of 100,000 or more as you would with a targeted print mail list of just 10,000. On the other hand, e-mail does permit quick testing of offers and lists. You know the same day how an offer has done, so you can roll out immediately to your best lists.

As we said about sending unsolicited e-mail newsletters above, although you'll be taking slightly less risk with an e-mail list that's very targeted to your offer and interest, it's still a risk. It amounts to targeted spam, and you may end up paying a higher price than you know in loss of trust and future opportunities. At the very least, explain why recipients are receiving this e-mail and provide a very quick-and-easy way for them to "unsubscribe." Usually, this is a matter of saying "Reply to this e-mail with 'unsubscribe' in the subject line." And make sure you unsubscribe them if they ask. Several newsletters I tried to unsubscribe from suddenly claimed they couldn't find my address. That's the same address they "found" in order to subscribe me in the first place(!?).

## The House List

Not surprisingly, the most effective e-mail marketing today is being done with house lists: those folks who have subscribed to your e-letter, responded to an offer, signed up as a member of your site, and/or agreed in some other way to receive e-mail announcements, etc. (It would be a mistake to assume that your newsletter subscribers, for example, are automatically accepting of any e-mail you care to send or that, even if they are, they will immediately recognize an e-mail as being from you. Care must be taken to be instantly identifiable to your list.)

In an e-mail announcement, the "Subject" line is your teaser, and you'll want to think long and hard about what to say there, or

> E-mail lists are even more unpredictable than postal mail lists, mainly because they deteriorate even faster.

risk being deleted before you're even read. We joke about people reading our direct mail packages over the trash barrel, but at least we get a chance to show a corner card, a teaser, and some sort of personality in the choice of envelope design. With e-mail, there is no envelope and just two precious lines, "From" and "Subject," in which to make it clear this isn't spam. (And never write, "This isn't spam," that's a sure way to get clicked off.)

For an e-mail to high school teachers I wrote this in the Subject line, "'A great teaching tool'–FREE!" Because this was targeted to teachers and I was able to tip the teacher off that this was addressed to her with the phrase "teaching tool," I used the "Free" word. But in e-mail, the word "Free" can be problematic, since so much of the spam offers free this and free that. Be careful with "Free" in this environment.

Then there are the quotes, which always get extra attention in print, and may lead one to wonder who's being quoted. They instantly denote a third-party endorsement for added legitimacy. Playing that out a bit further, I began the e-mail message with two quick testimonials from teachers to reinforce the third-party validation of the communication as well as the product.

Here's how the whole thing read:

From: The Highwired Classroom
Subject: "'A great teaching tool'–FREE!"

Here's what one teacher said about The Highwired Classroom:

"I would like to thank you for this opportunity to have our newspaper online. What a great teaching tool for the students . . . We greatly appreciate it."
—D.L., Sleepy Eye Secondary School, Sleepy Eye, MN

And another said:

"I think this concept is so timely in education for so many reasons . . . We love what you are doing for education."
—T.W., Fresno Christian School, Fresno CA

> The word "Free" can be problematic, since so much of the spam offers free this and free that. Be careful with "Free" in this environment.

These teachers, like many others, are raving about Highwired Classroom, the exciting new FREE service for teachers. As you read this, more than 1,500 schools are publishing on the Internet with Highwired.net. So can you. In a nutshell, Highwired Classroom:

- Requires no HTML—easy to learn and use.
- Empowers you to conduct Web-based projects, to showcase student work, and keep students and parents updated on classroom and school events.
- Use it from any Internet-connected computer.
- Includes a manual and supplementary materials to make curriculum integration a snap!

Just two quick steps to get started:

1. Sign up your classroom now at *http://www.highwired.net/classroom*, without cost or obligation of any kind.

And then—

2. SHARE THE NEWS with fellow teachers at *http://www.highwired.net/rewards!* in our "Share the News" Rewards Program.

You'll be doing teachers and students a favor. And just for forwarding this message to your colleagues, you'll be eligible for "Share the News" Rewards: A chance to win two round-trip tickets for two anywhere in the U.S. or a digital camera to enhance your Highwired Classroom site.

Our way of saying "thanks" for your help.

1. Sign up now at *http://www.highwired.net/classroom* and then
2. Share the News at: *http://www.highwired.net/rewards!*

Finally, this from L.H., Academy for Academic Excellence, Apple Valley, CA:

"Our principal thinks I'm a genius for having discovered you . . . "
Sign up now—and be the genius at *your* school!

Teachers are very responsive to the opinions of their colleagues. The testimonials provide support for reading the message and at least considering the proposition. The mention of 1,500 schools currently using the product is intended to reinforce the legitimacy of Highwired.net and of the idea of putting their classroom on the Internet. Remember, we're not only asking them to act on the proposition themselves; in an attempt at viral marketing, we're also asking them to refer this announcement to other teachers—something they would be very careful about, the reward notwithstanding.

Numbering the two offers helped discriminate between them. Also, since we needed to get these teachers to act, the enumeration made the double call to action as clear and simple as possible, even to the point of repeating it within the brief message.

## Give a Little, Get a Little

The Highwired.net e-mail admittedly took a chance on teacher interests, and played to their instincts. That can be a risky strategy for markets that are less reliable. For Cookn.com, for example, I wrote an e-mail that gives the recipient something of value—a recipe—in return for a few moments of their attention to a commercial message. Recipes are also what Cookn.com is all about—software that organizes recipes, and provides the customer with a monthly supply of fabulous recipes from the pages of *Cooking Light* magazine.

Giving the recipient something of value and appending your commercial message is a winning way to avoid the spam label. (There will always be some who label anything they receive as spam, but we can't let them run our lives, can we?)

To promote a new quarterly journal in the executive recruiting space, I wrote a subject line I felt would entice executive recruiters to check out the message and offered a few of the insights from the Premier issue with an invitation to get the issue Free.

> Giving the recipient something of value and appending your commercial message is a winning way to avoid the spam label.

Here's how they looked, the Cookn.com e-mail first. The Cookn recipe is longer than an ordinary e-mail should be, but if you're using a recipe as a teaser, you'd better give them all of it.

**Subject: Try this Luscious Recipe for Mocha Fudge Pie!**

**Mocha Fudge Pie**
INGREDIENTS FOR 8 SERVINGS:
$\frac{1}{3}$ cup hot water
4 teaspoons instant coffee granules, divided
$\frac{1}{2}$ (19.85-ounce) box light fudge brownie mix (about 2 cups)
2 teaspoons vanilla extract, divided
2 egg whites
Vegetable cooking spray
$\frac{3}{4}$ cup 1% low-fat milk
3 tablespoons Kahlua or other coffee-flavored liqueur
1 (3.9-ounce) package chocolate-flavored instant pudding-and-
pie filling mix
3 cups frozen reduced-calorie whipped topping, thawed
and divided
Chocolate curls (optional)

INSTRUCTIONS:
Combine hot water and 2 teaspoons coffee granules in a medium bowl; stir well. Add brownie mix, teaspoon vanilla, and egg whites; stir until well blended. Pour mixture into a 9-inch pie plate coated with cooking spray. Bake at 325°F for 22 minutes. Let crust cool completely.

Combine milk, 2 tablespoons Kahlua, 1 teaspoon coffee granules, remaining 1 teaspoon vanilla, and pudding mix in a bowl; beat at medium speed of a mixer 1 minute. Gently fold in 1½ cups whipped topping. Spread pudding mixture evenly over brownie crust.

Combine remaining 1 tablespoon Kahlua and remaining 1 teaspoon coffee granules in a bowl; stir well. Gently fold in remaining 1½ cups whipped topping. Spread whipped topping mixture evenly over pudding mixture. Garnish with chocolate curls, if desired. Serve immediately, or store loosely covered in refrigerator. Yield: 8 servings (serving size: 1 wedge).

Nonalcoholic Mocha Version: When making the pudding mixture, substitute 2 tablespoons 1% low-fat milk for the Kahlua. In the topping, omit the Kahlua, and dissolve the coffee granules in 1 tablespoon water.

Note: Store remaining brownie mix in a zip-top heavy-duty plastic bag in refrigerator; reserved brownie mix can be used for another pie or to make a small pan of brownies. To make brownies, combine reserved brownie mix (about 2 cups), ¼ cup water, and 1 lightly beaten egg white in a bowl. Stir just until combined. Spread into an 8-inch square pan coated with vegetable cooking spray. Bake at 350°F for 23 to 25 minutes.

NUTRITIONAL INFORMATION:
CALORIES 292 (22% from fat); PROTEIN 4.4g; FAT 7g (sat 5.3g, mono 0.1g, poly 1.1g); CARB 51.5g; FIBER 0g; CHOL 1mg; IRON 0.8mg; SODIUM 345mg; CALC 47mg

*Recipes Copyright ©Cooking Light Magazine*

When it comes to adapting an elegant hors d'oeuvre recipe for 40 guests, scaling down a favorite pasta dish to serve just the two of you, or looking for an unusual dessert to surprise your family, help is just a click away. Point your browser to *www.cookn.com* and see!

At Cookn.com, you'll also discover CookWare™, an innovative software program that allows you to collect and organize recipes with ease on your computer. Categories such as appetizers, breads, desserts, salads, and soups are accessed with easy-to-use, colorful button images. Try it yourself at *www.cookn.com*!

Or call Barbara Busenbark at 603-924-5224 for more information.
Cookn.com, 86 Grove Street, Peterborough, NH 03458
Here's the journal e-mail. This is closer to acceptable length.

**Subject: Executive recruiters have a powerful new weapon in the "War for Talent"**

- It includes a new understanding of what top executive candidates expect most from prospective employers . . .
- . . . anticipating the IT threat to the executive suite . . .
- . . . and re-ordering relationships to retain talent in a dot-com world.

Recruiters today are exploring critical issues like these and much more in an exciting new publication called—

**EXECUTIVE TALENT—**
**The Journal of Recruiting and Retaining Top Managers**

In the "war for talent," human capital has become both a critical success factor and a strategic resource, forcing companies into new methods of search and retention, especially at the highest executive levels.

*Executive Talent* takes you behind the scenes and into the boardrooms of the world's leading companies to reveal the "new rules" that are driving successful executive search, recruiting, and retention strategies for today's top managers.

Check out the new thought leader in executive recruiting at *www.kennedyinfo.com/executivetalent* and get the Premier Issue to examine without risk.

## Campaign Management

As with other e-commerce functions, there are agencies, like E-Dialog in Massachusetts (*www.e-dialog.com*), who can structure and manage an e-mail marketing campaign for you. At least at the beginning, it would be wise to use one, or at least hire one as a consultant, until you get your e-legs. One factor to consider is the relatively high percentage of bouncebacks you're likely to receive from any e-mail campaign. You'll want to be able to handle them, or they could crash your server. Your agency will set up a separate server to manage that traffic.

Increasingly sophisticated software tools are constantly being developed that help marketers leverage the e-commerce possibilities

## The Right Offer to the Right List

Electronic marketing can be effective when we meet the same basic requirements via e-mail that we strive for in regular mail: deliver the right offer to the right list. An example is a promotion for Harvard Business School Publishing (HBSP) conducted by E-Dialog, Inc. The first step was to develop and offer HBSP's customers and prospects an online newsletter on an "opt-in" basis. The subscriber list eventually grew to 90,000 e-mail names and addresses. The "unsubscribe" rate to the newsletter was less than 1%, a tribute to both E-Dialog's skill in creating a compelling newsletter, and Harvard Business School's strong credibility with this market. Step two was to use the newsletter list to offer a 30-day trial of a new CD-ROM to HBSP's upscale market of CEOs and COOs. E-Dialog's proprietary software product, QuickReply™, made it easy for recipients to reply with a single click and delivered the data directly to HBSP's database. The conversion rate for the e-mail test was 6.2%, versus 1.6% for fax, and 1.1% for direct postal mail.

of their sites and their various forms of communication. E-Dialog, for example, has a product called E-Append™ that can identify the addressing protocol of a company's e-mail and, given a roster of names, append accurate e-mail addresses to the list.

Another e-mail campaign agency is Bigfoot at *www.bigfootinteractive.com*, who promotes the concept as "e-mail campaign management" or ECM. Bigfoot's services include:

- E-mail delivery/campaign management (execution)
- File preparation, suppression, and hygiene
- File segmentation
- E-mail test/control matrix design
- Simple Text and HTML letters
- E-mail delivery
- Customer Response Management

When a visitor to your site presses the button and registers, you get two prospect names, FREE! Over time you build up an "account" of names that you can use at any time.

- High-performance delivery, algorithms
- Real-time, client-accessible campaign and individual-activity reporting
- Promotional/response history tracking
- Privacy/anti-spam protection

## Co-Ops Hit the Internet

In Chapter 11 we discussed co-op mailings in which several non-competing mailers participate by providing inserts for a single envelope mailed to a large consumer database. Now there's an online version of the co-op designed to deliver prospecting names via e-mail to marketers.

In this variation, a database compiler installs a button on your Web site offering various deals. When a visitor to your site presses the button and registers, you get two prospect names, FREE! Over time you build up an "account" of names that you can use at any time. And, of course, if you use up your accumulated names, the compiler will be happy to sell you more names at about $200 per thousand.

Major players in this e-mail name exchange include Worldata-Exchange (*www.worldataexchange.com*), NetCreations (*www.post-masterdirect.com*), 24/7 Alliance (*www.247media.com*), and YesMail (*www.yesmail.com*). Prices and terms of the deal vary a bit from company to company. Again, the caveats mentioned previously for any opt-in e-mail list apply here as well.

## A Final Note

Earlier I mentioned Dell's success at selling computers and peripherals online. The company motto, very much in evidence at Dell's Texas headquarters, is "The Customer Experience: Own It." The following is from the Fall '99 issue of *Net Company*, a sister publication to *Fast Company* magazine, which I highly recommend for anyone seeking to do business in the new century—online or otherwise:

"The customer experience. Building a great company on the Web isn't about 'aggregating eyeballs,' 'increasing stickiness,' or embracing any of the other slogans that masquerade as strategy. It's about rethinking the most basic relationship in business: the one between you and your customers. How well do you meet their needs? How smoothly do you solve their problems? How quickly do you anticipate what they'll want next? The real promise of the Web is a once-and-for-all transfer of power: consumers and business customers will get what they want. Jerry Gregoire, 47, chief information officer at Dell, puts it this way: 'The customer experience is the next competitive battleground.'"

As stated in a report on e-commerce from Kennedy Information Research Group, the products that sold initially on the Internet were, for the most part, commodity products: books, CDs, stocks, tickets, and the like—even software. Products that are safe—that are pretty much the same wherever you buy them. "Once one travels away from commodities, electronic commerce is not as effective a medium since a consumer must experience the product themselves to establish value," says the report. "Or, they must trust either the brand or the vendor."

Trust. A key ingredient of the customer experience. Dell built trust by allowing customers to configure their own products, and backed that up with killer support. If your product is at all unusual, you may have to go to a two-step model on the Web, even if it hasn't been necessary in other channels. Your offers and your customer service, and how people experience your Web site, are the ways you build trust.

The fall '99 issue of *Net Company* also quotes Jeffrey F. Rayport, a professor at Harvard Business School and the executive director of Marketspace Center, the e-commerce division of Monitor Co., a management consulting firm in Cambridge, Massachusetts. "Online, you don't differentiate yourself by what you sell," says

> Your offers and your customer service, and how people experience your Web site, are the ways you build trust.

Rayport. "You have to differentiate yourself by *how* you sell—by the experiences that you create around finding, trying, and purchasing. In the actual world, providing a bad experience is damaging. But people will keep going to the same supermarket, because it's on the way home. On the Web, a bad customer experience can be fatal."

The same holds true for any channel of direct marketing. As we've said before, the stimulus to response isn't the product, it's the offer.

> On the Web, a bad customer experience can be fatal.

## Online Resources

Small Business Advisor: *www.zdnet.com/smallbusiness*
*Inc.* Magazine Online: *www.inc.com*
AccuTips online newsletter: *www.accudata-america.com*
Web Referral Site: *www.recommend-it.com*
Advertising Learning Center and Site Promotion:
    *www.doubleclick.net*
Web Advertising Agency: *www.flycast.com*
Banner Exchanges/Site Promotion: *www.smartage.com*
Affiliate Programs: *www.linkshare.com*
Images and Web Design Tools: *www.mediabuilder.com*
E-Commerce Resources: *http://sellitontheweb.com*
Yahoo! Small Business: *http://smallbusiness.yahoo.com*
Web Site Tools: *www.websidestory.com*
Web Marketing Site & Newsletter: *www.wilsonweb.com*
BTB Web Auction Guide: *http://welcome/opensite.com/webmtg*
Web Marketing Tips & Newsletter: *www.infoscavenger.com*
Shopping Cart Guide: *www.onlineorders.net*
Web Digest for Marketers: *www.wdfm.com*
Web Data & Statistics: *www.usadata.com; www.nua.ie /surveys*
Search Engine Tool: *www.submit-it.com;*
    *www.virtualpromote.com*
Search Engine Placement Service: *www.websitepublicity.com*
E-mail Lists: *www.postmasterdirect.com; www.e-postdirect.com;*
*www.TargitMail.com; www.idg.net; www.venturedirect.com;*
*www.worldata.com (eSmart)*
Internet Sales & Newsletter: *www.audettemedia.com*

Web Marketing: *www.emarketer.com*
Web Marketing Articles: *www.searchz.com*
Banner Advertising Tips & Newsletter: *www.bannertips.com*
Domain Name Search & Site Registration:
    *www.networksolutions.com*
Web Site Journal Newsletter: *www.WebSiteJournal.com*
Web Site Tuneups: *www.websitegarage.com*
E-Commerce Support: *www.goselectsource.com;*
    *www.millard.com; www.catalogcity.com*
Web design tips: *www.lynda.com*

**Note:** The previous links are by no means definitive in terms of online sources of help for small business, but many of them carry links to other sources, which in turn will lead to still further sources. In addition, the inclusion of any link in this text is not intended as an endorsement of any Web site or service.

With the rapid growth of the Internet, and the Web in particular, however, some of these links and the services they connect with may be gone or changed by the time you read this.

You can keep pace with the latest Web marketing tools, how-to-help, and online solutions for small business by visiting the Web Marketing section of my Web site at–*www.duncandirect.com*

Use the following special "readers-only" User Name and Password to gain access. You may change them subsequently.

**User Name:** Streetwise
**Password:** marketer

> You can keep pace with the latest Web marketing tools, how-to-help, and online solutions for small business by visiting the Web Marketing section of my Web site at— *www.duncandirect.com*

---

For more information on this topic, visit our Web site at www.businesstown.com

# APPENDICES

**APPENDIX A** DIRECT MARKETING CHECKLISTS  **APPENDIX B** RECOMMENDED READING LIST
**APPENDIX C** DIRECTORY OF LOCAL DIRECT MARKETING CLUBS AND ASSOCIATIONS
**APPENDIX D** DMA ETHICAL GUIDELINES  **APPENDIX E** DMA PRIVACY GUIDELINES

# Appendix A

# Direct Marketing Checklists

Direct Marketing Checklists from the Institute of Direct Marketing (from the U.S., dial: 011 44 181 977 5705) has published a very useful booklet entitled "The Institute of Direct Marketing Pocket Organiser." It provides gems for anyone engaged in direct mail.

## #1. Direct Marketing Planning Checklist

A quick guide through the stages of planning and executing a successful direct mail campaign.

❐ Set Your Objectives—Be specific. State how many products you want to sell or how many leads per salesman you want, specify over what period of time.

❐ Set Your Budget—How much will you need to spend to meet the objectives?

❐ Outline Your Campaign Activity—Make sure you consider and plan for all the key stages—targeting, media selection, communication mix, print/production, fulfillment.

❐ Check on the Competition—Who are your competitors, what is their market position? What are they currently doing, what is their likely response?

❐ Identify Your Target Audience—What are their characteristics and attitudes? Existing customers or external lists that can match the profile of your target audience?

❐ Access Your Target Audience—Source the names for your direct mail. Select appropriate media. Identify any appropriate list or media opportunities.

❐ Develop Your Creative Approach—What message and offer do you want to communicate? What is the nature of the individual response you want? Again, identify any creative test opportunities.

❐ Design Your Mailing Package—What should the components be, e.g., letter, envelope, brochure, reply device?

❐ Draw Up Your Production Schedule—What are the timing requirements for this plan? Identify key tasks, responsibilities, and critical timings. Make sure all external suppliers are carefully briefed and schedules agreed.

❏ Brief Internal Personnel and Relevant Departments—Ensure all relevant departments are thoroughly briefed, e.g., customer service, order processing, warehouse; and that outline campaign details are generally communicated.

❏ Analyse and Evaluate Your Results—Once the campaign results are final, check them against your objectives. Check the results for statistical validity. Work through the financial implications of the results. What conclusions can be drawn and are there any lessons to be learned for future campaigns?

## #2. Mailing List Brief—Checklist

The list used in a direct mail campaign is the single most important variable. It's vital for briefs to be thorough and for subsequent list proposals to closely reflect the brief.

Here are a few pointers to help you structure your list brief.

❏ Product/Service Description—Briefly describe your product or service and outline product benefits and Unique Selling Proposition (U.S.P.).

❏ Target Market—What is your primary target market? Your secondary? What psychographic or demographic profile information is known about your target audience?

❏ Quantities Required—What are the minimum test sample sizes required? What is the roll-out potential of each list?

❏ Special Requirements—What special selections are required and what format will the list be supplied in, e.g., magnetic tape, disk, or labels? Do you want telephone numbers to be supplied with the list? Is the list required for one-time usage, multiple usage, or outright purchase? Can you address named individuals?

❏ Response Profile—How did the individuals on the list respond, by mail or telephone? How recently did they respond? What was the value of the transaction? Have they responded more than once?

❏ List Origin—How was the list originally built?

❏ List Quantity—How often is the list mailed? How frequently is it updated? Have Mailing Preference Service (MPS) names been suppressed from the list?

❏ Net Names—Are names available on a net names basis? Is it a set percentage quoted (85%) or is an actual figure negotiable?

❏ "Gone Aways"—What is the list owner's policy on undeliverable items? Is a rebate negotiable if the level of "gone aways" exceeds the generally accepted norm of 5%?

❏ Results/References—Who has used the list in the last six months and are results available to give an idea of the list's responsiveness? Are references available from satisfied customers?

❏ Rental Restrictions—Is rental subject to a minimum quantity? Is rental subject to list owner approval of the mailing package to be sent?

❏ The Cost of List Rental—What charges are included in the prices quoted? Are selection charges included? Are output charges extra (disk, labels, etc.).

❏ Lead Times—How soon can the list be supplied? Are selection counts readily available prior to order?

## #3. Creative Brief Checklist

The creative brief is critical to good creative input. Here is a checklist of headings and pointers to help structure a creative brief.

❏ Product/Brand—What is your product or service? Give a brief description with relevant and brief background information.

❏ Current Market Perception—How is your product or service perceived in the market place?

❏ The Objective—What do you want to achieve?

❏ Previous Communications—History and results, lists or media used, test results if appropriate. Include examples.

❏ Target Market—Who are you talking to? A "thumbnail sketch." Demographic and psychographic.

❒ Product Benefits—What are the key benefits? What are the secondary benefits?

❒ The Promise—What problem will it solve? What desire will it satisfy? (Rational or emotional.)

❒ The Offer—Price, incentive, terms.

❒ Any Special Offers—Discounts, special conditions, risk reduction mechanisms.

❒ Unique Selling Proposition (USP)—What are the unique characteristics that make your product/service better than the competition?

❒ The Competition—Who are you competing with? How does your product compare in strict production terms? How does the competition speak?

❒ Tone of Voice—Manner of communication: how should you speak to the target audience?

❒ Positioning—How you want the target market to perceive the brand tomorrow, relative to the competition—versus how you are perceived today.

❒ Media—Plan of likely media to be used—press, internet, TV, inserts, radio etc.

❒ Direct Mail
    a) Package contents (give example of similar elements)
    b) Size restrictions
    c) Response mechanism (telephone, coupon, order form, direct debit, bankers order, etc.)
    d) Test segments to be considered
    e) Total cost per thousand (including postage)
    f) Considerations—personalization details, etc.

❒ Budget—What financial restrictions are there on the creative work?

❒ Restrictions—Those governed by law, by client corporate guidelines, or by agency policy.

❒ Physical Requirements—Exactly what do you require from the creative team: scams, headlines, finished copy and visuals, storyboard, scripts?

❒ Timing—When is everything required by? Have you allowed adequate time for approval procedures and revisions?

## #4. Tips for Successful Direct Mail Letterwriting

The letter is the most personal part of the communication. Before you begin writing the letter:

a) Know your audience (talk to them). Think about their likes/dislikes, their problems and opportunities, their hopes and fears.
b) Translate the characteristics of your product into benefits for your audience.
c) Aim to establish one major benefit which will distinguish your product/service from the competition.
d) Use a P.S. in your letters. And a P.P.S. if you wish. The end of the letter is the most read part after the beginning.
e) Restate your benefits before closing.
f) Show others your letters and get their views and comments.

## #5. Printer Brief Checklist

Printer briefs must be consistent to ensure that you can compare alternative quotes and they must also be specific. The following checklist will help you with your print specification.

- ❏ Quantity—Have you specified how many pieces you want produced (and included an acceptable number of extra copies)?
- ❏ Type/Weight of Material—Have you specified what type and weight of material you want the job printed on?
- ❏ Colors—Is it a single, two, or four color job? Is it to be printed both sides?
- ❏ Flat Size—What is the flat size of the piece before and after trimming?
- ❏ Folds/Finished Size—Have you specified how the job should be folded? How many folds and the sequence? How many pages will the finished item have and what is the finished size?
- ❏ Special Instructions—Have you included clear details of any coding required? Any special finishing instructions: stitching, perforating, glueing, laminating, etc.?

❑ Reproduction—Are you supplying "trannies" or color "negs"? If so, what size and how many? Will tint-laying be required?

❑ Proofs—Do you want to see proofs? If so, is a prepress proof (running sheet) adequate?

❑ Timing—Have you agreed on a schedule with the printer stating:
   a) When artwork will be available?
   b) When proofs are required?
   c) Final delivery date?

❑ Delivery Instructions—Have you included clear packing (codes, quantities) and delivery (addresses, contacts) instructions?

## Tips for Better Print Buying

1. You can't be involved too early. By sitting in on preliminary meetings you'll have more time to critically assess the print requirements and maybe even prevent wasted effort on any unworkable scheme.

2. Keep a whole range of samples—formats, paper samples, special finishes. Get on printers' lists to stay up-to-date with the latest developments. Also keep notes of as many prices as you can get.

3. As far as possible work with standard sheet sizes. This reduces wastage. If you must use nonstandard sizes, use waste to print additional items at very little extra cost.

4. Your production schedule is king. Draw up a detailed schedule for every component in your campaign or mailing and then stick to it.

5. Watch the weight of the paper you choose and at an early stage make up a "dummy" of each item in a campaign using the actual materials being proposed. You will then be able to ensure that your package is within USPS allowances.

6. Make sure you use the right printer for the right job. The printer's machinery will dictate what they can and can't do cost-efficiently, so pick the printer with the most suitable machinery.

7. Keep tabs on your printers. Maintain details of their machines and samples produced by them. Make sure you visit them to check that they can offer all the services you require.

8. Having agreed the specification and the price with the printer, make sure you clarify terms of payment, ownership of materials (e.g., separated film), and the storage of the printed material.

9. Always insist on proofs and make sure you cut, fold, and paste them to ensure everything works as it should. Make sure all relevant people agree and clear the proofs.

10. If your job is printed both sides with one side of the sheet being exposed to the other by way of folds, cut-outs, etc., if budget allows, have backed-up proofs. Sticking two sheets together can have a wayward effect when checking positioning.

11. Consider different finishing processes. For example, an alternative fold may mean the difference between machine inserting and hand inserting into envelopes, resulting in considerable cost savings.

12. Check if your printer charges for overs. If so, consider changing your printer.

## #6. Layout/Stationery

A photocopy of the artwork will, hopefully, answer a lot of questions, but these points are given here as an indication of what to look for:

1. Is copy artwork available in advance showing laser position, toner exclusion area, perforations, peel-off stamps, cutouts, etc.?
2. What is the width and drop of each page of stationery?
3. Will text be rotated?
4. To ensure the lasered name and address fits into the window position, samples of the envelope should be provided.
5. Is the job one-up or more than one record per page?
6. Is there more than one stationery type for this job?
7. What type of stationery will be used?
8. Do you require samples?
9. Is bursting/trimming required?
10. What is to be done with excess stationery?

## #7. Text Processing

1. Is the printer required to set text for laser printing? Will proofs for preprint be required?
2. Does the text contain imbeds? How should these be shown on a plain paper proof?
3. What character style is required? Choice of style requires knowing if the job will be rotated, which in turn necessitates which rotation is required—90° or 270° (i.e., which edge of stationery will feed through first).
4. Will all the text be in the same style?
5. How should punctuation be handled (e.g., double or single spaces after full stops, etc.)?
6. Is page shaping required?
7. How many blank lines between paragraphs? (Norm = 1)

## #8. Defaults

Defaults are essential to ensure that there will not be unacceptable errors in the event of an omission of data on a disk. For example, if a name has to print, but there is no name present on the records, what is to be put in its place, if anything?

1. Default for the absence of a name?
2. Default for the absence of any other specifically referenced fields?
3. Can certain fields be expected to appear in the same position in each record (e.g name always in the same field)?
4. What action if text is too long for space (e.g., use a smaller character style)?
5. What is to be used as a salutation if the name is unsalutable? As an alternative to printing a default, records can be omitted and listed in an exception report is required.

## #9. Mailing House Brief Checklist

1. If it is a large-volume mailing, make sure the mailing house has been given plenty of advance notice (approximate mail quantity, pack description, mail date) so that they can build it into their production schedule.

2. Allow for delays. Late delivery of disks or printed material can mean missed mail dates. As the mailing house is at the end of the production process there is rarely flexibility if timing is tight.

3. Provide sufficient "overs" of all printed material. Avoiding inconvenient shortfalls in mail quantity more than justifies the low print run-on costs.

4. Clearly specify any special instructions prior to enclosing (e.g., folding, collating, hand matching, guillotining).

5. Make sure everything is coded. Where components are very similar, this should be emphasized even if codes are different.

6. Clearly specify the inserting sequence. A simple diagram can be used to illustrate the order in which components are to be inserted and which way they should face.

7. Provide the mailing house with dummy sample packs and ask them to provide you with sample packs once all components have been delivered (prior to enclosing). In addition, ask for "live" samples once enclosing is completed.

8. Clearly specify the mail date, or dates if the mailing is to be dropped over a period of time. Where test panels are included in the mailing, insist that they are mailed simultaneously to avoid possible timing bias.

9. Give clear postage instructions. Is the mailing to go out First Class, Second Class, or bulk rate? Does the outer carry a post-paid impression (PPI)? Do stamps need to be affixed or is the mailing to be franked? How is the postage to be paid?

10. Finally, once the mailing has been dropped, ask the mailing house to confirm the mail date/mail quantities, and advise them to store, return, or destroy any overs.

## #10. Response Guides

If you hear people in the Direct Marketing business quoting an "Industry Norm" of 2% response to direct mail, don't take them too literally. Chances are they have not been in the business very long. There are many factors affecting the response to a mailing campaign making it extremely difficult to give a meaningful statistic, even for a specific market. Note the following:

1. Market—Are you addressing business people or consumers?
2. Objective—Do you want them to buy, try, send for more details or simply give you information, e.g., return a questionnaire?
3. Do they know you?—Obviously, the better your relationship with them the better the response is likely to be. If they have heard of you—through advertising for instance—their response will be influenced by their opinion of that advertising. If they have never heard of you, this may affect their confidence in you and the likely response.
4. Targeting—How easy is it to seek out the actual individuals to whom you wish to speak? How accurately does your list selection locate them?
5. Offer—Are you offering them something in return for their response? A free gift, a discount, or a free sample can have a dramatic effect. Competitions or prize draws can greatly increase response from certain groups of prospects.
6. Timing—Is the mailing being sent out at a good time? This can simply be a factor of the buying pattern of the recipient (e.g., month end for salary customers, Financial Year start or finish for businesses), or may relate to other activities (e.g., an advertising campaign or perhaps a competitor's campaign or offer).
7. Creative—The caliber of your creative work. This is not simply a matter of originality or creative brilliance. The message must be clear, easily understood, and relevant. Size, shape, color and number of pieces enclosed, even a simple involvement device can appreciably affect response.
8. Outside factors—Major news events can have a big effect on response, for better or worse.

The above factors, though not an exhaustive list, give an indication of the difficulties of giving an overall response guide, even for a single medium like direct mail. Some of these factors will also affect response to other media such as Press, Inserts, Door-to-Door Distributions, Product Dispatches, etc.

## #11. How to Choose an Agency

1. Why do you need an agency? Have a clear idea of why you are hiring one in the first place.
2. Size. Ensure that the agency you choose is the right size to handle your account. Too small and it may not be able to cope with all your requirements, especially with regard to important staff being on holiday, etc., and staff turnover. Too large and the agency may not find your budget attractive enough.
3. Conflicting accounts. Be very wary if an agency is handling a conflicting or competitive account. Satisfy yourself that all necessary safeguards are taken.
4. Track record. How long has the agency been in business? What is their past performance in your particular area of business? Ask to take up references with their existing or past clients.
5. Areas of expertise. Has the agency experience in other markets which have relevance to your business?
6. Efficiency. What is your first impression of their offices and the agency representatives? How understanding were they of your industry and how sensitive to the issues you want to address? Will the commitment and enthusiasm initially shown carry on if they win the account?
7. Account Management. Do they genuinely expect to add to the marketing thought process? Do they fight their corner in a genuine disagreement or simply do as you tell them?
8. Above and below the line. Your direct marketing agency must be willing–and able–to work with other agencies in order that you benefit from fully integrated communications.
9. Finance. How does the agency charge for its services? Does it require a monthly fee, demand a percentage of the takings, want a mark-up on production, or a combination of all three? Closely study their Terms of Trade well before committing yourself.
10. Rapport. Do you instinctively trust and feel comfortable with the agency people? Are the people to whom you are initially introduced the same as those who will work on your account? This could be the most important factor of all.

## #12. Reasons Why People Buy

The psychology of selling and marketing is important. Research shows many reasons why people agree to or want to buy.

They Want to Gain:
- Popularity
- Praise from others
- Self-confidence
- Improved appearance
- Comfort
- Advancement: Social/Business
- Security in old age
- Leisure time
- Increased enjoyment
- Personal prestige
- Knowledge
- Power

They Want to:
- Express their personality
- Protect their family
- Satisfy their curiosity
- Win others' affection
- Resist domination by others
- Be fashionable
- Emulate the admirable
- Acquire or collect things
- Take advantage of opportunities

They Want to Avoid:
- Effort
- Risk
- Worry/self-doubt
- Embarrassment
- Uncleanliness
- Pain

Criticism
Losing face
Time wasting

They Want to Be:
Good parents
Attractive to the opposite sex
Successful
Enthused
Creative
Efficient
Recognized authorities
Up-to-date
Gregarious
Sure of themselves
Sociable
Healthy
Hospitable
Influential over others
Individual

## Further Information

If you would like to receive further information on this subject, please e-mail Martin Pollins at marketing@prbmp.com.

### Important Notice

Whilst PRB Martin Pollins and Better Results Corporation Limited of the United Kingdom have taken every care in the preparation of the content of this document, no representation or warranty, expressed or implied, is made as to its accuracy or completeness. You should neither act, nor refrain from action, on the basis of any information obtained from this document.

The information is relevant within the United Kingdom. You should take appropriate professional advice on your particular circumstances because the application of laws and regulations will vary depending on particular circumstances.

These disclaimers and exclusions are governed by and construed in accordance with English Law.

For more information on this topic, visit our Web site at www.businesstown.com

# Appendix B

## Recommended Reading List

One of the most creative and successful people in the direct marketing industry today is Alan Rosenspan. I have enjoyed his articles, his talks, and seminars for years, and have never failed to learn something from him each time we meet. When Alan offered his personal reading list in his monthly article in *Direct Marketing* magazine recently, I asked if he would let me share it with you.

Following is Alan's list, with some additions of my own. Most of the periodicals are listed elsewhere in this book, but I have listed them here for your convenience. Alan can be reached at Arosenspan@aol.com or by phone at 617-559-0999.

## Periodicals

1. *Direct Marketing* magazine, a monthly 80-page magazine available for $52 a year. Call 1-800-229-6700 for more information or to subscribe.

2. *Target Marketing*, a monthly that is probably the best "how to" magazine in the world of direct marketing. Call 215-238-5090. May be free to qualified direct marketers. They also publish:

3. *Who's Mailing What*, a monthly 15-page newsletter by Denny Hatch focuses on analyzing specific mailings and trends. It costs $168 a year, but you also get access to the Direct Marketing Archive.

4. *DM NEWS*, a weekly 60-page newspaper, free to qualified people. Fax your request to 609-786-4415. Very current source of news, new lists, job opportunities.

5. *Direct*, a monthly 80-page glossy, a lot like *Advertising Age*. Also may be free to people working in the field or students. Call 1-800-775-3777 for details.

6. *Marketing Tools*, from Cowles Business Media. Monthly, 64 pages. Specializes in database marketing tools and techniques, modeling and statistical analyses. $69 per year. Call 203-358-9900. They also publish an annual Marketing Tools Directory. Very helpful.

7. *Catalog Age*, also from Cowles. Monthly, news and articles for executives in catalog marketing firms. $74. 203-358-9900

## Books for Direct Marketers

1. *The One-to-One Future*, by Don Peppers and Martha Rogers. Their most recent book is called *The One-to-One Enterprise*. Both are excellent.

2. *Power Direct Marketing* by "Rocket Ray" Jutkins.

3. *Business to Business Internet Marketing*, by Barry Silverstein. This book is not only an excellent overview of Internet marketing, but also a valuable primer on direct marketing. Highly recommended.

4. *The Direct Marketing Handbook* also by Ed Nash, published by McGraw-Hill. Includes about 60 chapters, each written by a different direct marketing professional.

5. *Direct Marketing Management*, by Mary Lou Roberts and Paul Berger, published by Prentice-Hall in 1989. A 500-page book with real life cases, this is probably the most advanced (and useful) book available today.

6. *Commonsense Direct Marketing*, by Drayton Bird, published by the Printed Shop in the U.K. Difficult to get, but a wonderfully written, non-technical book with case histories mainly from overseas.

7. *Successful Catalogs*, by Steve Warsaw, published by Retail Reporting Corporation in New York (212-255-9595). Full of award winning catalogs and the techniques behind them. Very useful to catalog companies.

8. *Creative Strategy in Direct Marketing*, by Susan K. Jones, published by NTC Business Books (call them in Lincolnwood, Illinois for their comprehensive business books catalog). Focuses more on strategy than specific techniques. Worth reading.

9. *Winning Direct Marketing*, by Joan Throckmorton. Call the Direct Marketing Association in New York to find out where to get hold of this one. An excellent book that shows you how to write, art direct, conceptualize, develop, improve, and evaluate creative work in all media.

10. *MaxiMarketing*, by Stan Rapp and Tom Collins. Published by McGraw-Hill in 1987. One of the only books that shows how to integrate direct marketing into your entire marketing efforts. Their new book, also good, is called *Beyond MaxiMarketing*.

11. *Tested Advertising Methods*, by John Caples (or anything by the same author). 317 pages, published in paperback by Reward Books, a division of Prentice-Hall. The simple truths of this book have stood the test of time, plus you get excellent step-by-step instructions. Chapters include "32 ways to get more inquiries from your advertising" and "How to make small ads pay."

12. *Building a Mail Order Business*, by William Cohen, published by John Wiley & Sons. It's also called "A Complete Manual for Success" and you can't find a better one. 450 pages, complete with case histories and specific places to get even more information.

13. *Successful Direct Marketing Methods*, by Bob Stone. This has been called "The Bible of Direct Marketing." It's all in there, but it can be dry. Excellent reference book.

14. *Confessions of an Advertising Man*, by David Ogilvy. Or *Ogilvy on Advertising*. Two of the best books ever written by the man who built the agency that was referred to as "The University of Advertising." Either one is a "must read."

15. *Million Dollar Mailings*, by Denny Hatch, published by Libey Publishing based in Washington. A detailed analysis of the 74 most successful mailings of all time. Excellent, excellent, excellent!!

[To Alan's list "must read" list, I would add the following. GD]:

16. *The Lead Generation Handbook*, by Bernard A Goldberg, published by Direct Marketing Publishers, Yardley, PA (215) 321-3068. 838 pages, $89. An outstanding exploration of lead generation and database marketing. and *Business to Business Direct Marketing*, by Bernie Goldberg and Tracy Emerick.

17. *The Complete Direct Mail List Handbook*, by Ed Burnett, the "Father of List Management," published by Prentice-Hall, Englewood Cliffs, New Jersey. 774 pages of list expertise.

18. *How to Write A Good Advertisement*, by Victor O. Schwab, published by Melvin Powers, probably out of print.

19. *The New Rules of Marketing: How to Use One-to-One Relationship Marketing to be the Leader in Your Industry*, by Fred Newell, published by McGraw-Hill. The subhead says it all.

Now back to Alan's list:

## Just for Fun

No textbooks here, but a selection of books that I have found enjoyable to read and will give you a broader understanding of advertising and direct marketing.

20. *Positioning: The Battle for Your Mind* and *Marketing Warfare*, by Al Ries and Jack Trout.

21. *Advertising Pure and Simple*, by Hank Seiden.

22. *Success Forces* (The JS&A story—a great book), by Joe Sugarman. He just wrote three new books that are also worth reading.

23. *The Great Brain Robbery* and *Crowning the Customer* and anything by Murray Raphel.

24. *From Those Wonderful Folks Who Gave You Pearl Harbor*, by Jerry Della Femina.

25. *Swim with the Sharks Without Being Eaten Alive* and *Beware the Naked Man Who Offers You His Shirt* by Harvey Mackey.

26. *You Can Negotiate Anything*, by Cohen.

27. *How to Sell Yourself*, by Joe Girard.

## Government Agency Publications

28. Designing Letter Mail (Publication 25)—A technical guide to designing letter mail for automation.

29. Designing Reply Mail (Publication 353)—A step-by-step guide to designing Business Reply and Courtesy Reply Mail.

30. Postal Addressing Standards (Publication 28)—A guide to the various U.S. Postal Addressing Standards.

31. Address Information Systems (Publication 40)—A guide to products which improve the quality of address files.

32. Business Reply Mail Accounting System (Publication 46)—Describes a system to reduce costs for Business Reply Mail users.

33. National Change of Address (Notice 47)—Describes the NCOA system, which makes available current change of address information.

34. Metering Your Mail (Publication 125)–A pamphlet on how to obtain and use meters.

35. Addressing for Success (Publication 221) Addressing for compatibility with automated processing equipment.

### U.S. Postal Publications:

1. *Domestic Mail Manual*–Available by subscription. Contains official regulations, procedures and services.

2. *Postal Bulletin*–Available by subscription. Covers changes in regulations and new services.

3. *National Five-Digit ZIP Code and Post Office Directory* (Publication 65)–ZIP codes for every mailing address in the U.S.

4. Available from the Superintendent of Documents:

    U.S Government Printing Office
    941 North Capitol Street, N.W.
    Washington, D.C. 20402-9375
    *www.usps.gov*

And don't forget the terrific lineup of "Streetwise" and other books for small business published by Adams Media. You'll find them on the BusinessTown web site: *www.businesstown.com* and at *www.adamsmedia.com*.

For more information on this topic, visit our Web site at www.businesstown.com

# Appendix C

# Directory of Local Direct Marketing Clubs and Associations

One of the surest ways to become quickly immersed in direct marketing know-how is to join one of the many local DM clubs and associations located in major cities around the country.

These organizations hold regular meetings at which direct marketing issues are discussed and techniques are demonstrated. Most hold annual "Direct Marketing Days" or conferences of one sort or another which, together with the group's own membership, will introduce you to the suppliers and vendors of direct marketing services in your area.

This directory appears monthly in the listings pages of *Direct Marketing* magazine and is offered here with the publisher's permission. Remember that many of these groups change officers annually, so if the contact information provided is out of date, whoever answers will likely be able to refer you to the right people.

**Arizona**
Phoenix Direct Marketing Club—Pres. Andrew Yoelin
602-970-8643      Fax 602-804-1196
5524 East Waltann Lane, Scottsdale, AZ 85254-1701

**California**
American Telemarketing Assoc.—Pres. Margaret Leverence
818-766-5324  Fax 818-766-8168
4605 Lankershire Blvd., Suite 824, N. Hollywood, CA 91602-1891

DM Assoc. of Orange County—Pres. Roy Porter
714-776-4520 x 260
PO Box 27244, Santa Ana, CA 92799-7244

DM Club of Southern California—Pres. Jan Nathan
310-374-7499
627 Aviation Way, Manhattan Beach, CA 90266

Northern California Catalog Club—Pres. James West
510-682-5091  Fax 510-682-5091
4480 Treat Blvd. 348, Concord, CA 94521

North California Direct Marketing Club—Pres. Walt D. Abraham
415-434-1696  Fax 415-986-1848

c/o Communicator, 500 Sutter Street, Suite 906,
San Franciso, CA 94102

Western Fulfillment Management Assoc.–Pres. Jan Edwards Pullin
310-323-7231  Fax 310-323-7220
c/o BPA Int'l; Pacific Gateway II 19191, S. Vermont Ave., #350
Torrence, CA 90502

## Carolinas—North and South
Carolinas Direct Marketing Association–Assoc. Manager
800-377-2289  Fax 919-231-1299
PO Box 40523, Raleigh, NC 27629-0523

## California
Rocky Mountain DM Assoc.–Pres. Debra Jason
303-914-8407  Fax 303-969-8320
24595 Ammons Street, Lakewood, CO 80227

## Connecticut
DMA of Western Connecticut–Pres. Leslie Roger
203-452-2388  Fax 203-262-1261
PO Box 3586, Danbury, CT 06813-3586

New England Mail Order Assoc.–Pres. Ken Canaway
860-691-1290
14 Faulkner Drive, Niantic, CT 06357

## District of Columbia
Electronic Retailing Assoc.–Pres. Elissa Myers
202-289-6462
1225 New York Ave., Suite 1200, Washington, DC 20005

FMA Washington, DC Chapter–Pres. Joan Stalte
301-762-0564
PO Box 67, Hayattsville, MD 20781

Direct Mktg. Assoc. of Washington–Sherry Marshall, Exec. Dir.
703-821-3629
7702 Leesburg Pike #400, Falls Church, VA 22043

MASA Int'l–Pres. David Weaver
703-836-9200
1421 Prince Street, Suite 200, Alexandria, VA 22314

Advertising Mail Marketing Assoc.–Gene A. Del Polito, Exec. Dir.
202-347-0055
1333 F. St. NW 710, Washington, DC 20004-1108

Women in Direct Marketing Int'l-Washington–Pres. Donna Elek
703-451-7531
7923 Richfield Road, Springfield, VA 22153

### Florida
Florida Direct Marketing Assoc. State–Pres. Marge Rolfs
813-345-3271
c/o Direct Consulting Associates, 3160 Sunset Drive N. St.
Petersburg, FL 33710

Florida Direct Marketing Assoc., Gold Coast Chapter–
Pres. Betty Kaufman      954-472-6374  Fax 954-472-8165
8851 NW 10th Place, Plantation, FL 33322

Florida Direct Marketing Assoc., Sun Coast Chapter–Pres. BJ Ryan
813-855-4247
c/o Genesis Direct, 391 Roberts Rd. #1, Olsmar, FL 34677

### Georgia
DMA of Atlanta–Pres. Julie Henry
404-874-2333
229 Peach Street, Atlanta, GA

American Telemarketing Assn./Southwestern Chapter
–Pres. Roger Nunley, Co. Pres.      404-352-9291
17 Dean Overlook NW, Atlanta, GA 30318

### Hawaii
Direct Response Advertising & Marketing Assn.–Pres. Victor Fujita
808-545-1680  Fax 808-528-4293
Suite 315, 81 South Hotel Street, Honolulu, HI 96813

## Illinois

Business Management Association—Pres. Tom Carter
800-664-4BMA  Fax 312-409-4266
150 North Wacker Drive, Suite 1760, Chicago, IL 60606

Chicago Assoc. of Direct Marketing—Pres. Shelly Sable
312-670-2236  Fax 312-670-2239
435 North Michigan Avenue, Chicago, IL 60611

Women in Direct Marketing Int'l—Laura Johnson, Chicago Chapter Pres.
312-360-0381  Fax 312-360-0338
330 South Wells, Street 1422, Chicago, IL 60606-7107

## Indiana

Indianapolis Direct Marketing Assoc.
317-722-7220
PO Box 40112, Indianapolis, IN 46240-0112

## Kentucky

Louisville Direct Marketing Assoc.—Pres. Peter Wheeler
502-969-6300
PO Box 36034, Louisville, KY 40233-6034

## Maryland

Mail Order Assoc. of Nurseries—Pres. Ms. Camille Chioini
410-730-9713
PO Box 2129, Columbia, MD 21045

Maryland Direct Marketing Assoc.—Pres. Michael Lawson
410-267-7667
The McClure Group, 1319 Blackwalnut Court,
Annapolis, MD 21403-4660

## Massachusetts

New England Direct Marketing Assoc.—Pres. Chet Mattera
617-237-1366
6 Abbott Road, Wellesley, MA 02181-7517

### Michigan
Direct Marketing Assoc. of Detroit–Pres. Betsy DeLage
810-258-8803  Fax 810-258-0217
IBM, 18000 W. Nine Mile Road, Southfield, MI 48086

### Minnesota
Midwest Direct Marketing Assoc.–Pres. Donna Wald
612-928-4643  Fax 612-929-1318
4248 Park Glen Road, Minneapolis, MN 55416

### Missouri
Direct Marketing Assoc. of St. Louis–Pres. Marsh McConnel
314-291-3144
12686 Lonsdale Drive, Bridgeton, MO 63044-1507

Kansas City Direct Marketing Assoc.–Pres. Kristie McKabban
816-561-5323
638 West 39th Street, Kansas City, MO 64141-6264

### Nebraska
Mid America Direct Marketing Assoc.–Pres. Kerry Helnrich
712-323-2500, ext. 1740
5740 South 77th Street, Omaha, NE 68127

### New York
Assn. Of American Publishers–Jim Prendergrast, Exec. Dir.
212-644-8085  Fax 212-842-0270
PO Box 3139, New York, NY 10163-3139

Assn. of Direct Marketing Agencies–Jim Prendergrast, Exec. Dir.
212-644-8085  Fax 212-842-0270
PO Box 3139, New York, NY 10163-3139

Direct Marketing Association
212-768-7277
1120 Avenue of the Americas, New York, NY 10036

Direct Marketing Club of NY
516-746-6700
224 Seventh Street, Garden City, NY 11530

Fulfillment Management Assoc.–Pres. Andrea Reska Tome
212-532-7300  Fax 212-532-8771
60 East 42nd Street, Suite 1146, New York, NY 10165

Graphic Arts Professionals–Jim Prendergrast, Exec. Dir.
212-644-8085  Fax 212-842-0270
PO Box 3139, New York, NY 10163-3139

Hudson Valley DM Assoc.–Pres. Gail Henry
914-723-3176
c/o Marvel Assoc. 199 Sound Beach Avenue,
Old Greenwich, CT 06870

Long Island Direct Marketing Assoc.–Pres. Jeff Ehrlich
516-758-8300  Fax 516-758-8360
c/o Fulfillment Plus, Inc., PO Box 2181, Holtsville, NY 11742

Mail Advertising Service Assoc. of NY–Jim Prendergrast, Exec. Dir.
212-644-8085
PO Box 3139, New York, NY 10163-3139

Nat'l Assoc. of Publishers Representatives–Pres. Jim Predergrast
212-644-8085
PO Box 3139, New York, NY 10163-3139

Nat'l Business Circulation Assoc.–Pres. David Williams
212-714-3153
c/o K-Olll Directory Corp., 424 West 33rd Street,
New York, NY 10001

West Coast
414-905-2259

Upstate Direct Marketing Assoc.–Pres. Jim Della Villa
716-473-7300
Sigma Marketing Group, Inc., 1850 S. Winton Road,
Rochester, NY 14618

Women in Direct Marketing Int'l—Pres. Rosann Virgili
516-746-6700  Fax 516-294-8141
224 Seventh Street, Garden City, NY 11530

## Ohio
Cincinnati Direct Marketing Club—Pres. Tracy Burgoone
513-671-3811
11590 Century Blvd., Suite 211, Cincinnati, OH 45246

Direct Marketing Assoc. of Dayton—Pres. Marilyn Smith
513-294-4000
c/o Yeck Bros., 2222 Arbor Blvd., Dayton, OH 45439

Mid-Ohio Direct Marketing Assoc.—Pres. Chris McGovern
614-923-6000
PO Box 20284, Columbus, OH 43220-0284

## Oregon
Oregon Direct Marketing Assoc.—Pres. Nick Verlotta  503-239-8338
PO Box 2334, Portland, OR 97208

## Pennsylvania
Philadelphia Direct Marketing Assoc.—Pres. Shirley Taffe
215-619-3057
1787 Sentry Parkway West, Suite 1, Blue Bell, PA 19422

## Texas
Dallas/Fort Worth Direct Marketing Assoc.—Pres. Melitta Taylor
972-404-8345
4020 McEwen, Suite 105, Dallas, TX 75244-5019

Houston Direct Marketing Assoc.—Pres. Gale Kiester Pashia
713-690-8175
The Service Center

## Vermont
Vermont/New Hampshire Direct Marketing Assoc.—Pres. Kendra Fowler
603-225-9159
76 South State Street, Concord, NH 03301

## Virginia

Graphics Communications Assoc.–Pres. Norman Scharpl
703-519-8160
100 Dangerfield Road, Alexandria, VA 22314-2804

MASA International–Pres. David Weaver
703-836-9200
1421 Prince Street, Suite 100, Alexandria, VA 22314-2806

## Canada

Canadian Direct Marketing-National Headquarters–Pres. J. Gustavson
416-391-2392
#1 Concorde Gate, Suite 607, Don Mills, ON M3C 3N6 Canada

Canadian Direct Marketing Assoc./VAN-B.C. Chapter–
Pres. Theo Sanidas
604-681-4911
c/o Western Shores Direct Marketing Group, 200-1200 W. Pender
St., Vancouver, BC V5E 2S9 Canada

Canadian Direct Marketing Assoc./Calgary Chapter–
Pres. W. Gattinger
403-215-3200
c/o The Parker Group Comm., Inc., 833-4th Ave. S.W., Ste. 900,
Calgary, AB T2P 3T5 Canada

Canadian Direct Marketing Assoc./Manitoba Chapter–
Pres. Moe Levy
204-943-6766
c/o Winnipeg Fur Exchange, 314 Ross Ave.,
Winnipeg, MB R3A 0L4 Canada

Canadian Direct Marketing Assoc./Maritime Chapter–
Pres. F. Drinnan
902-827-2661
c/o DRM Database Marketing, PO Box 2336,
Dartmouth, NS B2W 3Y4 Canada

Canadian Direct Marketing Assoc./QU-Montreal Chapter
—Pres. R. Duhamel
514-289-9910
c/o G.T.C. Transcontinental Group, 1130 Sherbrooke St. W. Ste 620, Montreal, QC H3A 2MB Canada

Canadian Direct Marketing Assoc./Ottawa Chapter
—Pres. Bernie Forrestel
613-224-8487
c/o Mailtech

Direct Mktg. Assoc. of Toronto—Pres. Luci Furtado
416-502-0433
c/o DMAT, 200 Consumers Road, Suite 200, North York, ON M2J 4R4 Canada

Note: Call the operator for assistance with international calls.

## Austria
Direct Marketing Verband Osterreich
94 76 50        Fax 9112972
Linzer Strasse 357, 1144 WIEN

## Australia
Australian Direct Marketing Association
Fax 02-247-4919
Level 7, 22-30 Bridge St., Sydney, NSW 2000 Australia

## Belgium
Belgian Assoc. of Marketing Direct—Pres. Michael J.O. Sutherland
Fax 02-332-10-70
rue de Stalle 65, 1180, Brussels, Belgium

European Direct Marketing Assoc.—Pres. Michael J.O. Sutherland
322 21 76309
36 Rue du Gouvernement Prov., Brussels B1000, Belgium

## England

British Direct Marketing Assoc.–Pres. Colin Lloyd
Fax 71-321 0191, 71-321 2525 Haymarket House, 10 Oxendon
Street, London SW1Y 4EE

## Germany

German Direct Marketing Assoc.–Pres. Friedhelm Lammoth
0611-977930      Fax 0611-9779399
Hasengartenstrabe 14 D/65189, Wiesbaden

## New Zealand

New Zealand Direct Marketing Assoc.–Pres. Scott Fuller
+64 9-303-9470   Fax +64 9-303-4787
PO Box 47681, Ponsonby Auckland New Zealand

## Sweden

Swedish Direct Marketing Assoc.
Fax 46-8-662-76112
Box 14038, S-104, Stockholm Sweden

For more information on this topic, visit our Web site at www.businesstown.com

# Appendix D

## DMA Ethical Guidelines

## Outline of the Direct Marketing Association Guidelines for Ethical Business Practice

Revised August 1999

The Direct Marketing Association's Guidelines for Ethical Business Practice are intended to provide individuals and organizations involved in direct marketing in all media with generally accepted principles of conduct. These guidelines reflect the DMA's long-standing policy of high levels of ethics and the responsibility of the Association, its members, and all marketers to maintain consumer and community relationships that are based on fair and ethical principles. In addition to providing general guidance to the industry, the Guidelines for Ethical Business Practice are used by the DMA's Committee on Ethical Business Practice, an industry peer review committee, as the standard to which direct marketing promotions that are the subject of complaint to the DMA are compared. These self-regulatory guidelines are intended to be honored in light of their aims and principles. All marketers should support the guidelines in spirit and not treat their provisions as obstacles to be circumvented by legal ingenuity. These guidelines also represent the DMA's general philosophy that self-regulatory measures are preferable to governmental mandates. Self-regulatory actions are more readily adaptable to changing techniques and economic and social conditions. They encourage widespread use of sound business practices. Because dishonest, misleading, or offensive communications discredit all means of advertising and marketing, including direct marketing, observance of these guidelines by all concerned is expected. All persons involved in direct marketing should take reasonable steps to encourage other industry members to follow these guidelines as well.

### The Terms of the Offer

Honesty and Clarity of Offer—Article #1
Accuracy and Consistency—Article #2
Clarity of Representations—Article #3
Actual Conditions—Article #4

## Collection, Use, and Maintenance of Marketing Data

## Telephone Marketing

## Appendices

# DMA Ethical Guidelines in Detail

## The Terms of the Offer

### Article #1: Honesty and Clarity of Offer

All offers should be clear, honest, and complete so that the consumer may know the exact nature of what is being offered, the price, the terms of payment (including all extra charges), and the commitment involved in the placing of an order. Before publication of an offer, marketers should be prepared to substantiate any claims or offers made. Advertisements or specific claims that are untrue, misleading, deceptive, or fraudulent should not be used.

### Article #2: Accuracy and Consistency

Simple and consistent statements or representations of all the essential points of the offer should appear in the promotional material. The overall impression of an offer should not be contradicted by individual statements, representations, or disclaimers.

### Article #3: Clarity of Representations

Representations which, by their size, placement, duration, or other characteristics are unlikely to be noticed or are difficult to understand should not be used if they are material to the offer.

### Article #4: Actual Conditions

All descriptions, promises, and claims of limitation should be in accordance with actual conditions, situations, and circumstances existing at the time of the promotion.

### Article #5: Disparagement

Disparagement of any person or group on grounds addressed by federal or state laws that prohibit discrimination is unacceptable.

### Article #6: Decency

Solicitations should not be sent to consumers who have indicated to the marketer that they consider those solicitations to be vulgar, immoral, profane, pornographic, or offensive in any way and who do not want to receive them.

### Article #7: Photographs and Art Work

Photographs, illustrations, artwork, and the situations they describe should be accurate portrayals and current reproductions of the products, services, or other subjects they represent.

### Article #8: Disclosure of Sponsor and Intent

All marketing contacts should disclose the name of the sponsor and each purpose of the contact. No one should make offers or solicitations in the guise of one purpose when the intent is a different purpose.

### Article #9: Accessibility

Every offer and shipment should clearly identify the marketer's name and postal address or telephone number, or both, at which the consumer may obtain service. If an offer is made online, an e-mail address should also be identified.

### Article #10: Solicitation in the Guise of an Invoice or Governmental Notification

Offers that are likely to be mistaken for bills, invoices, or notices from public utilities or governmental agencies should not be used.

### Article #11: Postage, Shipping, or Handling Charges

Postage, shipping, or handling charges, if any, should bear a reasonable relationship to actual costs incurred.

## Marketing to Children

### Article #12: Marketing to Children

Offers and the manner in which they are presented that are suitable for adults only should not be made to children. In determining the suitability of a communication with children online or in any other medium, marketers should address the age range, knowledge, sophistication, and maturity of their intended audience.

### Article #13: Parental Responsibility and Choice

Marketers should provide notice and an opportunity to opt out of the marketing process so that parents have the ability to limit the collection, use, and disclosure of their children's names, addresses, or other personally identifiable information.

### Article #14: Information from or about Children

Marketers should take into account the age range, knowledge, sophistication, and maturity of children when collecting information from them. Marketers should limit the collection, use and dissemination of information collected from or about children to information required for the promotion, sale and delivery of goods and services, provision of customer services, conducting market research and engaging in other appropriate marketing activities. Marketers should effectively explain that the information is being requested for marketing purposes. Information not appropriate for marketing purposes should not be collected. Upon request from a parent, marketers should promptly provide the source and general nature of information maintained about a child. Marketers should implement strict security measures to ensure against unauthorized access, alteration, or dissemination of the data collected from or about children.

### Article #15: Marketing Online to Children Under 13 Years of Age

- Marketers should not collect personally identifiable information online from a child under 13 without prior parental consent or direct parental notification of the nature and intended use of such information online and an opportunity for the parent to prevent such use and participation in the activity. Online contact information should only be used to directly respond to an activity initiated by a child and not to recontact child for other purposes without prior parental consent. However, a marketer may contact and get information from a child for the purpose of obtaining parental consent.

- Marketers should not collect, without prior parental consent, personally identifiable information online from children that would permit any off-line contact with the child.
- Marketers should not distribute to third parties, without prior parental consent, information collected from a child that would permit any contact with that child.
- Marketers should take reasonable steps to prevent the online publication or posting of information that would allow a third party to contact a child off-line unless the marketer has prior parental consent.
- Marketers should not entice a child to divulge personally identifiable information by the prospect of a special game, prize, or other offer.
- Marketers should not make a child's access to a Web site contingent on the collection of personally identifiable information. Only online contact information used to enhance the interactivity of the site is permitted.

The following assumptions underlie these online guidelines:
- When a marketer directs a site at a certain age group, it can expect that the visitors to that site are in that age range; and
- When a marketer asks the age of the child, the marketer can assume the answer to be truthful.

## Special Offers and Claims

### Article #16: Use of the Word "Free" and Other Similar Representations

A product or service that is offered without cost or obligation to the recipient may be unqualifiedly described as "free."

If a product or service is offered as "free," all qualifications and conditions should be clearly and conspicuously disclosed, in close conjunction with the use of the term "free" or other similar phrase. When the term "free" or other similar representations are made (for example, 2-for-1, half-price, or 1-cent offers), the product or service required to be purchased should not have been increased in price or decreased in quality or quantity.

### Article #17: Price Comparisions

Price comparisons including those between a marketer's current price and a former, future, or suggested price, or between a marketer's price and the price of a competitor's comparable product should be fair and accurate. In each case of comparison to a former, manufacturer's suggested or competitor's comparable product price, recent substantial sales should have been made at that price in the same trade area. For comparisons with a future price, there should be a reasonable expectation that the new price will be charged in the foreseeable future.

### Article #18: Guarantees

If a product or service is offered with a guarantee or a warranty, either the terms and conditions should be set forth in full in the promotion, or the promotion should state how the consumer may obtain a copy. The guarantee should clearly state the name and address of the guarantor and the duration of the guarantee. Any requests for repair, replacement or refund under the terms of a guarantee or warranty should be honored promptly. In an unqualified offer of refund, repair or replacement, the customer's preference should prevail.

### Article #19: Use of Test or Survey Data

All test or survey data referred to in advertising should be valid and reliable as to source and methodology, and should support the specific claim for which it is cited. Advertising claims should not distort test or survey results or take them out of context.

### Article #20: Testimonials and Endorsements

Testimonials and endorsements should be used only if they are:
a. Authorized by the person quoted;
b. Genuine and related to the experience of the person giving them both at the time made and at the time of the promotion; and

c. Not taken out of context so as to distort the endorser's opinion or experience with the product.

## Sweepstakes

### Article #21: Use of the Term "Sweepstakes"

Sweepstakes are promotional devices by which items of value (prizes) are awarded to participants by chance without the promoter's requiring the participants to render something of value (consideration) to be eligible to participate. The co-existence of all three elements—prize, chance, and consideration—in the same promotion constitutes a lottery. It is illegal for any private enterprise to run a lottery without specific governmental authorization. When skill replaces chance, the promotion becomes a skill contest. When gifts (premiums or other items of value) are given to all participants independent of the element of chance, the promotion is not a sweepstakes. Promotions that are not sweepstakes should not be held out as such. Only those promotional devices which satisfy the definition stated above should be called or held out to be a sweepstakes.

### Article #22: No-Purchase Option

Promotions should clearly state that no purchase is required to win sweepstakes prizes. They should not represent that those who make a purchase or otherwise render consideration with their entry will have a better chance of winning or will be eligible to win more or larger prizes than those who do not make a purchase or otherwise render consideration. The method for entering without ordering should be easy to find, read, and understand. When response devices used only for entering the sweepstakes are provided, they should be as easy to find as those utilized for ordering the product or service.

### Article #23: Chances of Winning

No sweepstakes promotion, or any of its parts, should represent that a recipient or entrant has won a prize or that any entry stands a greater chance of winning a prize than any other entry when this is not the case. Winners should be selected in a manner that ensures fair application of the laws of chance.

### Article #24: Prizes

Sweepstakes prizes should be advertised in a manner that is clear, honest, and complete so that the consumer may know the exact nature of what is being offered. For prizes paid over time, the annual payment schedule and number of years should be clearly disclosed. Photographs, illustrations, artwork, and the situations they represent should be accurate portrayals of the prizes listed in the promotion. No award or prize should be held forth directly or by implication as having substantial monetary value if it is of nominal worth. The value of a non-cash prize should be stated at regular retail value, whether actual cost to the sponsor is greater or less. All prizes should be awarded and delivered without cost to the participant. If there are certain conditions under which a prize or prizes will not be awarded, that fact should be disclosed in a manner that is easy to find, read and understand.

### Article #25: Premiums

Premiums should be advertised in a manner that is clear, honest, and complete so that the consumer may know the exact nature of what is being offered. A premium, gift, or item should not be called or held out to be a "prize" if it is offered to every recipient of or participant in a promotion. If all participants will receive a premium, gift or item, that fact should be clearly disclosed.

### Article #26: Disclosure of Rules

All terms and conditions of the sweepstakes, including entry procedures and rules, should be easy to find, read, and understand. Disclosures set out in the rules section concerning no-purchase option, prizes, and chances of winning should not contradict the overall impression created by the promotion. The following should be set forth clearly in the rules:

- No purchase of the advertised product or service is required in order to win a prize.

- Procedures for entry.
- If applicable, disclosure that a facsimile of the entry blank or other alternate means (such as a 3" × 5" card) may be used to enter the sweepstakes.
- The termination date for eligibility in the sweepstakes. The termination date should specify whether it is a date of mailing or receipt of entry deadline.
- The number, retail value (of non-cash prizes), and complete description of all prizes offered, and whether cash may be awarded instead of merchandise. If a cash prize is to be awarded by installment payments, that fact should be clearly disclosed, along with the nature and timing of the payments.
- The approximate odds of winning each prize or a statement that such odds depend on number of entrants.
- The method by which winners will be selected.
- The geographic area covered by the sweepstakes and those areas in which the offer is void.
- All eligibility requirements, if any.
- Approximate dates when winners will be selected and notified.
- Publicity rights regarding the use of winner's name.
- Taxes are the responsibility of the winner.
- Provision of a mailing address to allow consumers to receive a list of winners of prizes over $25 in value.

## Fulfillment

### Article #27: Unordered Merchandise

Merchandise should not be shipped without having first received the customer's permission. The exceptions are samples or gifts clearly marked as such, and merchandise mailed by a charitable organization soliciting contributions, as long as all items are sent with a clear and conspicuous statement informing the recipient of an unqualified right to treat the product as a gift and to do with it as the recipient sees fit, at no cost or obligation to the recipient.

### Article #28: Product Availability and Shipment

Direct marketers should offer merchandise only when it is on hand or when there is a reasonable expectation of its timely receipt. Direct marketers should ship all orders according to the terms of the offer or within 30 days where there is no promised shipping date, unless otherwise directed by the consumer, and should promptly notify consumers of any delays.

### Article #29: Dry Testing

Direct marketers should engage in dry testing only when the special nature of the offer is made clear in the promotion.

## Collection, Use and Maintenance of Marketing Data

### Article #30: Collection, Use, and Transfer of Personally Identifiable Data

Consumers who provide data that may be rented, sold, or exchanged for marketing purposes should be informed periodically by marketers of their policy concerning the rental, sale, or exchange of such data and of the opportunity to opt out of the marketing process. Should that policy substantially change, marketers have an obligation to inform consumers of that change prior to the rental, sale or exchange of such data, and to offer consumers an opportunity to opt out of the marketing process at that time. All individual opt-out requests should be honored. Marketers should maintain and use their own systems, policies, and procedures, and at no cost to consumers refrain from using or transferring such data, as the case may be, as requested by consumers.

List compilers should maintain and use their own systems, policies and procedures, and at no cost to consumers refrain from using or transferring data, as the case may be, as requested by consumers. For each list that is rented, sold, or exchanged, the applicable DMA Preference Service name removal list (e.g., Mail Preference Service, Telephone Preference Service) should be employed prior to use. Data about consumers who have opted out of use or transfer should not, per their requests, be used, rented, sold, or exchanged. Upon request by a consumer, marketers should disclose the source from which they obtained personally identifiable data about that consumer.

### Article #31: Personal Data

Marketers should be sensitive to the issue of consumer privacy and should only collect, combine, rent, sell, exchange, or use marketing data. Marketing data should be used only for marketing purposes. Data and selection criteria that by reasonable standards may be considered sensitive and/or intimate should not be disclosed, displayed, or provide the basis for lists made available for rental, sale, or exchange when there is a reasonable expectation by the consumer that the information will be kept confidential.

### Article #32: Promotion of Marketing Lists

Any advertising or promotion for marketing lists being offered for rental, sale, or exchange should reflect the fact that a marketing list is an aggregate collection of marketing data. Such promotions should also reflect a sensitivity for the consumers on those lists.

### Article #33: Marketing List Usage

List owners, brokers, managers, compilers, and users of marketing lists should ascertain the nature of the list's intended usage for each materially different marketing use prior to rental, sale, exchange, transfer, or use of the list. List owners, brokers, managers, and compilers should not permit the rental, sale, exchange, or transfer of their marketing lists, nor should users use any marketing lists for an offer that is in violation of these guidelines.

## Telephone Marketing

### Article #34: Reasonable Hours

Telephone contacts should be made during reasonable hours as specified by federal and state laws and regulations.

### Article #35: Taping of Conversations

Taping of telephone conversations by telephone marketers should only be conducted with notice to or consent of all parties, or the use of a beeping device, as required by applicable federal and state laws and regulations.

### Article #36: Restricted Contacts

A telephone marketer should not knowingly call a consumer who has an unlisted or unpublished telephone number, or a telephone number for which the called party must pay the charges, except in instances where the number was provided by the consumer to that marketer. Random dialing techniques, whether manual or automated, in which those parties to be called are left to chance should not be used in sales and marketing solicitations. Sequential dialing techniques, whether a manual or automated process, in which selection of those parties to be called is based on the location of their telephone numbers in a sequence of telephone numbers should not be used.

### Article #37: Use of Automated Dialing Equipment

When using automated dialing equipment for any reason, telephone marketers should only use equipment which allows the telephone to immediately release the line when the called party terminates the connection.

- ADRMPS (Automatic Dialers and Recorded Message Players) and prerecorded messages should be used only in accordance with tariffs, federal, state, and local laws, FCC regulations, and these guidelines. Telephone marketers should use a live operator to obtain a consumer's permission before delivering a recorded message. When using any automated dialing equipment to reach a multi-line location, the equipment should release each line used before connecting to another.

### Article #38: Use of Predictive Auto Dialing Equipment

Repeated abandoned "hang up" calls by individual marketers to consumers' residential telephone numbers are seen as offensive by consumers and should be eliminated. Marketers who use predictive auto dialing equipment to contact consumers' residences, and those on whose behalf those contacts are made, should:

- Set a company-wide standard that requires that every effort is made to have a live operator converse promptly with the consumer who answers the telephone. Abandoned or "hang up" calls should be kept as close to 0% as possible, and in no case should exceed 5% of answered calls per day in any campaign.
- If a live operator is unavailable to take any call generated by the dialer, abandon the call and release the line after not more than two seconds.
- Not abandon the same telephone number more than twice within a 48-hour time period and not more than twice within a 30-day period of a marketing campaign.
- If further calls are placed to a telephone number that has been either abandoned by the marketer twice in the same month of a marketing campaign, or twice during the past 48 hours for any marketing campaign, then any additional calls must be connected promptly to a live operator.
- Not knowingly call anyone who has an unlisted or unpublished telephone number unless calling an existing customer or in support of an existing marketer-customer relationship, and not knowingly call anyone who is on the marketer's do-not-call list.
- Use the DMA's Telephone Preference Service name-removal list prior to using any outbound calling list of prospects (not existing customers).
- Allow the predictive dialing system to ring at least four times or for 12 seconds before disconnecting.

Companies that manufacture and/or sell predictive auto dialing equipment should:

- Design the software with the goal of minimizing "hang up" calls to consumers. The software should be delivered to the user set as close to 0% as possible.
- Distribute these Guidelines for Users of Predictive Auto Dialing Equipment to purchasers of predictive dialing equipment and recommend that they be followed.

- The predictive dialing equipment's software should include reporting capability that would 1) allow prospective buyers to compare products, and 2) permit the user of the equipment to substantiate the manner in which the equipment is used. At a minimum, the software should be capable of providing the following information:
  calls attempted—numbers
  calls answered—numbers and percentage
  calls connected—numbers and percentage
  calls passed to agent—numbers and percentage
  calls capturing previous do-not-call requests

### Glossary of Terms Used

Predictive Auto Dialing Equipment—any system or device that initiates outgoing call attempts from a predetermined list of phone numbers, based on a computerized pacing algorithm.

Abandoned Call—a call placed by a predictive dialer to a consumer, which, when answered by the consumer, breaks the connection because no live agent is available to speak to the consumer.

Abandon Rate—the percentage of leads that are brought up by the dialer which are not then transferred to a live operator (does not include calls to answering machines).

Answered Calls—calls which are answered by a live consumer (not an answering machine).

Marketing Campaign—a marketing effort carried out by marketers to consumers, or by service agents on behalf of marketers, during a specific time period, and in which a list of prospective customers is used to sell the same products or services.

Report—reportable information that should be made available which contains key points, including the percentage of abandoned calls, call attempts, call delays, and other statistics.

### Article #39: Use of Telephone Facsimile Machines

Unless there is a prior business relationship with the recipient, or unless the recipient has given prior permission, unsolicited advertisements should not be transmitted by facsimile. Each permitted transmission to a fax machine must clearly contain on each page or on the first page, the date and time the transmission is sent, the identity of the sender, and the telephone number of the sender or the sending machine.

### Article #40: Promotions for Response by Toll-Free and Pay-per-Call Numbers

Promotions for response by 800 or other toll-free numbers should be used only when there is no charge to the consumer for the call itself and when there is no transfer from a toll-free number to a pay call. Promotions for response by using 900 numbers or any other type of pay-per-call programs should clearly and conspicuously disclose all charges for the call. A preamble at the beginning of the 900 or other pay-per-call should include the nature of the service or program, charge per minute, and the total estimated charge for the call, as well as the name, address, and telephone number of the sponsor. The caller should be given the option to disconnect the call at any time during the preamble without incurring any charge. The 900 number or other pay-per-call should only use equipment that ceases accumulating time and charges immediately upon disconnection by the caller.

### Article #41: Disclosure and Tactics

Prior to asking consumers for payment authorization, telephone marketers should disclose the cost of the merchandise or service and all terms and conditions, including payment plans, whether or not there is a no refund or a no cancellation policy in place, limitations, and the amount or existence of any extra charges such as shipping and handling and insurance. At no time should high pressure tactics be utilized.

### Article #42: Fund-Raising

In addition to compliance with these guidelines, fundraisers, and other charitable solicitors should, whenever requested by donors or potential donors, provide financial information regarding use of funds.

### Article #43: Laws, Codes, and Regulations

Direct marketers should operate in accordance with laws and regulations of the United States Postal Service, the Federal Trade Commission, the Federal Communications Commission, the Federal Reserve Board, and other applicable federal, state, and local laws governing advertising, marketing practices, and the transaction of business.

# Appendices

## Appendix 1: Other DMA Resources

- Marketing Online Privacy Principles and Guidance
- Privacy Promise to Consumers Member Compliance Guide
- Mailing List Practices Guidance
- Screening Advertisements: Guide for the Media
- Mail Preference Service and Telephone Preference Service Subscriber Brochures
- A Business Checklist for Direct Marketers
- Recommended Practices for Customer Service

The DMA can also provide your company with information on the following Federal Trade Commission (FTC) and Federal Communications Commission (FCC) regulations and rules affecting direct marketers:

FTC:
- Mail or Telephone Order Merchandise Rule
- Telemarketing Sales Rule
- Negative Option Rule
- Guides Against Deceptive Pricing
- Guarantees and Warranties
- Equal Credit Opportunity Act
- Fair Debt Collection Practices Act
- Telephone Disclosure and Dispute Resolution Act

FCC:
- Telephone Consumer Protection Act
- The U.S. Postal Service's Fighting Mail Order

- Fraud and Theft; Best Practices for the Mail
- Order Industry Reference Guide is available, as well as other DMA and government titles, and a variety of consumer education brochures. Contact the Ethics and Consumer Affairs Department in Washington, D.C., for more information.

## Appendix 2—DMA Interpretations Under the Ethical Guidelines

The Direct Marketing Association's Guidelines for Ethical Business Practice are principles that direct marketers should follow to ensure that they are conducting their business in an ethical manner. Guidelines, by their very nature, are meant to be general tenets. However, sometimes more specific guidance is needed to address various marketing practices. When such situations arise, the DMA issues specific guidance which expands on the ethical guidelines. "Interpretations" are used to respond to consumer and regulatory concerns regarding specific issues and to educate industry members on acceptable industry practice. As other interpretations of the guidelines are issued, they will be included herein.

### Appendix 2—#1: Interpretation on Use of Automatic Number Identification and Caller ID Under Ethical Guideline #36

The Direct Marketing Association (the DMA) recognizes that the proper use of technology such as automatic number identification (ANI) and Caller ID benefits consumers. The DMA also acknowledges the privacy concerns that may arise with the use of such technology. The DMA Guidelines for Marketing by Telephone require that telephone marketers who receive or collect consumer data as a result of a telephone marketing contact, and who intend to rent, sell, or exchange those data for direct marketing purposes should notify the consumer of that fact. Consumer requests regarding restrictions on the collection, rental, sale, or exchange of data relating to them should be honored. Telephone marketers using Automatic Number Identification (ANI) should not rent, sell, transfer, or exchange, without customer consent, telephone numbers gained from ANI except where a prior business relationship exists for the sale of directly related goods or services.

### Appendix 2—#2: Interpretation on Use of Financial Information by Direct Marketers Under Ethical Guidelines #30 and #31

The DMA considers credit card numbers, checking account numbers, and debit account numbers to be personal information and therefore should not be transferred, rented, sold, or exchanged when there is a reasonable expectation by the consumer that the information will be kept confidential. Because of the confidential nature of such personally identifying numbers, they should not be publicly displayed on direct marketing promotions or otherwise made public by direct marketers.

### Appendix 2—#3: Interpretation on Use of Social Security Numbers by Direct Marketers Under Ethical Guidelines #30 and #31

The DMA considers Social Security numbers to be personal information and therefore they should not be transferred, rented, sold, or exchanged for use by a third party when there is a reasonable expectation by the consumer that the information will be kept confidential. Because of the confidential nature of Social Security numbers, they should not be publicly displayed on direct marketing promotions or otherwise made public by direct marketers. The DMA acknowledges, however, that Social Security numbers are used by direct marketers as part of the process of extending credit to consumers or for matching or verification purposes.

### Appendix 2—#4: Interpretation on Disclosure of Health and Medical Data Under Ethical Guidelines #30 and #31

Direct marketers understand the sensitivity of collecting and using certain types of data, including health-related data. In the management of health-related data, fair information principles outlined in the DMA's Guidelines for Personal Information Protection would apply. Information derived from the relationship between a patient and a medical care provider should never be disclosed or used for marketing purposes. Health and medical data not derived from the provider-patient relationship should nonetheless be considered sensitive and personal in nature and should be rented, sold, transferred, or exchanged only where appropriate privacy safeguards are in place. Such data may include, but are not limited to, data voluntarily provided by the consumer and compiled by way of questionnaires and/or compiled list methods and marketed with the knowledge of the consumer. Consumers who provide health and medical information that may be rented, sold, transferred, or exchanged for marketing purposes should be informed at the point of providing the information of the potential for the rental, sale, transfer, or exchange of such data. Marketers should offer an opportunity to have a consumer's name deleted or suppressed upon request.

Marketers should ensure that safeguards are built into their systems to protect health and medical data from abuse, theft, or misappropriation. The text and nature of solicitations directed to consumers on the basis of health-related data should take into account the sensitive nature of such data.

## The DMA Ethics and Consumer Affairs Department

In its continuing efforts to improve the practices of direct marketing and the marketer's relationship with customers, the DMA sponsors several activities in its Ethics and Consumer Affairs Department.

- Ethical guidelines are maintained, updated periodically, and distributed to the direct marketing industry.
- The Committee on Ethical Business Practice investigates and examines mailings and offerings made throughout the direct marketing field which are brought to its attention.
- The Ethics Policy Committee revises the guidelines as needed, and initiates programs and projects directed toward improved ethical awareness in the direct marketing area.
- "Dialog" meetings between direct marketing professionals and consumer affairs and regulatory representatives facili-

tate increased communication between the industry and its customers.

- DMA's ConsumerLine (formerly Mail Order Action Line) assists consumers in resolving direct response complaints. MPS (Mail Preference Service) offers consumers assistance in decreasing the volume of national advertising mail they receive at home. TPS (Telephone Preference Service) offers a decrease in national telephone sales calls received at home.
- The Sweepstakes Helpline offers assistance regarding sweepstakes issues.

For additional information contact the DMA's Washington, D.C., office at:

1111 19th Street, NW, Suite 1100
Washington, D.C. 20036-3603
202-955-5030
fax: 202-955-0085
e-mail: consumer@the-dma.org
sweepstakes@the-dma.org
consumer@the-dma.org

Copyright ©1999 Direct Marketing Association, Inc.
Used with permission.

# Appendix E

# DMA Privacy Guidelines

# Responsibly Conquer a New Frontier with the DMA's Marketing Online Privacy

While the DMA's Guidelines apply to marketing in all media, the following principles and illustrations highlight issues unique to online and Internet marketing. They cover:

Online Notice and the Means of Opting Out,

Unsolicited Marketing E-Mail

Online Data Collection From or About Children

All marketers operating online sites, whether or not they collect personal information online from individuals, should make available to consumers their information practices in a prominent place. Marketers sharing personal information collected online should furnish individuals with an opportunity to prohibit the disclosure of such information.

## The Online Notice

The notice should be easy to find, easy to read, and easy to understand. A marketer should post its notice so as to readily enable the consumer to learn about the marketer's information practices in a manner that permits a consumer effective choice over the collection and disclosure of personal information.

For example, a marketer operating a World Wide Web site that collects personal information from individuals who visit it could post notice of its information practices on its home page or on the page where information is collected (e.g., survey questionnaire). A marketer could provide an icon on its home page that, when clicked, will furnish the consumer with access to additional screens disclosing the marketer's information practices.

The notice should identify the marketer, disclose an e-mail and postal address at which it can be contacted, and state whether the marketer collects personal information online from individuals. If the marketer collects personal information online, the notice should contain disclosures about: the nature of personal information collected with respect to individual consumers

Depending on the circumstances, information collected about a consumer may include:

1). Contact or locator information (such as name, postal, and e-mail addresses),

2). Billing information (such as financial accounts and credit card numbers),

3). Transactional information (such as data on purchases a consumer makes),

4). Navigational information (such as data revealing consumers' preferences or the choices they make among the range of products, services, or sites, and the times of day purchases are made), and 5). the content of correspondence or messages directed to a marketer.

For example, a marketer could include language such as: "We keep the information you provide in responding to our questionnaire." Or, "We maintain your name, postal, and e-mail addresses, telephone number, and payment and order processing information. We also may keep information on your communications with our customer service representatives." Or, "We collect information on the times and ways you use our Web site."

### The nature of uses of such information

The information may be used, for example, to ensure that a consumer is properly billed, for marketing by e-mail, or for evaluating and understanding consumer reactions to content, services, or merchandise offered online. It also may include using the consumer's name and address for marketing by mail or other media. For example, a marketer could include language such as: "We will use your e-mail address only to contact you about merchandise or services you have indicated are of interest to you." Or, "We use information for billing purposes and to measure consumer interest in our various services or pages."

### The nature and purpose of disclosures of such information, and the types of persons to which disclosures may be made

This may include disclosure of names, postal and e-mail addresses to other merchants for marketing purposes, or to firms that conduct market research for the marketer, or disclosure of additional information for bill collection purposes.

The mechanism by which the individual may limit the disclosure of such information. An opt out will traditionally be the means offered to consumers to limit the disclosure of information collected about them.

## The Means of Opting Out

All marketers sharing personal information collected online should furnish consumers with the opportunity to opt out from the disclosure of such information. The notice and opt out process should enable consumers to request their personal information not be rented, sold, or exchanged. Marketers' notices should clearly and accurately inform consumers of their opt out choices (e.g., transfer of all information to third parties, contact by third parties in a particular medium, re-contact by the marketer, etc.). Marketers should suppress in a timely fashion the personal information of individuals who request that their personal information not be rented, sold, or exchanged.

Whenever possible, marketers should provide consumers with the opportunity to opt out via e-mail. In opting out from lists used for online solicitation purposes, consumers may also seek to opt out from solicitations in other media, such as mail or telemarketing. Marketers should honor these consumer requests for opt outs from solicitations in other media. The DMA's notice is limited because the type of consumer information collected at the site is limited. If, for example, sales were transacted or a chat room were sponsored at the site, then the notice would require additional disclosures.

## Unsolicited Marketing E-Mail

Online solicitations should be posted to newsgroups, bulletin boards, and chat rooms only when consistent with the forum's stated policies.

To facilitate adherence to this principle, forum operators should publicize their policies regarding solicitations in their forums. For example, "We would like to send offers for valuable services and products that may be of interest to consumers." Marketers should inquire about the forum's policies before directing online e-mail solicitations to the forum. Online e-mail solicitations should be clearly identified as solicitations and should disclose the marketer's identity. Marketers using e-mail should furnish consumers with whom they do not have an established business relationship [mask] with notice and a mechanism through which they can notify the marketer that they do not wish to receive future online solicitations. Marketers using e-mail should furnish consumers with whom they have an established business relationship with notice and a mechanism through which they can request that the marketer suppress their e-mail addresses from lists or databases rented, sold, or exchanged for online solicitation purposes.

Online solicitations should be identified in a way that allows recipients to readily recognize them as solicitations. For example, a marketer should use clear language, such as "End-of-Season Sale," that ensures that—without reading more than the first paragraph—a consumer will recognize the e-mail message as a solicitation. The identifying information in the solicitation should include the name of the marketer making the solicitation and an e-mail address, postal address, and telephone number where the marketer can be contacted.

For example, a marketer could say, "Here's how you can reach us . . . (name, address, etc.)." Marketers should have systems in place that will honor consumer requests to not receive future online solicitations or, in the case of consumers with whom they have an established business relationship, to have their e-mail addresses removed from their lists or data bases that are made available for rental, sale, or exchange for online solicitation purposes. For example, a marketer could say, "We value our relationship with you and if you wish to opt out of receiving further e-mail advertisements, let us know. To get on our opt out list, all you have to do is send an 'unsubscribe' message to . . . ."

Whenever possible, consumers should be provided with the opportunity to opt out via e-mail. Marketers should identify where consumers are invited to send such opt out e-mail requests, particularly if the e-mail address is different than the one from which the marketing e-mail solicitation is sent.

Because of the unique characteristics of automated mailing lists (e.g., listservs), subscribers to such lists cannot individually opt out if the list manager permits online solicitations to be directed to its subscribers. This prevents a marketer from suppressing online solicitations to some subscribers of a listserv but not to others.

Consequently, a marketer directing online solicitations to subscribers of an automated mailing list should honor the list manager's stated policies regarding online solicitations. To facilitate adherence to this principle, managers of automated mailing lists should identify themselves and make their policies known to marketers and their agents prior to a solicitation. Marketers should also ask about policies that effect them. Any person who uses for online solicitation purposes e-mail addresses or screen names, collected from the online activities of individuals in public or private spaces, should see to it that those individuals have been offered an opportunity to have this information suppressed. Ideally, marketers using e-mail addresses and related information they have harvested should provide consumers with an opportunity to opt out prior to using the information for online solicitations. For example, a marketer could say, "We see that you frequent the (XYZ Corporation) site—we'd like to send you offers of (computer equipment). If you don't want to receive these offers, just let us know."

When using lists of e-mail addresses harvested by others, marketers should ensure that consumers have already been offered an opportunity to have their e-mail addresses and related information removed. Marketers should contractually require the sellers of harvested lists to contain the e-mail addresses only of persons who did not respond to a notice and opportunity to opt out. Marketers who operate chat areas, newsgroups, and other public forums should inform individuals using these spaces that information they voluntarily disclose in these areas may result in unsolicited messages to those individuals by others. For example, a marketer may inform visitors to a Web site with a message that reads: "You should be aware that when you voluntarily disclose personal information (such as your screen name) in our message boards or other public areas, your information can be collected and used by others."

Marketers should also support industry and other efforts to help educate consumers about ways to protect their privacy online. All persons involved in the use, rental, sale or exchange of lists and data for online solicitation purposes should take reasonable steps to ensure that such sharing of lists and data adheres to these industry principles. Industry groups should take appropriate steps to encourage their members to follow these principles. For example, marketers should incorporate these principles into their list rental contracts and should furnish these third parties with a copy.

## Online Data Collection From or About Children

This section contains additional principles that apply to online activities directed primarily at children who, more so than adults, may not understand the nature of information elicited from them nor the uses to which the information may be put. Because of this difference in maturity, marketers operating online or Internet sites directed primarily at children should encourage parents to share in and monitor their children's online experiences. In making decisions whether to collect data from or communicate with children online, marketers should take into account the age, knowledge, sophistication, and maturity of their intended audience.

For example, marketers should encourage young children to obtain their parents' permission, using language such as, "Your mom or dad should say it's okay for you to answer these questions."

Marketers should be sensitive to parents' concerns about the collection of their children's names, addresses, or other similar information, and should support the ability of parents to limit the collection of such data for marketing purposes through notice and opt out.

Marketers should encourage children to consult with their parents before furnishing data.

Marketers should also support industry and other efforts to help educate parents about ways to protect their children's privacy online, including informing them about software tools and parental access controls that prevent their children from disclosing their name, address, or other personal information.

The DMA's Web site, for example, hosts a special "For Parents" section on its Consumer Assistance page, which informs parents of the various software packages available for helping parents provide a kid-friendly Internet for their children. Marketers could hyperlink to this page.

In conjunction with supporting the ability of parents to limit the collection of such data online, marketers should limit the use of data collected from children in the course of their online activities to the promotion, sale, and delivery of goods and services, the provision of all necessary customer services, the performance of market research, and other appropriate marketing activities.

Marketers should also effectively explain that the information is being requested for marketing purposes. For example, a toy manufacturer's disclosure to young children might state, "If you give us your e-mail address, we will tell you when the new toy arrives at the stores, but it's important that you ask your parents if this is okay." The same toy manufacturer's disclosure to parents might say: "Information collected from children at this site is used only to understand their preferences among products and to notify the children of new toys." Marketers should implement strict security measures to ensure against unauthorized access, alteration, or dissemination of the data collected online from children. Marketers should consult the DMA's Guidelines for Personal Information Protection (Articles 7, 8, and 9) for suggested measures that should be taken to ensure security. These articles lay out the guidelines direct marketers should follow for the security of personal data, for authorization of visitors to areas where personal data is processed and stored, and for secure transfer of data.

# DMA Privacy Guidelines

For more information contact:

Direct Marketing Association
1120 Avenue of the Americas
New York, NY 10036-6700
Phone: 212-768-7277
Fax: 212-302-6714
E-Mail: consumer@the-dma.org

For more information on this topic, visit our Web site at www.businesstown.com

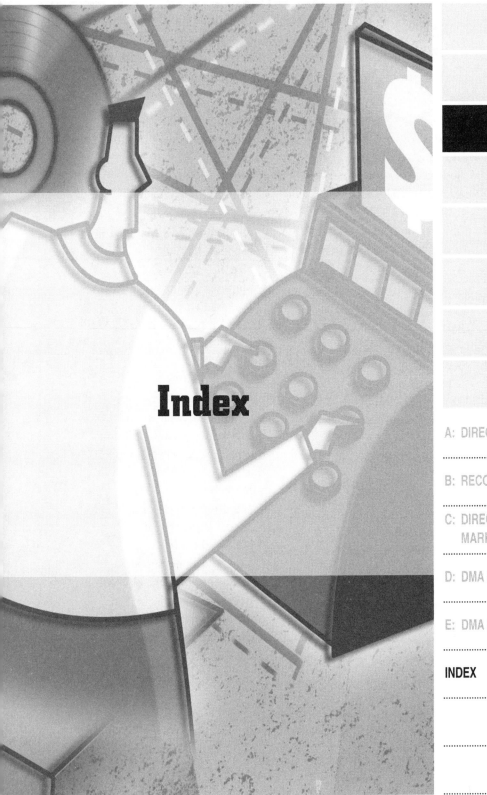

# Index

# FIND MORE ON THIS TOPIC BY VISITING
# BusinessTown.com
## The Web's big site for growing businesses!

- ☑ **Separate channels on all aspects of starting and running a business**
- ☑ **Lots of info on how to do business online**
- ☑ **1,000+ pages of savvy business advice**
- ☑ **Complete web guide to thousands of useful business sites**
- ☑ **Free e-mail newsletter**
- ☑ **Question and answer forums, and more!**

**Accounting**
Basic, Credit & Collections, Projections, Purchasing/Cost Control

**Advertising**
Magazine, Newspaper, Radio, Television, Yellow Pages

**Business Opportunities**
Ideas for New Businesses, Business for Sale, Franchises

**Business Plans**
Creating Plans & Business Strategies

**Finance**
Getting Money, Money Problem Solutions

**Letters & Forms**
Looking Professional, Sample Letters & Forms

**Getting Started**
Incorporating, Choosing a Legal Structure

**Hiring & Firing**
Finding the Right People, Legal Issues

**Home Business**
Home Business Ideas, Getting Started

**Internet**
Getting Online, Put Your Catalog on the Web

**Legal Issues**
Contracts, Copyrights, Patents, Trademarks

**Managing a Small Business**
Growth, Boosting Profits, Mistakes to Avoid, Competing with the Giants

**Managing People**
Communications, Compensation, Motivation, Reviews, Problem Employees

**Marketing**
Direct Mail, Marketing Plans, Strategies, Publicity, Trade Shows

**Office Setup**
Leasing, Equipment, Supplies

**Presentations**
Know Your Audience, Good Impression

**Sales**
Face to Face, Independent Reps, Telemarketing

**Selling a Business**
Finding Buyers, Setting a Price, Legal Issues

**Taxes**
Employee, Income, Sales, Property

**Time Management**
Can You Really Manage Time?

**Travel & Maps**
Making Business Travel Fun

# Also available from Adams Media Corporation

# Streetwise Books

**Relationship Marketing
on the Internet**

$17.95, ISBN 1-58062-255-0

Repeat customers are your most profitable customers. But how do you create and implement a customer-focused strategy for the Web? This book is filled with creative, low-cost ideas to turn browsers into loyal customers. Whether you have an existing web business or are considering starting one, *Streetwise Relationship Marketing on the Internet* will give you the tools you need to develop a site that customers will return to again and again.

## Also available in this series:

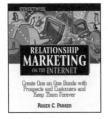

**Relationship Marketing
on the Internet**
$17.95
ISBN 1-58062-255-0

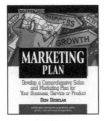

**Marketing Plan**
$17.95
ISBN 1-58062-268-2

**Do-It-Yourself Advertising**
$17.95
ISBN 1-55850-727-2

**Get Your Business Online**
$19.95
ISBN 1-58062-368-9

**Maximize Web Site Traffic**
$19.95
ISBN 1-55850-369-7

**Available wherever books are sold.**

## For more information, or to order, call 800-872-5627
## or visit www.adamsmedia.com

Adams Media Corporation, 260 Center Street, Holbrook, MA 02343

# Adams Streetwise books for growing your business

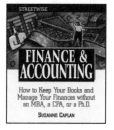

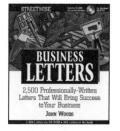

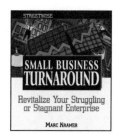

## About the Author

George Duncan is a national award-winning direct mail writer and consultant in Peterborough, New Hampshire. He is frequently listed among the top direct mail copywriters in the country. Following sixteen years in key positions with such major direct marketers as Ziff-Davis, Columbia House, and Xerox, he founded Duncan Direct Associates in 1976. Duncan Direct provides a full range of consulting and creative services to a national roster of publishers, software companies, and individual marketers of business-to-business and consumer products and services in both print and electronic media. He can be reached via e-mail at duncandirect@pobox.com or by phone at 603-924-3121. Further information, how-to articles, and updates to the material in *Streetwise Direct Marketing* are available on his Web site at *www.duncandirect.com*.

Duncan Direct Associates provides clients with direct marketing strategies, copy and design, consulting, creative direction and execution for effective direct mail, response advertising, Internet, database marketing, and sales promotion programs. We work closely with selected agencies and designers who understand the unique dynamics of interactive principles and techniques to deliver finished art on disk—or we'll submit copy and copywriter's rough layout with design recommendations for your designer or in-house design facility. Formats include sales letters, direct mail packages, self-mailers, product and company brochures, space advertisements, catalogs, action cards, and Web sites. We also assist with integration of such related support services as list acquisition, telemarketing, database development, Web site development, and more.